A LAWYER FOR ALL SEASONS

A LAWYER
FOR ALL SEASONS

Tales of celebrated trials
and famous sporting personalities

Ronnie Teeman

Scratching Shed Publishing Ltd

First published by Scratching Shed Publishing Ltd in 2011
Registered in England & Wales No. 6588772.
Registered office:
47 Street Lane, Leeds, West Yorkshire. LS8 1AP

www.scratchingshedpublishing.co.uk

ISBN 978-0956478788

Cover illustration by John Ireland
www.john-ireland.co.uk

A catalogue record for this book is available from the British Library.

Typeset in Cheltenham Bold and Palatino

Printed and bound in the United Kingdom by
L.P.P.S.Ltd, Wellingborough, Northants, NN8 3PJ

This book is dedicated to my daughter Miriam, fed from birth on a diet of legal tales which ensured her future membership of the profession and the ability to tell her own; to my son Brian, who at an early age suffered from legal indigestion which drove him to the internet and websites and afforded him recognition by his peers as a champion blogger – and my grandson, Leo, who enthuses in everything the family does. Finally, to my wife, Shirley, who cared for us all and kept our feet firmly planted with kind words, not only of encouragement when needed but of chastisement when deserved.

Acknowledgements

My thanks go to my secretary Sarah Wood for her patience in sorting out the manuscript, and to my colleagues at Ford Warren Solicitors for their inspiration.

Contents

*

Foreword
by David Oxley, CBE
- former Secretary General of the
Rugby Football League

In common with many people, I owe a great deal to Ronnie Teeman. That is why I am delighted to have the privilege of providing this foreword.

From my earliest days at Rugby League headquarters in the mid-1970s, Ronnie proved to be a staunch friend, a wise counsellor and a fine advocate, whose skills were as influential within the game as they were celebrated in the courtroom.

Shortly after my arrival at Chapeltown Road, I met Ronnie for the first time at the Queens Hotel, Leeds, the revered venue of the late Eddie Waring's famous 'Friday Night Club'. Privileged to be invited into this convivial but exclusive company, I quickly realised it would pay me to be a receptive listener, learning lessons which prevented me making serious mistakes at the outset of my career, throughout it and, indeed, beyond.

A Lawyer for all Seasons

In 1973, Ronnie played a leading and inspirational role in helping to establish the New Hunslet club following the sad and controversial demise of the famous old Hunslet RLFC. I particularly recall two characteristically innovative initiatives Ronnie masterminded as he strove to place the fledgling club at the centre of a sceptical rugby league public's attention.

Having secured a home ground at the old Leeds Greyhound Stadium in Elland Road, he installed tuning fork-shaped goalposts like those used in American Football. At first, the governing body raised no objection but visiting clubs soon did, claming their ace goal kickers were severely disadvantaged when aiming at – and too often missing – the unfamiliar target. So the posts had to go, to be replaced by some of conventional design.

Then, later, Ronnie hired a helicopter to hover low over a badly waterlogged pitch in a brave attempt to dry it sufficiently to allow a tasty and potentially lucrative Challenge Cup tie to go ahead. The resulting publicity, on a national scale, which these two brainwaves attracted, was manna from heaven as the struggling, embryonic club battled to establish itself.

The game at large also has much to thank Ronnie for. For instance, it was he who, in 1986 following conversations Manchester United's chairman, Martin Edwards, first suggested that the RFL should stage major matches at Old Trafford, the venue still proving to be a fitting climax to the Super League season. Ronnie's powers of persuasion were seen at their highly impressive best as he 'sold' the idea to RFL Council members, who were not merely sceptical but largely hostile to the bold proposal, it proving to be a huge success.

Also around that time, a number of high profile transfers involving star players threatened to blow wide open the long-standing but by then totally illegal 'retain and transfer' system under which clubs virtually owned the players on their respective registers. An inevitably successful challenge in court would have caused chaos. Playing contracts, clearly setting out the rights and obligations of both the players and their clubs were desperately needed.

Appointed by the governing body, Ronnie worked tirelessly ensuring every club was fully educated about the new system and producing a standard contract which the wise clubs immediately adopted and the recalcitrant soon realised they must follow. It was a crucial landmark in the game's long history, a monumental piece of work for which the sport should be eternally grateful.

Ronnie Teeman possesses and is always willing to share, a warm generosity of spirit, a calming sense of proportion and deep-seated wisdom and clear-sighted vision, all offered with his characteristic, eye-twinkling sense of humour.

DAVID OXLEY, CBE

1

*

That Damned United

No matter which football team you supported in the sixties and seventies, John Giles was a great player. Tough, competitive and yet with the most cultured of passes, he was both lionised by the fans of the clubs he played for and vilified by those he didn't, a sure fire sign of abilities and standing.

I doubt whether there has ever been a more explosive period of employment in the world of sport than the 44 days that Brian Clough spent as manager at Leeds United, a club that had been crowned League champions the previous season. His short tenure of office played a prominent part in the lives of so many people not least his own, the financial settlement he received from the Elland Road club setting him up for life while he went on to have a brilliantly successful career with Nottingham Forest, the climax being consecutive victories in the European Cup. The episode also helped establish David Peace, a West Yorkshire man living in Japan, as a writer of critical acclaim when he turned the events into a novel, entitled *The Damned Utd*. John Giles, a football genius but not a man of letters who was at the centre of the brilliant Leeds team of the time is described in the book as a key figure in the sacking of Clough.

Giles was angry and distressed that the book portrayed him as a disruptive influence and as the players' ringleader against Clough. He said it gave the impression he plotted the downfall of Clough and had his own personal agenda to become the manager himself. Since his active participation in soccer ended, Giles has become an admired and respected sports journalist and television pundit, appearing regularly in the Republic of Ireland as an expert analyst of the English Premiership; the European Champions League and international games. For almost 30 years he has had a prime role as a panelist and could justifiably be described in Ireland as a national treasure. John said his reputation was damaged by the false references to him in the book.

The Damned Utd was classified as a work of fiction, which has an Oxford dictionary definition as: 'an inventive idea; statement or narrative .... describing imaginary events and people.' As all the people referred to in the book did actually exist and all the material events set out did actually take place, its genre was flawed. The apparent success was in the main due to the fact that it was not fiction. Indeed, the author states in it: 'This novel is another fiction, based on another fact,' and then recites the sources to which he has referred. They included an assortment of books about Leeds United, its then players and biographies of Brian Clough.

One omitted from the list was John Giles. He was able to indicate which passages in the book were inaccurate and had been either manufactured or distorted to paint him in an unfavourable and damaging light and so instructed me to act for him saying, 'If what was said of me was true, I would have hated myself.'

I was, at the time, a consultant with Ford & Warren, one of the oldest firms of solicitors in the north and staffed by a team of highly talented litigators headed by Nick Collins, who agreed to conduct the litigation on John's behalf. Nick, an excellent lawyer, was both knowledgeable and thorough and began assembling a case against both the publisher, who had a made a substantial investment in their author, and the writer, who was by then the darling of the literary press. A quarter of a century earlier I had acted for Giles' skipper and similar icon, Billy Bremner, devising a protocol for such sports-based libel proceedings. Nick also took into account that a film based on the book was already in the pipeline.

All the purported conversations which David Peace claimed John had had with Clough were hurtful but there was one that was more wounding than the others. He describes a training session when Giles and Norman Hunter were on one team and Clough had lined up with the opposition. Peace wrote that Giles passed the ball short to Hunter and when Clough went for it they deliberately crunch tackled him with the intention of causing him injury.

John was shattered by the assertion, believing that nothing could be more damaging to his reputation in the game than the inference that he would deliberately try and injure his boss, especially one older than him. Moreover, that everyone sympathised with the fact that Clough's illustrious playing career had been prematurely curtailed at its peak by an on-field accidental collision, literally added insult to injury. I have no doubt that the entire episode from which that passage is an extract, is a brilliant piece of descriptive writing; colourful, tense and dramatic and designed to show how Clough would be mentally affected by it. However, the reader could, quite reasonably, be expected to believe that Giles, the perpetrator, was indeed, 'a cruel and vicious bastard.'

A Lawyer for all Seasons

There was no question that David Peace also painted a dark picture of Clough, profiling a great man crumbled who resorted to drink and acts of physical violence and that his inevitable downfall at Leeds was caused by his own actions – but that was of little consolation to John. But if he begs for sympathy for Clough, should he do it at the expense of others? In my view he had a responsibility to those – alive and well known – who he used as a mouthpiece for his narrative to make sure that the facts were right and not merely distorted for dramatic effect.

Nick Collins listened patiently to the reasons given by the publisher as to why they urged the material was not defamatory and that excused liability. Football journalist Owen Slot, reviewing the book in *The Times*, said that because it used the authorial voice with such 'originality', he appreciated that Peace left no-one in any doubt that Clough was the architect of his downfall. He concluded his piece by questioning how anyone could, 'stick with Clough for long' but also said that Peace portrayed, 'The supporting cast at Leeds, from the Board to the playing staff, as such a rich and dark company of villains that Clough nevertheless wins our sympathy.' John took some solace from the fact that a professional writer from inside the game had a similar view as his to the author's intent and his recourse to legal action was vindicated when the case was won.

After the settlement of the claim was made public, the rights and wrongs of action was discussed, including on *The South Bank Show*, a champion of the arts. The most forthright supporter of Peace was another sports writer from *The Times*, Matt Dickinson. He pulled no punches in his article in defence of the author and, as he showered praise on the work of a genius, had to find a villain to castigate. Referring to the description of Giles by Peace, he wrote, 'Even the portrait of him as quick-witted but opinionated

16

and highly confrontational is likely to strike anyone who had met Giles as true to character.' On reading it Giles told me, 'You know I am the longest serving TV analyst in the British Isles and I am paid well for opinions. As for me being highly confrontational, I cannot remember playing against Dickinson,' he added with a grin.

Dickinson aimed a further dart at the Giles heart suggesting, 'It is just as well he is not the censor-in-chief or we would have been denied the movie *The Queen*.' John's reply was fired off to me just as quickly, 'If Tony Blair had been depicted untruthfully as being disloyal to the country and given voice to a wish to overthrow the monarchy in that film, I have no doubt whatsoever that his lawyers would have 'gone to war' on his behalf against the film makers.' John held firmly to the view that he had maintained throughout. 'I was not prepared to accept untrue statements put into my mouth and being painted as disloyal, untrustworthy and a plotter,' he told me. 'People should be made aware that I put at risk my own money against a large publishing company. If they and the author thought that right was on their side, all they had to do was defend themselves and let the High Court decide. Instead they decided to pay up and apologise.' When the second edition of the book – amended as directed and agreed by Nick Collins – was released it, not surprisingly, contained a glowing endorsement by Matt Dickinson.

In December 2010, Giles put out a book of his own, *A Football Man* and reviewer Tom Dart of *The Times* interviewed him and posed the question, 'Is *The Damned Utd* the greatest football book or a stinking gust of creative flatulence. The truth is --- what?' John, quick as a flash, gave him a wonderful line, 'I thought it was all arty farty stuff.' Tom Dart describes Giles as a crusader against tall tales of all kinds and someone bold enough to see a half-truth and call it a half-lie. Simon Barnes, the chief sports writer at 'the Thunderer' then had his turn and in the final paragraph of his weekly column wrote, 'I was intrigued to read in these pages John Giles' measured condemnation of the bizarre book *The Damned Utd*. Normally I am in favour of all kinds of freedoms for all kinds of writers – believing the only immorality is to tell a bad tale, but *The Damned Utd* gets its edge, its power from the fact that its subject, Brian Clough, was real, and because the team he managed briefly, Leeds United, was full of real people. This is fiction that works - because it is not fiction. It seems to me – well – a bit of a cheat.'

Nick Collins did not have an easy ride with the publisher's solicitors, who 'reluctantly' agreed to give a written apology, pay a substantial sum by way of compensation and legal costs but - of vital importance – the removal of the passages that John Giles considered offensive to him as well as being inaccurate. He had the support of specialised counsel from the excellent Jonathan Crystal, who has a wealth of experience of sport – some very personal to him – but it is ultimately the relationship between solicitor and client that is the determining factor. Only the solicitor knows how much resilience his client has and how far he can go in the delicate art of negotiation where fine judgements and assessments have to be made. In John Giles' case, money was secondary to withdrawal of all the offending passages and receipt of an apology, showing the world that he was not the, 'despicable, vicious plotter' as depicted.

Nor was that the end of it. Nick was faced with a similar *cause célèbre* when the film came out and former Scotland international and Spurs and Derby favourite Dave Mackay considered that he had been defamed. Dave, who by then was 76 years of age, had been described by Clough as the best of his signings. 'He had everything as a player and he was the ideal skipper,' he noted. As part of his armoury, he was not a man to be messed with and is remembered at Leeds for a famed dust up with fellow irascible Scot Billy Bremner, a famous photograph showing Dave with hand around the throat of the then youthful pretender to his throne. The film script for *The Damned United* was written by Peter Morgan, adapted from Peace's novel and BBC Films had a role in the production. It was not surprising to observe that the role of John Giles in the downfall of Clough was very slight in comparison with the book although I have to say that my abiding memory of the film was that the great star-studded Leeds United team was depicted as if they were a pub side playing in a Sunday league.

What Dave MacKay and his family complained of was a scene about the resignation of Clough and Taylor where a Derby player is reading a petition from the dressing room to the Board reiterating their support and respect for Messrs Clough and Taylor and asking for them to be reinstated. A list of players who have signed the petition is read out and the character playing Peter Taylor says, 'But not Dave Mackay' and continues, 'He just accepted the job.' Michael Sheen as Clough shows his anger shouting, 'I signed the fat f**k – saved his professional life – gave him two years as a player – he wouldn't dare.' That scene was intended to make Dave appear treacherous, the skipper taking the job behind the back of his team mates. Unfortunately for the film maker, MacKay had left Derby two and a half years before Clough and Taylor departed.

John Giles was contacted by Dave Mackay's daughter, Val, and he pointed her towards me. We spoke that night and I asked her to make contact with the office which she did and Nick Collins steered the ship from that point until it reached its port in a calm sea, with the generous help of the

A Lawyer for all Seasons

Professional Football Association. Dave Mackay always maintained that if he had been at Derby at the time of Clough and Taylor's departure, he would have joined the campaign to save them from the sack and certainly would not have taken the job in those circumstances.

I wonder if the eminent writers who rushed to the aid of David Peace when under fire from Giles consider that to put an untruthful 'fact' into an actual situation should be permissible. Dave Mackay existed, the meeting took place, the petition was prepared but the events did not go together. Why should the writer escape liability because it's a work of fiction, you use real people at your peril.

When Giles' supposed *bête noir* Brian Clough's family were traumatized by what Peace had written about their beloved husband and father, they turned to John for assistance and, again, he referred Barbara Clough to my practice. Furthermore, he willingly appeared on the brilliant documentary that ITV produced, which was shown at the same time the film was released, and depicted much of the brilliance of Clough and his achievements while recognizing his weaknesses.

John's autobiography was extremely well received and reviewed. In it he makes mention of me and how we met and expresses his gratitude in rather lavish terms surrounding the assistance I gave to him which frankly would have made me blush if I was capable of it! He became a client of mine in 1970 and over 40 years on still is and has become a great friend. The diminutive Irishman, who was the midfield general of the great Leeds United team, was destined for stardom. Two friends of mine introduced me to him. One was his golfing partner, solicitor Stuart Crossley who was a property lawyer and the other a mutual friend, Turkish born Tunos Osbay, the proprietor of the Nouveau, a nightclub and restaurant for the 'sophisticated' in the centre of Leeds.

John had entered into a partnership – not a limited liability company - with an Irish insurance broker in Leeds when in his late twenties, to develop what John considered was a niche position in the pension industry. He neither obtained nor sought independent legal advice. The concept was that their brokerage would arrange pensions for professional footballers who would be able to deduct tax from their wages for the pension payments they made. With a typical earning span in their chosen profession at its peak for only a few years, footballers began to realize that provision needed to be made come the day they were released back into the labour market, possibly unskilled. When it was announced that the Inland Revenue accepted that the normal retirement age for a footballer was to be 35, United Insurance Brokers enthusiastically moved into the market. Obviously through John's contacts many doors were opened and within a short time they had on their books a number of the players at Leeds United and Arsenal. Managers indeed welcomed them, anything that made football stars responsibly save money for their future was to be commended and encouraged.

John played little part in the day to day running of the business, his partner being in total control and apparently doing a good job, constantly reporting back their excellent progress which enabled him to become a leading personality in the commercial and charitable life of the City. Indeed, his work for the Leeds chapter of the Variety Club of Great Britain, which did such valuable work for underprivileged children, was recognised when he became chairman-elect. Satisfied, John did not take one penny piece from the business but his cohort relied upon the business for his living and drew weekly wages. John was encouraged by the healthy noises relayed to him and it was, therefore, a tremendous shock to hear that the business had a liquidity problem and people were knocking on his door for money. Even worse than that, monies received by the company for client's premiums had been used up and the Insurance companies had not had transferred what was due to them. My partner in our legal practice, Leslie Gould, was also a keen Variety Club member and conceded that many of their members were attracted by the glamour of associating with the leading lights in commerce and showbusiness did not have the monies to match the big shots but still tried to do so.

John was staggered. His first thought was for his soccer friends who had handed over relatively large sums although he was relieved to discover that they were all personally safeguarded. His partner quickly revealed that he had no funds and did not hang around long in Leeds, doing nothing to help clear up the mess and made no contribution to the losses sustained. As an aside, at one meeting with the creditors, I was amazed at the information one insurance company manager had of John's contract with Leeds United, not only the salary but also the bonuses paid. That information could only have come from the club. I was incensed and made enquiries at Elland Road. I was surprised to discover - but really should not have been – that a director had obtained the information for a friend who had passed it on. The insurance companies were looking to only one man to redress the balance and one with a very high profile in the city.

My first in-depth discussion with John is imprinted on my memory. He asked the right questions and speedily accepted his own position. 'It's down to me alone - isn't it?' he asked and I confirmed that legally it was. He continued, 'Let's find out first what it's going to cost and then we'll discuss finding the money and, by the way, if I pay up, the business is mine isn't it?' His summation was accurate and prescient. Quickly we quantified how much the insurance companies required although attitude-wise, I was a little surprised how some of their local managers, who had previously fallen over backwards to meet sporting celebrities, became hardhearted and confrontational overnight. John told me how much he could muster and I suggested the balance be obtained from Leeds United by way of a loan to be approved of by the Football Association and re-payable within a relatively short period, which would mean not taking a rise from his next playing contract. He was reluctant but I told him he would be surprised how many of his contemporaries borrowed money from their clubs. I spoke to the club chairman, Percy Woodward, who served with me on Leeds City Council and, seeing it was in Leeds United's interest, it did not take long to give the nod to my request. I was then able to revert to the insurers and when they confirmed that John was entitled to future commission on renewals as well as new business, we were able to conclude a deal. While I was working on that aspect, I was preparing the way for John to recoup some of his outgoings. I made an approach to an independent insurance broker of standing in the City. He saw the prospective value of the business and I recognised that he had the necessary skill and the organisation to move it forward. A deal was struck, United Insurance Brokers were no more and John could sleep easily at night. To raise additional finance I arranged a summer playing contract for him in South Africa which Leeds manager Don Revie approved.

Stanley Rostron, the principal of the new brokers, took the business under his personal control and, as he knew his trade well, was able to increase the client base considerably while also nurturing the existing policy holders so it turned out to be a win-win situation. Some of the investments made for footballers saw them receiving pensions of over £10,000 a year as their policies subsequently increased by five per cent annually. Considering that the amounts invested were small in those days – a good First Division player earning no more than £300 a week - the pension must have been a godsend to the players of that generation. I was full of admiration for the way John bore his troubles and concentrated on his football regardless and, indeed, enjoyed the best period of his soccer career. Without rancour he faced the future and, where many would have stumbled and had reason for complaint, he stoically accepted what had been happened in his name, accepted responsibility and moved on. Many I have known, when faced with such a financial setback sit back and surrender while others bathe in self pity, John took everything in his stride. Icy determination and dogged persistence were his valuable assets. The analytical and constructive mind he used on the football field served him well, he could make decisions and make them quickly. Despite a lack of formal education, he had a great intellect which was recognised by his peers in the sport. He was a thinker, a student and a doer and it was easy to understand why others in soccer, not only from the ranks of his own team but elsewhere, turned to him for guidance. From the field of play he went on to management at both club and international level and was hugely regarded for his thoroughness.

He became an authoritative commentator in the press and on television. Unlike many on the box who think they must state the obvious and chatter incessantly, John gave his sage perceptive comments so that the viewer could comprehend the game better. My association with John took me to many countries in Europe and to North America. He was also the source of numerous sportsmen coming to my legal practice, my waiting room often appeared to be an alternative dressing room for soccer stars. Though many of the gentlemen of today's press never saw him on the pitch, that did not prevent them from making references to him and although giving a grudging mention of his brilliant skills would, at the same time, if not directly accusing him of being a 'dirty player', one who, 'had a mean streak in him'. In his defence, as he stoutly maintains, during his many years at Leeds in league matches he was never sent off, nor did he accumulate sufficient disciplinary points to warrant suspension.

Less than five feet five and just over ten stone, he was one of the small but skillful artists of his time, a playmaker gifted with two good feet with an uncanny ability to pass accurately long or short. As a result, he was the target for his opponents, 'Stop Giles and you're on your way to stopping Leeds' was the shout. In an early game in his career he was seriously injured by an opponent's violent act and resolved there and then that it would not happen again. He developed, as one contemporary commentator said, 'a fierce determination to defend himself'. Historians of the game tell us that in his era the tackle from the back had not been outlawed and that 'over the top' collisions were prevalent. Furthermore, each club had at least three notorious 'hard men' on the field. Giles survived all this and played at the top level until his late thirties. He made no secret of his frustration with those writers who emphasised the negative while neglecting the positive side of his play and would consult me when he thought his critics had failed to make that distinction.

2

*

Captured by the Law

I t is unlikely now, in my 81st year, that I will find myself across the console from the delightful Kirsty Young discussing my *Desert Island Discs* choices and how my life in the law came about. Assuming she had asked how it all began, the trail goes back to the War years in 1943. We lived in a semi-detached house in Leeds. I attended Roundhay School, a local authority grammar school and was not the most assiduous of pupils. The homework schedule was always heavy but the distractions even more onerous.

I'd completed my homework one evening and went to bed. The following day the police were at the house. We'd had a midnight intruder and I was instructed not to go into the dining room where my books were stacked on the dining room table as the fingerprints experts were coming. Sent to school, my Latin master, Mr. G.G. Hall, noted for his quick temper and humour, came round to collect in the previous evening's efforts. Explaining my situation, he snorted, 'Don't tell me, laddie that burglars came to your house to steal your miserable Latin homework!' I pleaded that I couldn't give any other explanation than the truth, to which he retorted, 'Ronald when you leave this school there is only one career for you and that's to become a lawyer.'

I am known for downplaying my lack of public school education by describing myself as an Old Cowperian, having attended the friendly neighbourhood Cowper Street Primary school in Chapeltown from the age of five. It was a mixed school of Jewish and Christian children of the predominantly upper working class. The teachers were kind, caring and enthusiastic and whenever I meet old school friends, we always speak endearingly of Miss Beevers and Miss Owen, two ladies who played an important part in our formative days.

Among my classmates was Gerald Kaufman, part of a large family that lived next door to my grandfather and we saw a lot of each other. He achieved fame as a distinguished politician and a member of the kitchen cabinet of Harold Wilson but later fell out with the Jewish community and they with him, more is the pity. Gerald, being the youngest, was to some extent spoiled and addicted to the cinema, probably because his sisters would give him a copper or two to get out of the house in the evening and give them some peace. He was not interested in sport but he would sometimes come with me and climb the wall that gave us free entry to Bracken Edge, the home of the Yorkshire Amateurs FC on a Saturday afternoon.

I was the only son in what was a traditional, strictly kosher although not Orthodox Jewish home. My father was a first generation immigrant, his parents having arrived from Russia in the 1880s, met in this country and married. They had eight children, two of whom were girls. All the boys, apart from Louis the youngest, volunteered and served in the British Army in the First World War and it was somewhat unique that a quintet from one family all returned home at the cessation of hostilities. Father served in the Royal Artillery and was injured in the first battle of Ypres, returned to England, was operated on and when fit – after a few weeks – returned to the battlefield in time to fight in the second battle there. I learnt nothing from him about the horrors, he would not talk about it. All he would say was, 'it was a hell hole.' And we never pushed him on the topic.

When on holiday, if the weather was hot, he never wore shorts or swimming trunks, the reason being that he had quite an ugly hole in his right buttock. That prompted mother to remark, 'Your father had his back to the fighting'.

Looking back on my childhood, I appreciate that I came from an affluent home, a terraced house in a tree lined road with gates at one entrance. We had a maid and my sister, Marjorie, went to private school. Almost the entire summer was spent in St Anne's on Sea, father coming up at weekends and we then moved further northwards to a newly built home with a large garden facing farmland in the northern suburbs of Leeds.

My father worked on the racecourse as clerk to a leading firm of bookmakers, Tattersalls. He was a human ready reckoner and his handwriting was immaculate and stylish. He loved sport, cricket being his favourite closely followed by rugby league and was a great walker. He also spent time in the family woollen waste business buying 'clips' from tailors which were recycled into shoddy cloth. Demand diminished when synthetic fibres replaced the wool. He was a quiet man and would have a pint but seldom more on his way home. He liked his food and enjoyed Jewish traditional occasions, in particular Friday night Sabbaths and the other feasts in the calendar. I inherited his love of sport but not his neatness, precision and discipline. He had a remarkable memory for events, particularly of a sporting nature.

A Lawyer for all Seasons

Mother was a few years his junior, not the many she would often claim. She was born in Poland and, as a toddler, was brought to England where her family settled in Leeds. A natural blonde and petite, she was known as 'Little Eva'. Fluent in Yiddish, she did well at school and her father, a Hebrew scholar, bought her a fruit and sweet shop near to Millgarth Street police station in the centre of Leeds when she was 14. She worked long hours, frequently closing after 9pm, staying open just in case people returning home from a night out wanted some cigarettes or sweets. She was very funny but not intentionally so and her gaffes were legendary. Like so many small in stature, she had a lot to say and would insist on saying it. A good cook and hostess, she was extremely popular especially among my sister's friends.

After Cowper Street and our move, I went to Talbot Road School where I was inspired by the enthusiastic head teacher, Bertha Calvert and her maxim, 'Whatever is worth doing – is worth doing well.' At Roundhay I passed the school certificate with three distinctions and six credits and went on to the sixth form where I encountered serious academic problems. The first year seemed good but when I returned in September to complete the studies, my form teacher advised me to get a job instead of wasting my time there. I immediately applied to the Faculty of Law at Leeds University. Father paid the entrance fee of 15 pounds 15 shillings for the year and I was duly admitted. He also spoke to his solicitor and secured articles for me although it cost a further £350 premium. I was nearly 17 but I was up and going.

I draw a heavy curtain over the degree course at Leeds University. Firstly, I was only 16 when I started there and was not sufficiently mature to accept unsupervised and uncontrolled study. Secondly, I was only a part-time student attending the University two days a week with the rest of the time being spent at my principal's office. Added to that, some of the subjects were totally irrelevant to me; Roman Law, Legal History, Constitutional Law and Private International Law amongst them. The lectures consisted of an entire class of students taking down notes that were dictated mechanically. Questions were not encouraged, there were no tutorials and I lost interest after a term. I took the advice of my principal, Ernest Wurzal, who told me to get any sort of a degree and, thereby, exemption from the Law Society Intermediate exam.

I ended up with a second class degree for very little work and went on to a 'crammers course' at Gibson and Weldon's Guildford HQ for my Law Society finals. I spent four months in digs with ten other students who had similar objectives. The firm was a private enterprise whose sole aim was to get names on the pass list. No discussions, no tutorials, no academics just endless swotting with a test every few weeks to show your progress – or lack of it.

I met some great folk at the university and retained their friendship after we all left for the outside world. One of Britain's most eminent barristers, the late Gilbert Gray, converted from Theology to Law. Eric Orbaum, who shared a desk with me at Wurzal's and who my sister had the good fortune to marry, sadly passed away at 60 in the prime of his life. Stanley Berwin was a bright hope for the Liberal Party and secured articles to a leading firm of solicitors in Leeds. At University, Stanley did not take kindly to examinations but did grant them the courtesy of answering some of the questions – allowing him to leave with an Ordinary degree. In the meantime, he fought the 1950 General Election for the Wakefield constituency held by leading Labour figure Arthur Greenwood. I learned my trade as a speaker by helping his campaign, sometimes speaking at three meetings a day at various locations. The main support speaker in the campaign was of course Gilbert Gray. He could, and would be heard above the sound of traffic. He was also one of the comedy stars – alongside future entertainer Frankie Vaughan – then an Art student – in the student review which ran twice nightly for six nights at the local Music Hall.

I did, however, get a twinge of conscience that I had wasted father's hard-earned cash and decided to do some post graduate work and, in deference to him, sought permission to write a thesis on the, 'Attitude of the Judiciary to Contracts by way of Gaming and Wagering.' I was assigned a tutor, the excellent, tolerant Law lecturer Geoffrey Hornsey, whose enthusiasm for research infected and inspired me. I was awarded an LLM Degree and recall my oral examination vividly as Professor James put me at ease by his first question. 'Before we start,' he said, 'what will win today's big race?' The only horse whose name I had seen in the papers was Tulyar. I trotted it out and it duly won.

W hen my career as a defence lawyer passed its shelf life and I said my farewells with a party for colleagues, they recognised the occasion by inaugurating the Ronald Teeman Trophy.

This was to be presented to the most prominent male and female advocate of the year at an annual get-together I had started a couple of years earlier, the 'Not the Law Society Dinner'. I had no desire to be sidelined from the profession and thought the occasional stint for the Crown Prosecution Service would be a novel experience for one that had done nothing else during his entire career in court but defend. It was a chilling, exciting ride. Picking up a bundle of files before 9am on the date of a hearing was nerve wracking but improvisation, procrastination and obfuscation were my stock in trade. Defence advocates were generally and surprisingly less prepared than the Crown Prosecution Service presenter. A file well prepared by an intern at the CPS office was easy meat for an experienced lawyer. Either side of the fence, I encountered a range of characters some of whom left a huge impression.

The first lady stipendiary magistrate in the city was Penelope Hewitt. I came to know her better over the years as we breakfasted together frequently at a local café. She was liked by everyone, even the accused were charmed by her. I was present when Romany James, a serial attendee for a miscellany of petty offences and, arguably, the mainstay of the practice of solicitor Graham Parkin of Hyams & Co, proposed marriage to her from the well of the court. She politely but firmly declined. When she was called to London to take up a much more senior position, there was much sorrow in Leeds.

From time to time sheer boredom creeps into the style of the district judge. Listening to monotonously similar cases each day with an inevitable ending is not stimulating nor is seeing and hearing the same advocates who have not the wit to change, if only slightly, their language and approach. I recall one such advocate claiming, 'It is three years this month since my client's last conviction and he has not re-offended since.' 'Of course he hasn't,' the stipendiary magistrate retorted in exasperation, 'he was sentenced to four years imprisonment then and was only released a few weeks ago.'

Tom Feakes was the Leeds clerk to the justices when I first started practice in 1953. Unqualified but with a lifetime of experience in the court system climbing the ladder, he was a martinet and could be seen running round the corridors at 'curtain up time' to ensure all courts were running before returning to his own. He could see the strengths and weaknesses of his magistrates at close hand and he was also a brilliant communicator, he knew of their problems and difficulties and had ears that listened. Once, local solicitor Peter Fingret had an application for a regularly granted liquor licence at the Odeon cinema, who were hosting the Red Army choir, inexplicably turned down by a particularly truculent magistrate. Tom tried to seek redress but on countering the adjudicator was given short shrift and told that the decision was *res judicata*, a decreed judgement meaning another court could not change it. Tom knew he was not out to win a battle of minds, how to get out of the mess was of more importance. As the application was for half an hour before the concert, during the interval and the same time after the performance, Tom made the suggestion that Fingret should go to another court and ask for a licence covering three quarters of an hour. He did, it was happily approved and the problem solved.

Peter Whitehead then became the first solicitor to be appointed C to J for Leeds and a magnificent job he made of it. A training and recruitment campaign for clerks and magistrates was commenced, training for court chairmen introduced and similar courses for new appointees. A breath of fresh air blew all the cobwebs away. Youngsters could see a professional career and structure ahead, the whole place buzzed.

Peter had the support of his chairman Dr Roy Hullin, a biochemist from Wales who made a great contribution I understand in the development of lithium salts in mental cases. Roy's work behind the scenes did not go unnoticed, indeed his court appearances were welcomed by solicitors as he was innovative, understanding and tolerant and had a sympathy for those human beings who had been cast aside by society. Similarly, John Power was a deeply religious bachelor who was kindness personified in the juvenile court but could come down hard on the little miscreants when required.

Arnold Ziff, an industrialist who supported good causes to all sections of the community was appointed a JP at a young age and had an old fashioned view of charity and public service. Although a member of an orthodox synagogue, he once sponsored a performance of Handel's *Messiah*, my favourite choral work, which I attended at the Town Hall. That was typical of his generosity and when I told some of his colleagues they said with a laugh, 'Arnold probably thought it was written about him.' His good deeds were not always performed in the public spotlight and each Christmas or Easter when one court at least had to be manned, he would attend so that his Christian colleagues could celebrate the holiday with their families.

There were those on the magistrate's bench who made a career of their appointments. Experience brought them many mannerisms that even the most theatrical judges would not display. The most dangerous are those who are insecure and uncomfortable in their own skins but display a desire to play a role where the camera is focused on them and the spotlight gives brilliant illumination to their egos. I have to say they are becoming fewer, thank goodness. One who was a perfect fool – save that no one is perfect – got a degree of comeuppance at a charity ball at the Queens Hotel, Leeds. A solicitor was standing at the bar awaiting his wife's arrival and was confronted by the said magistrate and his good lady. 'Oh good to see you, how are you keeping?' said the magistrate. The solicitor responding only perfunctorily but the magistrate went on, 'Damned interesting case you had last week.' Again the solicitor merely shrugged his shoulders. 'Ah well' the magistrate sighed and suddenly realizing he had not introduced his wife added, 'Oh, I must apologise to you dear boy, this is my wife.' The solicitor, by this time desperate that the unwelcome companion would leave retorted, 'There's no need to apologise, I've seen worse.'

There were days when the Leeds Law Society played a vital part in the life of the city. Indeed when their annual dinner was held at the banqueting suite of the Queens Hotel, it was so heavily subscribed that guests who had to be rationed to two per member. It was indeed rumoured that one firm near Park Square employed more solicitors just before the dinner so they could have the largest table in the room. The much smaller civic hall is now used and the event has to be marketed and members pressurised to attend. The local political parties were headed by solicitors as were the churches and synagogues, the panoply of political and spiritual issues in Leeds were determined by lawyers. The profession even provided a leader for the temperance movement. Mr Morrish of the firm that bore his name objected to each and every application for a drinks license which came before the magistrates court in Leeds. I am pleased to note, however, that the present partners of that firm, take their libations at the Town Hall tavern and have eschewed that practice.

Nowadays I look in vain for evidence of solicitors playing a similar role in the life of the city and our local Law Society is in no way representative of the profession – the major firms show little interest and the smaller outfits accept that its activities have little impact on their professional priorities. It is some years since I started the 'Not the Law Society Dinner', an evening of good fellowship and cheer with no outsiders to impress but a gigantic dose of good old fashioned banter dispensed and it is a popular date in the solicitor's diary.

In September 1993, I received the legal business magazine *The Lawyer*, a rather upmarket journal aimed at the 'better end' of the profession. I must confess when reading it to a feeling of being an intruder. On the front page there were two large portraits of local solicitors Robin Smith and Paul Rhodes under the banner headline, 'These Men Will Eat You For Lunch - How Aggression Pays at Dibb Lupton.' The inside copy was even more exciting, dramatic and full of bile and angst. The author Catrin Griffiths had been to a bash at the Cutlers Hall in Sheffield to celebrate a partner's retirement. In her opening paragraph she wrote, 'It is an evening of fine wine, champagne and forced conviviality...,' before continuing, 'The Dibb Lupton culture is not one of aristocratic leisure - it is a culture that is, in a nutshell, irreverent, boisterous and hardnosed by turn, where partners openly and obsessively speculate about the sexual antics of their colleagues and expectations, and compete against each other for a bigger slice of the equity cake.' 'The only thing we've got in common is greed,' quips one partner.

That article to my mind detailed the worst facets of a legal practice imaginable. It boasted of their present income and the projected increase. It explained how success was rewarded and that those who stood still were quickly moved out. As the author so dramatically explained, 'the pressure on this money-orientated success culture has not been to everyone's taste.' Intimate areas of the firm's activities were divulged including the firm's in-house magazine which, jokingly of course, urged fee earners when sending bills to clients, 'to include all disbursements – especially those lunches which the client thinks we were paying for.' I do not to this day know or could even guess the motives of the two lead partners in permitting or even encouraging a journalist to portray them in a way that would heap ordure on them.

I have never met Rhodes but I knew, or thought I knew, Smith well. He was a local man and at the time the article appeared, president of the Leeds Law Society and had been a long serving member of the Council of the Law Society in London. When I started my practice in Leeds in 1956 Dibb Lupton were a small firm specialising in conveyancing and probate. I seem to remember that their main client was the Yorkshire Conservative Newspaper Ltd, who published the *Yorkshire Post* and *Yorkshire Evening Post* and they had, as a result, an effective debt collecting department which kept them active in the county court and in the insolvency world. Robin Smith, I remember from his early days in the profession and also as a keen attender at Headingley for both cricket - he became president of Yorkshire CCC - and rugby events. Just as he succeeded to the chair of the Leeds Law Society by dint of service so he was expected to receive the mantle of president of the Law Society but left the council chamber before that could be placed on his shoulders.

I found the article both insulting and degrading and a derogation of the ideals of our chosen profession. I did not recognise my profession or my role in it from the most disturbing prose I have ever read concerning solicitors. On the 23rd September, 1993 I wrote to Robin Smith and a day or so later decided to circulate copies to the many solicitors I knew in the city. The effect was dramatic. Those who read my letter phoned to say they shared my views and others mentioned that they would now read the article. Other lawyers and that included several members of the judiciary to whom I had not written, asked for copies and the letter became a collector's item. Robin did reply, saying that innocent remarks at a convivial evening had been taken out of context although one former partner of the firm sadly confirmed to me that the article accurately conveyed the atmosphere there at the time.

The period when that article was written heralded a

complete change of attitude as an enterprise culture was created around the law which did not have a high regard for previously long held ethics or concepts. It is with profound sorrow that I dwell on that piece which reflected the depths to which the great profession had plunged. The lawyer on the front line dealing with the man in the street and his traumas and who is dependent on public funding for access to the law is a casualty. In my considered opinion, the standards in the lower courts are now worse than they have ever been partly because the clever university graduate is dazzled by the bright lights and promise of considerable financial rewards offered by major commercial firms and practices. Who wants to do crime, matrimonial, immigration and employment law? Only those who cannot achieve a training contract with a major player.

It is an inevitable result that we do not produce advocates because those major firms do not practice that skill. It has always been my platform that advocacy training should be an integral part in legal learning even in the office of city lawyers. The ability to present your client's case in a persuasive manner and to detract from that of your opponent is a fashionable piece of furniture and if it is polished so much the better. An advocate of quality has the ability to think on their feet, is seldom fazed and rarely brow-beaten. Put an advocate with such experience in a commercial scenario; that gift together with their specialist knowledge of company and commercial law puts them in an advantageous position. It is not only verbal reasoning that a sound advocate has in their armoury but also the ability to compose written arguments with the force of reason behind them.

All legal practices now see the need to market, target, advertise and involve themselves in public relations and it works. No longer is the accepted 'do not tout' the norm.

A Lawyer for all Seasons

When my profession gave up the standards and ethics that had served them well for centuries, they forfeited the respect and on some occasions the reverence with which the solicitor was held in society.

In my early days the golden rules set up by Thomas Lund, the secretary general of the Law Society, were sacred. It was explained to me that you put your client's interests before your own and ensured that their money was preserved. My principal during my training said that you could enjoy any consensual sexual familiarly known to man with a lady client, at night, during the day, be it in the office, in the home or in the open air and as often as you wished, with one proviso that the intimate moments you enjoyed did not under any circumstances touch her fortune. It was forbidden to advertise your wares or to suggest that you had talents that other colleagues might not. Offering inducements to outsiders to supply you with instructions or entering into agreements with clients for the sharing of the spoils of victory were all the vices of yesteryear yet are the pleasures and profits of today.

In 1960, I was invited by the *Yorkshire Evening Post* to contribute, without fee, an explanatory article of the proposed new Betting Gaming and Licensing Act. The Law Society refused me permission to use my name so it was authored anonymously. Similarly, when the celebrated BBC satirical programme *That Was The Week That Was* featuring David Frost invited me to appear live, the Law Society said I could not be described in the programme as a solicitor but it would not offer any objections if I was described as an academic when doing battle with Bernard Levin. The motives of the Law Society were as praiseworthy as they were simple. We were a profession and a noble one at that so we had integrity, commitment and dedication to our clients, whose interest we put first. We were not tradesmen nor were we men of commerce; we were a profession who had standards of behaviour and conduct that we demanded of ourselves and enforced.

A sound legal practice now looks at promotions and slogans. I knew of someone who was advised to use the mantra, 'Tomorrow's Lawyer' on his business card and advertising material. It seemed quite a brilliant idea until he attended a hearing a day late and was told by the judge caustically that he may consider changing to 'yesterday's man.' The one-man-band today is a rarity if not an impossibility. It is discouraged by the Law Society which is a pity for a sole specialist can provide a useful service not only to the public but to the profession. At the age of 24, I was operating my own practice, developing it slowly from personal contacts, family connections, kind hearted solicitors who had a surplus of work and the courts who found it difficult to persuade solicitors to appear without a fee.

The most important development of my practice, however, was recommendation from clients. I still have a filing cabinet under lock and key in which rest old files of solicitors I represented. The offences ranged from dishonesty to drunk and disorderly, drunk and incapable, driving whilst under the influence, attempting to pervert the course of justice, violent and sexual assaults, 'flashing' and 'cottaging.' Some of the names were convicted – others acquitted. All were contrite, humble and grateful for not only my expertise but the compassion and understanding shown to them. I have had my spats with judges, magistrates and fellow professionals. I have been provocative and acted in cases that were truly sensational, eventually becoming the subjects of books and plays and which, 30 years later, are still being discussed. I have represented some of the great international sportsmen and travelled around the world pursuing their causes. I have brought and defended actions in the High Court relating to defamation which have been headline grabbing. It is no wonder I found the profession exciting and challenging.

I still act for many of my older clients and their children but I have found a new client base, fellow solicitors who suffer from the consumer driven society which believes that when something goes wrong someone must be to blame and who, then, are subject to complaints. We are governed by a Law Society that connived at the payment of 'bungs' to get work using the phrase 'referral fees' and that sat back allowing legal firms to exploit coalminers' compensation claims. Nevertheless, it is the common apathy of me and others like me that is to blame. The percentage of members voting on issues that concern the profession is laughable.

I recognise that advancing technology and global commercialism have inevitably meant a change in legal practice. Parliament has increased its output of reforming legislation and keeping up-to-date is now almost a full time occupation. Back in 1954, the lease of a shop in the centre of Leeds was usually six to eight pages in length, now it would be at least ten times as long. What remains is what it takes to be a good lawyer, which has not changed. For me, it is good judgement. The rest can be found in books.

3

*

Brady, Jordan and the Italian Job

The capture of orchestrating Arsenal midfielder Liam Brady by the Juventus club of Turin in the summer of 1980 ranks as the sporting equivalent of the most successful jewel heist in history.

Under European Law at that time, a player had the right to move from his club at the end of his contract to one in another EEC country which only had to pay compensation based on a formula calculated on his age and the use of a multiplier applied to his last salary. The younger the player, the higher the multiplier. While Arsenal could expect to receive well in excess of £1,500,000 on the English market, his value to them would be around £600,000 on the continent. The deal with Juventus was a slow and tortuous process, the Italians - although attracted by him being just 24 – wanted to pay much less than the market valuation. I am convinced that English clubs believed the regulations did not apply to them and were shocked when it dawned on them.

Liam was recommended to me by John Giles who was his

manager at international level. John was a great admirer and awarded him his first cap against Russia in Dublin. Arsenal had recruited well from that fair city, capturing Brady, David O'Leary and Frank Stapleton and they were all making an impact in the First Division. Brady had a driving ambition to play in Italy and Giles agreed with him that the freedom to creative midfielders offered by their style of play would suit his ability to run with the ball and pass accurately, both short and long. I agreed to represent him but warned he would have to be patient, especially as that trail had gone cold around that time.

I first advised him to be let it known that he saw his future in Italy, giving his reasons for that choice but to make it clear that if he stayed in England he would not wish to play for any other club than Arsenal. Ken Fryer at Highbury did everything he could to persuade Liam to stay. I attended meetings galore at which Ken put forward financial schemes to titillate the young maestro, one of which had been prepared by a leading tax barrister. It was all to no avail as Liam's mind was made up and I was eventually contacted by Gigi Peronace, the man who took the gentle Welsh giant John Charles from Leeds United to Juventus, a couple of decades earlier.

For many years Gigi had lived in Twickenham and had a loose association with the Italian Football Association and the national team. He followed English football in general and Arsenal in particular. When we spoke I warmed to him. He oozed enthusiasm, 'Yes – I am sure my country would love Brady – he is the tonic that Italian football needs,' he said. I had meetings with him at his London home where his wife's cuisine was superb and he and his secretary, a well spoken efficient upper-class English lady seemed to live on the phone. At his behest I met representatives of many Italian clubs – one from Napoli arriving in Manchester airport for a chat while his plane refuelled - but still nothing positive arose. I could see Liam was becoming impatient and understandably so, and his unease was exacerbated by other agents sympathising with him in his predicament and simultaneously extolling their own abilities to place him.

A plan was hatched to let the Italians know that they did not have the field to themselves and it worked. The press reported that Martin Edwards of Manchester United and his manager Dave Sexton were showing keen interest in Liam's future and, eventually, they admitted their interest. Picked up by their voracious daily sport's papers, it did seem to galvanize the Italians into immediate action. Gigi urged me to be cautious when dealing with Manchester United, telling me that the money they would offer was *pocco* to what was available in Italy. But protocol and courtesy determined that I see Manchester United. The chairman and manager came over to my house in Leeds but the offer they made was underwhelming and I said we would consider it. Within 24 hours Dave Sexton phoned and said that he thought the chairman would increase his offer to Liam if any real interest was shown.

I was now getting phone calls from Italian football journalists based in London. Their readers, apparently, could not get enough news about Liam Brady and which clubs there were interested, but the important call I awaited did not come until a day or so later. Gigi phoned and said, highly excitedly, 'Ron, Juventus want Liam.' He explained their offer was of a signing-on fee and a contract for three years with excellent wages and bonuses. Liam was on holiday in Majorca with his wife and when he phoned me at his usual time in the early evening I gave him the good news. I told him that there was still some way to go as their offer fell short of what I thought was reasonable compared to the salaries of similar players in Serie-A. Eventually I had a satisfactory offer on the table which I recommended to Liam, who was by then back at Arsenal starting pre-season training.

It was arranged that I would travel with Gigi to Turin on Monday 29th July to conclude an agreement with the Juventus Management as Liam was still under contract to Arsenal until the next day and their president Boniperti – a former Juventus and Italian international who was a team mate of John Charles – duly signed the agreement. I did on behalf of Liam and I remember joking that Juve had just bought an unfit, overweight lawyer, not quite 50 but it did not go down well. The phone call to Arsenal was more enervating. I spoke to manager Terry Neill to tell him out of courtesy that Liam had signed for Juventus. 'But he can't Ron. He's out here training with me,' was his response.

On the Wednesday, Liam arrived in Italy to a tumultuous reception. My Secretary had the English papers waiting for my return and I was disappointed to read the comments of Arsenal chairman Dennis Hill Wood. 'All English football stars will go abroad when their contracts are up unless they have an interest in English football or loyalty to their club. It is a ridiculous state of affairs brought about by our inflationary transfer market and the freedom of contract. It was an absolute disaster when it went through, though there was nothing we could do legally to stop it. It means that most of our very best players will move abroad at a time when our game needs them most. It could kill the game here. I'd much rather he stayed in England from his own point of view, Old Trafford would have done him more good than Italy – it's a lovely club to play for.'

Liam had two great years with Juventus winning the 'Scudetta' (the League championship) in both. He then moved to Sampdoria for two years and then Inter Milan for a further couple. Six years in Italy brought him much joy on and off the field. He gained the experience of life in a different country and culture and soon had the ability to speak a new language very well. In the early days of his Italian adventure, Liam was enjoying the lifestyle of a *Calcio* star with great food, weather and form on the pitch making life wonderful. Suddenly his peace was disturbed by a letter from the publisher of a book he had written before he left England entitled *So Far. So Good.*

In retrospect, he conceded that it was a stroke of vanity that prompted him to pen it when he was not yet 25 years old. Agents had however persuaded him, holding out a pot of gold, and he succumbed to their blandishments. Stanley Paul's were publishers of repute in the field and a ghost writer was commissioned to deliver the copy. I doubt whether Liam paid heed to the small print but concentrated on the financial aspects of the deal. I did not see the contract and the first I knew of the book was when Liam sent a draft of it to me for my comments.

I was fascinated to read it and, not being much of a fan, realised that the inside story would delight his fans. His story was not exceptional but I told him that I thought his views of Terry Neill were strong, although he was entitled to his opinion. I asked him if the facts upon which he based his comments were true and he confirmed they were. He took that as a green light, the book was published and I believe it sold reasonably well. At that time the standard player's contract had a clause preventing a player from making public comment without the club's approval, however I doubted whether Arsenal – as opposed to the manager – would take any action because he had not consulted them. Terry Neill, I understand, was disappointed by the comments Liam made but took no action.

Where he did run into trouble was in re-telling a story about the fractious relationship between footballers and some journalists, illustrating the point with a tale about renowned striker Malcolm Macdonald. Liam recalled there had been a news bulletin on the radio which said that a Malcolm Macdonald had been killed in a road traffic accident. An alert newspaper reporter made the assumption that the person referred to in the bulletin was 'Supermac' and no doubt wishing to obtain a scoop, promptly drove to his home. Malcolm's wife answered the door and was asked to comment and the poor woman broke down. The reporter left her in a distressed state but some hours later Malcolm walked in and on hearing what had happened blew his top.

The newshound concerned took exception to the story being printed in public and, with the financial assistance of the newspaper and their lawyers, commenced proceedings to recover damages for defamation from Liam. When a publishing contract is entered into, there is one clause that is of vital importance to the publisher. In essence, the author is asked to warrant to his publisher that the contents of the book are true and that if any matter is libellous, the author will indemnify the publisher from all the consequences thereof such as damages, legal costs, a re-print if necessary as well as the cost of books that are withdrawn from the shelves.

Stanley Paul acted within the terms of the agreement and Liam was faced with defending a libel action in the High Court at his own cost. I advised Liam that to succeed with the defence of justification he had to prove that the story was true and it was essential that we had the Macdonalds on board. They were cooperative, gave statements and agreed to give evidence and the trial took place before a jury in the High Court in London. The Macdonalds could not be shaken in the witness box and, after a short summing up, the jury returned with a verdict which vindicated Liam. His counsel, Richard Rampton, after the foreman had announced their decision said, 'Members of the jury, if you remain in the box for a few moments, I am sure Liam Brady will sign his book for you.'

Joe Jordan, a future Scottish international centre forward, arrived in Leeds from relatively unheralded Morton, recommended by a fellow Scot who had put the Elland Road side on the road to glory, Bobby Collins.

Joe was welcomed into Don Revie's family where he quietly started re-learning his trade. Full of determination and oozing with fitness, he did not have to wait long to make his debut and his enthusiasm and total commitment allied to selfless bravery was sometimes frightening to behold. He quickly became a favourite of the crowd.

Senior players recalled that Joe was always questioning and seeking guidance on how he could improve. He was joined at Leeds by fellow Scot Gordon McQueen, and they became great friends and eventually as bachelors shared a flat together before moving on to Manchester United which tarnished their worth in the eyes of some blinkered Leeds fans. Anxious to learn his trade, Joe followed the old maxim, 'If you pick brains, make sure they are good ones' and was neither a card player nor a drinker. He formed a firm friendship with John Giles, who was willing to listen to the difficulties faced by young players, went out of his way to resolve problems and took delight at the progress his junior colleagues made. When Joe was invited to sign a new contract with the club he consulted Giles. Joe was worried not so much about the terms offered but queried whether the club would not only maintain its present position but make further progress because many of its star names were coming to the end of their careers. Furthermore, the club was under the new and yet unproved management of Jimmy Armfield.

A Lawyer for all Seasons

After deciding to wait a while before signing, he maintained his enthusiastic commitment to the club but before Christmas 1977 he was 'tapped up' on the phone by a Dutch journalist saying that their top club Ajax were interested in him. Joe, by nature often taciturn, was his non-committal self but intimated that he would listen leading to the Ajax president making contact with Leeds chairman Manny Cussins, a deal maker by instinct and application.

I believe he agreed a transfer with the Amsterdam outfit with Leeds receiving a handsome fee and then broke the news to Joe who remained guarded. He contacted me and we received notification that the Ajax key people were flying to Leeds/Bradford airport and wanted to meet at the hotel there at lunchtime. On arrival, with Mr Cussins's car conspicuous in the car park, Joe and I were directed towards one of the lounges where we were joined by the Dutch party led by Ajax president Jaap Van Praag. They made it clear that they were keen to sign Joe but made a wage offer that was only slightly higher than that still on the table from Leeds even though it would, apparently, have made him the highest paid player on their books. The upshot was that Joe politely thanked them for their interest, said he was flattered by it but that he thought he should remain where he was for the time being.

Manny was quite angry saying that the offer was a generous one and that Leeds had done their best for Joe. The press were assembled outside the hotel waiting for news. I believe that when they arrived they thought it was a done deal and, having been given the thumbs down by Manny, demanded a response from us. Reading the papers the following day I learned for the first time that the fee agreed between the clubs was £350,000, which was a large one in those days.

Leeds were anxious to recruit new players to rejuvenate

their ageing squad and were short of cash. My view was that the offer was not right for Joe and other interested parties would now be alerted both at home and abroad and, not long after, he found a new home at Old Trafford. I kept in contact with him and he certainly enjoyed life at Manchester United under two completely different managers, studious Dave Sexton and the flamboyant Ron Atkinson. His international career blossomed and the fans warmed to him especially after baring a mouth full of gums for a lager advert. Joe, by then a family man with his schoolteacher wife Judith, who he had met in Leeds, often returned to the city and we met up from time to time.

With the success of Liam Brady's move to Italy and my specialist knowledge of European employment law, clubs there were anxious for more players, particularly as they represented a cheap investment once out of contract. Aged 29 and at the end of his deal, Joe became an understandable target. Interest was heightened by the placing of a discrete story by me with a journalist friend that hinted he could be on his way there. AC Milan made contact, keen to regain their place in Serie A after what was called 'serious manipulation of matches' which had seen them relegated. They were still a great club and desperate to fight their way back to the top. Their negotiator, a director of a large trading company in Milan, came over with a generous offer and the contract was drawn up there and then in a well known Italian restaurant in Leeds. It was translated by an Italian waiter who was so overwhelmed by the large amounts Joe was to receive that he could barely contain himself.

The contract was made subject to Manchester United agreeing the terms of compensation under the EEC Regulations and giving Joe clearance to UEFA. I then phoned their secretary to inform him of the deal and to ask him to provide the necessary figures and documentation. Joe and I went to Italy and he was taken around the club's trophy room which contained a large picture of the side that had beaten Leeds United in Salonica in the Fairs Cup final, a notorious game in which Joe played and the Greek referee was later banned for life for alleged bribery. Joe could not contain his fury, turning to their director of football - who had actually played in the match - and said, 'It was bent.....crooked.' The Italian obviously understood for his response was a shrugging of his shoulders and mumbled *pocco*, which translates as a little.

Joe settled in very quickly despite a coach/trainer who was renowned for the severity of his regimes. The crowds at San Siro took to him and gave him the nickname El Squalo, the Shark. A year later they were back in the top flight and Joe's contribution was considerable. He was determined to make the best of life there, he learned the language and appreciated the culture developing a love for opera and made many friends. When he left, having also assimilated much of the playing and coaching style and fitness regimes, his parting shot was, 'I learned so much I should have paid them.'

After a season with Verona he was courted by Lawrie McMenemy, the manager at Southampton, who was a firm believer in having a core of old pros with good habits in his squad. I negotiated that contract and the compensation for Verona and Joe then moved on to Bristol City as player manager. I then acted for him when he was invited by Scottish entrepreneur Wallace Mercer, in the summer of 1990, to take over as manager of famous Edinburgh club Heart of Midlothian. He was given a three-year contract with generous side benefits and approached his new task with enthusiasm but I always thought that the job was not as rewarding in the football sense as he anticipated.

Joe had an older sister and a brother John, several years

younger, who would flit in and out of Joe's life. John played football for fun and was a happy-go-lucky character with wanderlust. Pop culture was his life; he would follow groups around Europe eking out a living by selling souvenirs and memorabilia. Tragedy befell him. He was travelling as a passenger in a car in Sweden which skidded on a patch of ice, was thrown out of it and pronounced dead at the scene. Joe went over there with his parents to investigate and make the necessary arrangements and seemed to be gone a while. Understandably, he took his brother's death badly and was numbed by it. He was always worried about John's well being and was desperate that he put roots down and got a 'proper job' but it was not to be.

Joe was regularly phoning me from Sweden keeping me informed of his enquiries and when he told me of the circumstances of the accident, it was apparent that John's death had been caused by negligent driving. Because John was single and with no known dependants, any claim for damages would, in financial terms, be very small. However, we found out, that John had a one time girlfriend, Kathy, with whom he had had a baby girl. They had remained friends and John was extremely fond of the child. Joe pursued the claim for the benefit of John's daughter Vicky and his patience and concern were rewarded when my office reached a suitable financial settlement with the insurers of the driver at fault. Joe grieved for a long time, as did his elderly parents although his mother gained a great deal of consolation in her declining years from her association with her newly-found grandchild.

Joe lived for football and I was delighted to be able to negotiate a book deal for him and introduce him to well known journalist James Lawton of *The Independent* who assisted Joe in recording his life story. It was no chore for him to attend a match wherever it was being played and when not working he could be irritable and restless. He filled in his time with match analysis for radio and television and as an expert commentator on Italian games which were then covered on English stations. But there was no substitute for an intimate involvement, even writing detailed analysis of teams for managers was only passing the time. It was the atmosphere around a club and in the dressing room that he missed.

His managerial experience at Huddersfield Town was disappointing and reflected little credit on the club or its then chairman David Taylor. The manner of its termination was sordid and undignified leaving Joe with no other alternative but to bring that former great club before an industrial tribunal. Prior to 2001, the Terriers had been in the first division but when Joe joined as assistant to Lou Macari, a former colleague of his at Manchester United and in the Scottish team, they were already in the second division and finances under strain with wages from those headier days still high. David Taylor, a chartered accountant, was part of the consortium which acquired control of the club in January 2002.

Joe's contract with Huddersfield began on 1st November, 2000 and continued until 31st May, 2002. Neither Mr Taylor nor anyone else in authority did anything about renewing it in the month of its expiry. Joe went into hospital to have his hip repaired and then carried on working during the closed season and even had discussions with the club secretary as to a pre-season venue for training. Though Joe took his holiday on 12th June, a week, the same day the directors met to dismiss the coaching staff. On Tuesday 14th June, Taylor wrote to Joe saying, 'At the meeting of the 12th June it was decided that your fixed-term contract having come to an end would not be renewed. He did not receive the letter until his return to the UK on 19th June but was so conscientious and loyal that even during his absence he had made telephone calls to the club and no-one ever mentioned his supposed departure. A local reporter contacted him for his reaction to the sacking but he could not comment as he had not yet received the letter. On his return from leave, Joe came over to see me. The upshot was that a claim was made for unfair dismissal.

At the opening of the case the club withdrew any allegations concerning Joe's capabilities but the tribunal found it hard to agree with any of Taylor's assertions, notably that, on the day of the takeover before a match against Colchester, he had told the management team how important it was for the club to return to the top as soon as possible. He claimed that he made it clear he expected good results, an attractive playing style and, in addition, the development of their own players. Both Macari and Joe were adamant that such a conversation had not taken place. Similarly, having heard a rumour on the grapevine that the club were looking for a new management duo, Joe confronted the chairman who rejected it out of hand. Again the tribunal favoured Joe's version. Taylor then gave evidence that at the beginning of March, just before playing Swindon, he told the pair that if promotion was not achieved there would have to be a parting of the ways, an assertion that was also denied.

The eventual decision of the tribunal made extremely interesting reading. They accepted that Joe was handicapped by the timing and manner of his dismissal especially as there had been no previous warning or any indication that his contract would be terminated. He had not had the opportunity of looking elsewhere nor been able to take any action to try and retain his position with the club and that his reputation had been unfairly harmed. The unanimous decision was in favour of Joe, he had been unfairly dismissed. In March 2003, the tribunal ordered the club to pay Joe £31,000 in compensation but he did not receive a penny piece. Taylor's party was over and Town went into administration. His was not one of the protected debts. Such practices are now even more commonplace. Football management is not always a picture of brilliant colours, there are times of gloom, doom and wrongdoings to counterbalance the glamour. The crowd and cheers of the fans, magnified by newspaper headlines intoxicate the sports star but, ultimately, it is how they react to adversity which reveals whether they are deserving of greatness. It is a results driven business and managers and their staff are constantly aware that the axe could fall at any time. A manager is held in the highest regard and is at his strongest on the day he signs a contract and, as I once said to the press when another Leeds stalwart Allan Clarke was sacked, 'a football manager's contract should have a health warning attached.'

Joe and I had been together for 30 years and there has never been a signed contract between us. I regard him not only as a valuable client but as a good friend. The experiences we shared over the years have, like life itself, had high and low points but we do have one thing in common, namely our respect and affection for our chosen careers and would not have chosen differently. You can not keep a good man down. Joe turned down several offers on my advice before accepting one from Harry Redknapp, then manager of Portsmouth, to join him as first team coach. It was a tremendous success, including a Cup final triumph. When Spurs offered Redknapp the vacant position there, he sought out Joe's services and he is helping them make an impact in Europe after a long time in the doldrums. How wise he was to study for his international coaching badge.

4

*

Laughter in Court

I hate to admit it but the legal profession does not have a particularly enlightened sense of humour, they are good at making jokes at the expense of others while struggling to retain their mirth if it is on them.

Women were virtually excluded from a career in the law until the latter three decades of the twentieth century and when their prominence did rise, they had to work even harder to earn their reputations.

In a male dominated enclave, used to heavy drinking, horseplay and often ribald songs, the ladies had, in reality, little place and there developed a breed of barristers who considered the 'weaker sex' inferior. Fortunately, I saw many receive their deserved comeuppance. A 40-plus year old high flying barrister with a severe narcissus problem, exacerbated when he became a QC before his 38th birthday, was seen examining the notice board outside the principal court.

'Ah,' he said to his junior. 'I see we are second on – there is an application to be heard before we start'.

A Lawyer for all Seasons

A sweet demur voice from a petite, rather glamorous barrister said, 'Nothing to worry about Mr Barker-Young, I am in it and I assure you it will take less than five minutes'.

Barker-Young, speaking straight through the person who had had the temerity to address him, turned to his junior and snorted pompously, 'I cannot stand those women who say they will only take five minutes and then go on for hours.'

The lady sweetly and quick-wittedly responded, 'And I can't stand those men who say they can go on for hours and are finished in five minutes.'

My chance to serve my own ends came when I was prosecuting John Robertson who was asking for the restoration of his driving license having served two years of a three-year ban. There were compelling reasons advanced for its return not least that he was a window cleaner and without a vehicle had to leave his ladders outside the last house. I, as prosecutor that day, thought it my duty to probe the evidence by adding some searching questions.

'How many houses do you do a day?' I enquired, followed by 'What do you charge?' How long does it take you to do a house?' was my next searching probe, 'And do you work areas of large houses?' The stipendiary magistrate was bored to tears. 'How is this going to help me, Mr Teeman?' he wearily protested. My reply was quick. 'Sir, I really don't know but if you give me another five minutes there is an excellent chance my family will obtain the services of a quality window cleaner at a reasonable price.'

The public perception of the lawyer is mainly acquired by how he is portrayed in the media. Years ago, he or she would be seen as a sober, upright citizen, devoted to clients and their wellbeing. Their word was their bond and actions beyond examination. Honest, of course, respectable certainly and free from vice; a person in whom you could place trust and confidence. Today, in the pecking order, the lawyer has been downgraded and they have a place alongside tradesmen and those of commerce. One reason for the drop in status, in my opinion, is that years ago lawyers remained apart from society's hunger for status and fame. Today they are not only in the race but at the very heart of it.

The courtroom advocate is the glamour side of the profession, their image fashioned by depiction in the press, film or on television. Imagine Charles Laughton, in the Patrick Hastings classic courtroom drama *Witness for the Prosecution* or Michael Dennison, debonair and charming as the barrister in many legal situations written for theatre or screen and the template is set. Even the local solicitor enjoyed celebrity status when newspapers published daily a multitude of local cases.

The creation of the lovable, eccentric, populist Rumpole of the Bailey was welcomed in general by the profession. Rumpole dealt with genuine people in real situations. He had a generous heart and compassion and fought the good fight and stood against the Establishment while remaining in the centre of it. He was a trier, the little man's champion, the fighter for the underdog. He was not just a hero of the working class he went far beyond such distinctions, readers and then viewers could readily identify with him.

Before he achieved enduring fame with Rumpole, the writer John Mortimer had a reputation as a hard working, utterly dependable defence barrister, usually on obscenity cases. His theatrical accomplishments as an author, included the moving play *Dock Brief*. The public are frequently attracted to tales from the law courts and Mortimer was able to capitalise on the perceived glamour of the advocates, a market at one time exploited by Henry Cecil, a former county court judge. Mortimer would not deny that his experiences at the bar, both legal and in the pub, and the retelling of gossip and stories from the circuit gave him much of the material for his tales and his characters. Every solicitor with a criminal practice would have a 'Rumpole' on their own patch, viewed with a combination of pity and admiration for their endurance and fortitude and envied for having been blessed with a thick skin.

I first heard Mortimer at Leeds Crown Court in January 1969 when he was instructed by a colleague to defend a Bradford book seller, Arthur Dobson, who had printed and circulated Walter's *My Secret Life*, first published at the end of the nineteenth century. They contained the sexual diaries of a civil servant whose exciting pastimes encompassed a variety of hideous and, occasionally, grotesque activities with prostitutes and under-age girls. It was never seriously suggested that Dobson's motive in publishing was a desire to educate and illustrate life in the raw in the Victorian age but Mortimer in his defence urged that the book was a work of serious historical interest.

Seeing him on the first day of the trial, his appearance and demeanour did not equate to the impression I had of him. His voice was soft and not commanding and its tone did not vary. He did not follow the tradition of the London silk when making a rare appearance in the provinces which normally centred on exhibiting both elegance and arrogance. His gown appeared well worn, covering a morning suit, the front of which looked distinctly untidy and his wig was slightly askew and yellow. He came with a reputation not only as a confirmed and persistent objector to all the laws of obscenity but much more glamorously in being a 'man about town', friendly with a variety of famous ladies of the stage and screen while having a well known theatrical wife at home.

After the formal business had been swiftly dealt with,

Mortimer made his first application. He said the jury should read the book in its entirety. He submitted that it was totally unsatisfactory for them to be told of assorted passages in the book which the prosecution considered to be obscene and in breach of the Act. He argued that if he was to succeed in his submission that it was both a work of literary merit and historical interest he would be deprived of the argument's main thrust if extracts were taken out of context. It was an argument that on the face of it had considerable attraction and merit and so the judge, Mr Justice Veale - who had been a member of Leeds chambers until his elevation to the bench – found in his favour, although not to his liking.

The judge, in allowing the jury to receive the full version of the book, ruled that they should read it not in their own time but in the jury room and that he required some guidance from counsel as to the length of time that would be required. Mortimer's protest was fierce, arguing that a person would not normally read a book in a room with eleven others and that no-one could read a book if a time limit was imposed on them.

'It was not satisfactory,' he argued. 'Every person had a different reading speed and different concentration and comprehension levels, nor would they achieve the experience that a member of the public would by reading the book privately.' He posed the question, 'How does the average person read a book generally?' proffering the view it was, 'In the tranquillity and privacy of their own home.' The judge accepted the proposition and ordered a week's adjournment for the members of the jury to take the book home and he advised them that they should discuss it with no-one else.

I guess that the prosecution counsel would have been wounded by the adjournment, for it was doubtful that they would be able to get any gainful work for that week, one of the perils of legal practice. A week later, I was in the corridor outside court number two at Leeds Town Hall and saw the jury assembling ready to make their entry, book in hand and coats folded. I heard a middle-aged Yorkshireman smile at his colleague of a similar age and say, 'Well, what you think of it?' There was a pause as his fellow juryman listened, allowing the question to sink in. 'What do I think? What do I think?' he repeated. 'I'll tell thee this, I wouldn't let my fucking dog piss or shit on it.' It looked like being a difficult case for Mortimer.

I was not in court throughout the entire time, but at irregular intervals. Mortimer called many witnesses, all experts with an axe to grind or a jaundiced view of the law. One was the celebrated Montgomery Hyde, who wrote a fascinating account of the life of Oscar Wilde, and another Steve Marcus. One witness described himself as a lecturer in prudery and I must confess I'd not heard of the subject area previously, nor which University had a 'prudery faculty'. There was one witness, who after giving his name and address, was asked for his qualifications. He said firmly that he was 'auto-didactic' and then proceeded to give a long lecture. While I was in court, no-one, not even the judge, challenged him but his description of his abilities was most seductive, if not informative. It was a posh way of saying self-taught but what the jury made of him I know not. There were long discussions over the meaning of the word fuck, its origin and the date when it was first used. The jury bought in a verdict of guilty and the sentence was two years in prison plus a fine and an order to pay costs.

I read and re-read many of Mortimer's works and, if I was unable to see an episode of *Rumpole*, I would record it for later consumption. I recognised quite a few old chestnuts that were taken from the archives before being recounted by a master story teller. In 2002, the premier of Mortimer's play

Naked Justice was performed at the Playhouse in Leeds before its transfer to the West End. Its star was Leslie Philips, the suave comedy actor of Mortimer's vintage. Mortimer came to Leeds and agreed to give a talk to his interested public on the stage a couple of hours before the performance. He was interviewed by Jude Kelly, the director of the Playhouse. It was sad to see a man in physical decline but, nonetheless, pleasing to hear him at his acerbic best.

After his dissertation, he retired to the theatre bar and the old Mortimer sparkled, supported by two young ladies. I approached him and asked if he remembered Leeds Assizes and Walter's *My Secret Life*. 'I certainly do', he said with a chuckle. 'Were you there?' I related the tale of the juryman's succinct views on the book before hearing the case.

'Ah yes,' Mortimer mused. 'I did not know that but typical of how the man in the street reacts to obscenity. When wishing to give an adequate reflection of his own views, he himself resorts to obscenities when ordinary language could not portray his feelings.' He continued, 'The judge was hopeless and never gave the defence a chance or listened to the witnesses I called.' I asked him how many auto-didactic witnesses he called and with a smile he answered, 'Quite a lot.'

The play received a courteous welcome in Leeds but most of the audience thought that it lacked bite, sparkle and credibility. Mortimer, I think, was not satisfied himself and rewrote the play. It then re-opened in Birmingham but never made the West End. The varied works of Mortimer and his serious contribution to the arts were recognised belatedly by a knighthood on his 75th birthday and he died a few years later. He left us Rumpole and much laughter at the expense of his profession.

A Lawyer for all Seasons

His Honour Judge Dermot Oswald McKee, a former member of the Bar with chambers in Park Square, Leeds, was appointed a county court judge in the early fifties.

Highly popular, he was a clubable man and it was a shame that my first ever rebuke by the judiciary should come from him. The cause of the anger was a divorce petition that I had personally drafted. More often than not my colleagues would go to counsel to undertake the task and they would charge £2.4/6 for adultery, and £3.5/6 for cruelty. I thought that as the petitioner had to pay and because many of my clients had limited resources, it was just as easy for me to do the drafting and save them a bob or two. I seldom had any problems. When a barrister drafted a petition and it was typed, his name as the author would be added at the end of it but not so a solicitor who would merely sign. My typist, for reasons best known to herself, adopted a practice of typing my moniker.

For several years I had no problems until one day 'DOM', as he was affectionately known, looked at it disapprovingly. Quivering with rage he shouted, 'Who does he think it is – this is ridiculous – I want this man to come before me and explain his conduct.' My articled clerk, Peter Fingret returned to the office hot foot and perspiring, as he always did when we had a problem, and reported that I had been ordered to appear at court the following Monday. I duly attended wearing best suit and looking suitably humble, forlorn and chastened. I said I regretted what I had done, that it would not be repeated and asked for my sincere apology to be accepted. He looked me up and down and said 'Well, you can go now – I am sure you won't do it again.'

Within a day or so there was a message from the divorce court asking me to return the following Monday as his Lordship wanted to see me again. I spent an uneasy weekend and turned up apprehensively at the appointed time. This time he seemed to be in a more jovial mood. 'I myself behaved badly last week, Mr Teeman,' he said. 'Since then I have looked at the regulations and there is nothing at all to prevent a solicitor having his name typed on a petition – it is just a convention of the Bar. I do apologise most profusely for the embarrassment I caused you and the criticism I made of you in public and I trust that you will accept this apology in the spirit it was given.' I bowed and said 'I did.' Just as I was turning my back to leave the witness box he enquired, 'Before you go, just wait one moment. As you were in the right, please tell me why on earth did you apologise?' I looked up from the well of the court and said meekly, 'My Lord, I am a coward.'

I do recall one lady magistrate remonstrating with me for apparently sleeping while my opponent was addressing them. I had to concede that my eyes were closed and explained, as patiently as I could, that I was only resting them and certainly no discourtesy was intended to the court or to my opponent. Indeed I recited to her the last three submissions he had made during the time I was alleged to have been sleeping. I was able to do that because my opponent invariably made the same submissions each time he addressed a Bench.

My most important and celebrated argument attracted not only the attention of the local press but all the national newspapers including *The Times* and *The Guardian* who each devoted an editorial to it and its significance. It all started with misbehaviour in a working class area inhabited by a large number of recently arrived Asians. Leeds is a city with a history of tolerance towards immigration, whether from the Russian pogroms of the nineteenth century or the Nazi persecution which started in the 1930s. Post-war immigration from the West Indies and the Indian sub-continent followed.

The latter groups were not victims of oppression but had arrived in the UK seeking better conditions for their families and to enjoy an enriched life. It would be erroneous to pretend that there were not pockets of distrust of the new immigrants and some resentment of their presence.

Similarly, many new arrivals without much education, believed that the only jobs made available to them were those that the local population considered 'dirty'. In the summer of 1969 – and it is remarkable how tensions increase when the weather is hot - arising out of incidents on the 27th and 28th of July, three youths were arrested and charged with using threatening behaviour where a breach of the peace might be caused, under the Race Relations Act and the Public Order Act. It was suggested that the charge arose, 'out of racial disturbances'. Solicitor Michael Lawrence representing 17 of the accused told the magistrate that the apparent 'boiling cauldron' mentioned at an earlier hearing was a figment of someone's imagination. I was appearing for a further three of the men charged – all living in the Burley Road district. One of them was a well-known amateur rugby league player and I made an application for bail for two of the men which was not opposed by the police.

The other application was strenuously resisted. On the Bench was Mr Gilbert Parr, a regular court chairman and one of the most experienced magistrates in the city. Sitting with him was Mrs Diane Phillips who originated from the West Indies and was the city's first and only coloured magistrate. I gave, cogently I thought, the reason why 19-year old Terence Drury should be admitted to bail and the Magistrates retired for ten minutes or so to consider. On returning, Mr Parr announced that he was granting bail for my client and said that he had excluded Mrs Phillips from his decision for, 'obvious reasons.' I left the courtroom utterly astonished. Composing myself I returned to court and waited for Mr Parr to conclude the case before him and said to him, 'When you said that you had excused Mrs Phillips from your deliberation I was lost for words. I would like to say, Sir, that on mature reflection it does not invalidate the decision you made, but it would be wrong in future to exclude a magistrate for this particular reason.'

I was more concerned in case anyone might have thought that I, as a defence advocate, might have asked that a coloured magistrate should be excluded from the judgement in a case which involved a conflict between different racial groups. I told the court that, 'We as lawyers practicing in these courts and you as magistrates, both approach our duties with the same objective task'. I continued that I had had the pleasure of appearing before a Bench on which Mrs Phillips had sat and that I was confident that, 'She would approach her duties in the same way as you and your other colleagues.'

Mr Parr, a postmaster by trade in west Leeds and a considerate man, confirmed my view and then rather put his foot in it by saying that it was his thought that, 'It would be in your favour Mr Teeman, for it could be thought to stand against you if Mrs Phillips gave any decision in this particular matter'. I repeated that, 'I should make it clear that any decision Mrs Phillips makes in any case would be free from prejudice and we as advocates would not ever give a thought to her being prejudiced'. While this debate was going on, Mrs Phillips and the other male on the Bench said nothing.

The editorial in *The Guardian* was to the point and the writer's case that her possible exclusion was prejudice was indisputable. But Mrs Phillips was placed in an unfortunate position and I speculated how others with limited legal experience would have stood up for her right to participate.

Some weeks later I was given a sharp reminder of the

magistrate's concern to be seen as being both unbiased and fair. Gordon Newman, a senior court clerk, was in attendance when I was commencing the defence of an employee stealing some perfumes and toiletries, the employer being a part of Great Universal Stores, probably at that time the country's leading retail merchandiser. The magistrate and Gordon Newman whispered together and eventually Newman then addressed me and my client. 'The chairman wanted you to know, Mr Teeman, that he has a shareholding in the company who owned the goods alleged to be stolen. What do you think he should do?' He faced me as he spoke but his look gave his own views away thinking that it was an irrelevance. I had no hesitation in replying that, 'The magistrate should sell his shareholding – the market is in a bear situation at the moment.' The chairman's two colleagues were seen with their hands in front of their faces.

A good advocate makes it absolutely clear that his mitigations are not aggravations and I have a similar view towards correspondence. A letter can add fuel to the fire rather than be placatory or consoling and I am firmly of the view that many are written in the heat and anger of the moment and the author, if he or she had undertaken a period of reflection, would have produced a more mature and responsible reply. A very newly qualified solicitor wrote a letter to the president of the Leeds Law Society criticising my behaviour towards him which, in his view, was not justified. I read the letter which was well composed and set out the facts upon which he founded his complaint with clarity and accuracy and in no way could I demur from it. There are many occasions where it is better to confess and avoid rather than have direct confrontation and this was one of those cases.

The facts were simple, I had been away from the magistrates courts for two or three years devoting myself to the creation of what became a successful commercial practice, but was passing the building which contained the court on my way to a commercial bank. Old habits die hard and I headed for the crypt in the town hall where solicitors gathered for coffee and chats. The building was empty apart from two lawyers who I did not know. I asked where everyone was and one pointed to a part of the room that was curtained off where there was a sign that read 'advice room'. It was known to us as 'the tent' and the local law society had a rota of solicitors who would dispense advice freely to members of the public.

I popped my head in and came across a young man who I had never seen before and I was about to make my exit when he promptly said, 'Come in and sit down - can I help you?' Devilment took over and I said, 'Yes you can. I am alleged to be a fraudster and I expect to be charged any day and it could be one of the longest trials ever in the city. I am absolutely penniless and I would need legal aid as well as a very good brief.' As I was talking, I realised I had a very receptive audience and he eagerly responded, 'Well you've come to the right person, it's just my cup of tea.' I immediately countered, 'It's certainly my lucky day meeting you'.

There then followed a catalogue of advice including the do's and don'ts at police interviews, some of which was correct, other parts doubtful. It dawned on me that this young man thought I was not only the dish of the day but someone who was going to adorn his own table with rich pickings. I decided to beat a hasty retreat, made my excuses and left. I was about to exit the building at street level when I was button-holed by a senior court clerk who had been a very good friend of mine. We exchanged pleasantries and some gossip and the young man from the tent then walked past and did a double take, turned round looked at me and said, 'You've just been talking to me haven't you?' I couldn't deny it and was about to give him an explanation when he shouted, 'You'll hear more of this' and disappeared.

The letter of admonition came from Shirley Schofield, the first lady president of the Leeds Law Society and a charming sound lawyer as well, of my own vintage. She asked for an explanation and I wrote as follows:

Dear Miss Schofield,

Thank you for your letter.

The facts outlined in the complaint are totally correct. I entered the tent to see whether it was staffed by any of my contemporaries and found your correspondent who was unknown to me. Let me say, I was one of the founders and authors of the Legal Advice scheme in the magistrates court and it was supported by all the major firms with criminal law practices.

The purpose of the scheme was that experienced practitioners would, on a rota basis, staff the centre and give advice and, if required, represent the visitor. Firstly, I was concerned to see a very youthful solicitor who, secondly, claimed to be able to advise on one of the most complex areas of criminal law, commercial fraud. That would be beyond the capabilities – by sheer scale of operation - of the majority of practices in the city.

My visit, unannounced and spontaneous was justified. I would urge that the Society takes steps to redress the position and ensure that the function of the advice centre is correctly addressed to serve the public's need for which it was designed.

Yours sincerely

Apart from an acknowledgement and a friendly word from Shirley on the phone saying, 'I take the point' I heard nothing else, but I learned that thereafter the tent was occupied by experienced practitioners with a trainee or a young solicitor looking on to gain experience.

Hardly a day passes by now without a solicitor receiving a letter asking if he has a vacancy for a youngster who wants work experience. In the current economic climate it is almost impossible to satisfy the requests and, if one does find a place for a student on a very nominal expenses-only basis, the schools put you through the hoop. They want to know about your facilities, the programme available, the supervision, the health and safety arrangements and so it goes on. When you are trying to be helpful, this looking over your shoulder mentality is self defeating.

My first work as an unpaid articled clerk - whose father had paid a £350 premium to a Leeds solicitor, in the days when a teacher only earned £225 a year – I found horrific. My initial job was to hand-deliver at least 50 letters to solicitors, accountants and barristers in the city. I then had to place labels on envelopes that had been opened so that they could be re-used. No paper was thrown out that could be re-used and the headed notepaper was only given in small quantities to the secretaries as and when requested. My third task was to enter neatly in a book the names and addresses of those outside Leeds who had letters posted to them, together with the amount of the stamp. After that it was to go to the post office with the mail that had to be sent by registered delivery. Finally, I had to return to the front step all the empty milk bottles having first washed them thoroughly with warm water.

'Was this what the Law was about?' I mused as I made my way home on the tram following several days of such monotony. After about a month I plucked up courage and addressed my employer in halting tones. 'Sir, I am not going to learn much law with this programme,' I said. 'Teeman' he replied, 'Do not be impatient. How will you ever know where all the professional offices are in this place if you do not deliver to them?' Things would improve he told me. He did show a little more interest and invited me to travel with him to out of town courts. This I discovered, however, was not for the purpose of me gaining experience in the courtroom but because he had such bad eyesight. I was like a guide dog, telling him when to turn and when to stop.

I did, however, learn to appreciate the value of a sheet of solicitor's notepaper because of an incident that happened to a friend of mine. He was young, recently married and received a letter with a London post mark. When he opened it there was a missive from a well known firm of city solicitors which read:

> Dear Sir,
> Our client, Sarah Jones, gave birth to a female child on the 27th June this year. She instructs us that you are the father of the child.
>
> Would you please let us have your proposals to the maintenance of the child within seven days of this letter and so avoiding the necessity of proceedings being commenced in the magistrates' court against you.
>
> Yours faithfully

His hand was shaking as he passed the letter to his wife. She cried, 'Oh, how could you do this?' and the greater he protested the more distressed she became. His protests were to no avail. Finally she told him that he had better seek legal advice from her father who was a very senior court officer. When the father read the letter and heard his son-in-law's protests, he brushed them aside saying, 'These London solicitors don't make mistakes.' He did add, though, that he would pass it to his own solicitors for them to reply. That was the office of my employer, who replied:

> Dear Sirs,
> Your letter of the 6th instant written on behalf of Sarah Jones to our client Mr .... has been passed to us with instructions to act.
>   Our client denies he is the father of the child and any proceedings instituted by your client will be strenuously defended.
> Yours faithfully

The response from the capital came a few days later.

> Dear Sir,
> We have your letter of the 20th instant. Could you please quote our reference so that we can pass the letter to the person who has the conduct of the file.
> Yours faithfully

Matters were solved when the alleged father received a visit from his 'best man', who worked in London. His first greeting was, 'Hey mate, what did you think of my letter?' and all was then revealed. The 'best man, had apparently found a sheet of the London solicitor's notepaper in a book he had borrowed from a library and hatched the ill-conceived plan. The culprit then came to our office to own up and was instructed by my superior to immediately pen a humble apology and to undertake not to do anything similar again, which he did. By return of post he received a letter from the London solicitors:

> Dear Mr....
> We have your letter of apology. Your actions caused this office unnecessary time to be expended. Accordingly we

enclose our bill for 5 pound 5 shillings for our aborted services.

Yours faithfully

A poorer but wiser man returned to London.

I had few articled clerks in my career but I did give work experience to two sixth formers, both of whom chose the law as a career but not with me- a sad reflection, I feel sure, of the experience I gave them.

The tale of Anthony John Sugare is a cautionary one. He was in the upper reaches of Leeds Grammar School when his mother persuaded me (perhaps pressurised might be a more accurate expression) to give him a holiday job. He was a lanky lad with a mop of unruly red hair which he was constantly brushing out of his eyes. If I had needed to file a report card at the end of his experience it would have said, 'enthusiastic, energetic and enterprising.'

We decided to give him a testing time. After lunch he was asked to go to the post office to purchase four verbal agreement stamps, each of two shillings six pence denomination. When he had not returned within two hours we became anxious. My secretary said, 'Perhaps he has found out that he has been duped and thrown himself in the river.' I retorted, 'Don't be so dramatic, he's hardly likely to do that without returning the one pound we gave him for the stamps.'

Just before 5pm a breathless Anthony arrived back and said, 'Sorry about that but I have been to four post offices and not one of them had any of these stamps in stock.' Seeing the obvious look of discomfort on my face he added, 'Don't worry Mr Teeman, I have been to the central post office and spoken to the boss there and he's going to phone you.' Those words had hardly left his lips when the telephone rang. It was the head postmaster himself. After a few pleasantries he said, 'I'll be frank, Mr Teeman. Since I have been in Leeds I have not seen any verbal agreement stamps but I have spoken to my colleague in Manchester who usually has quite a few in stock and he will send them over by courier in the morning.' I told him I was most grateful for his assistance.

Turning back to Anthony I told him, 'You've done a good job. Collect the stamps tomorrow and stick them on the verbal agreement.' It was when I asked him to 'stick them' and the girls in the office laughed that he released he had been fooled by us and he had in turn duped someone else. He dashed out of the office and he never came back.

It did not surprise anyone that he later became a most resourceful solicitor with a quiet but effective gift of persuasion in the magistrates court and recently completed 40 years service there. But you can still see him bristle when anyone talks about entering into a verbal agreement.

5

*

The Art of Advocacy

A good advocate possesses skills which are honed over the years and witnesses, even if telling the absolute truth, can be easily at a disadvantage when challenged by a skilful exponent.

In 1947, when I was a 17-year-old having entered into articles, I was fortunate that my principal was a fine exponent with a quiet yet forceful manner and whenever he was in the magistrates court I went with him. I was a keen onlooker as well as an enthusiastic questioner. What was noticeable was that the regular court protagonists were confident, composed and carefree. They stood up, spoke up and shut up, wasted little time and were careful to be both precise and concise because time cost money.

An incentive to acting in the magistrates court was the free publicity in the local evening papers – the *Evening Post*, *Evening News* and *Telegraph and Argus*. Advocates quickly learned to use fulsome expressions and headline grabbing language and needed the ability to think on their feet. The lawyer of today does not know how fortunate he or she is. The defendant has a right to bail and the burden moves over to the prosecution to prove a remand in custody is necessary. Advance disclosure of the prosecution case is served on the defence and statements of prosecution witnesses similarly handed over. A defence lawyer can take full instructions from the accused, plan tactics and prepare the case at leisure. The element of surprise has gone.

The Crown Prosecution Service is now independent of the police and has the responsibility for bringing wrongdoers before the court and prosecuting them and they only deal in near certainties. But is the plea bargaining in the interest of justice or the public? Recently, a very good looking hairdresser went out on the town on a Saturday night, drank far too much and was staggering about. Told by the constabulary to stop shouting abuse, it had no affect and indeed her language worsened. She was arrested and fought like a tigress with the officer concerned. Taken to the cells she was charged with being drunk and disorderly and bailed several hours later when she had sobered up.

She consulted me and I accompanied her to court. We were handed the statements of three witnesses which she quickly read through, dismissed and said she was pleading not guilty. The court clerk asked if we could fix a trial date. I said I would require all the prosecution witnesses and I would be calling the defendant and perhaps one other witness and that the estimated trial would take at least one and a half days. The prosecuting solicitor immediately offered that he would withdraw the charge if she agreed to be bound over to keep the peace, which is not a conviction. My client agreed and she walked out of court with no costs to pay and no criminal record. It is no wonder we are developing a generation of courtroom lawyers who do mitigations and tick boxes.

In the sixties, recently qualified solicitors were put on the right path by the stipendiary magistrate, Ralph Cleworth QC. He loved the law and those who practiced it and anyone who was about to embark upon a legal career received his enthusiastic encouragement. He always attended the annual dinner of the Leeds Law Students Society. They were his blood brothers, he was never condescending and always made himself available for a quiet word. Patience personified, the local solicitors spoke in hallowed tones of him. When he retired, at his own expense, he threw two large parties one for the court administrators and the prosecution and the other for the defence lawyers.

One occasion when I was in Mr Cleworth's debt was when I appeared for George Tootle. Everyone south of the river Aire knew George, who was then old and blind. In his younger days he had been a prominent rugby league player with Hunslet and a professional boxer in the light-heavyweight division. It was clear that in both careers he had taken far more punishment than was good for him and life thereafter had not given him many happy moments. He was in court because of his dog, a black mongrel. Clearly this animal had not come to him as a gift from 'Guide Dogs for the Blind' but had been trained by him. The two were inseparable and as George and pet stumbled along the road, locals would pause for a chat. Sadly the dog took a bite of flesh from a passerby's leg who complained to the police and an application for the dog to be destroyed was made to the court.

George was inconsolable and a compassionate court clerk asked me if I would appear for him under the OPA – the 'old pals act'. I agreed and saw George and prepared my mitigation. George and the dog stood forlornly in the well of the court as I addressed Mr Cleworth. I cannot recall what I said but I conveyed to him that the dog was not dangerous and, extending my hand, claimed that it was quite docile. Without warning he lunged forward and took as a prize my first finger of my left hand in his mouth. Blood flowed and Mr Cleworth came down from the bench and extended his hand to the mongrel who wrapped his tongue around it. 'See Teeman,' he said 'it was the sudden movement of your hand that caused the dog to bite.' George and the dog happily left the court together and the press had a field day at my expense. I mentioned the episode to a local hack who retorted that it would have been a much better story if you had bitten the damn dog.

In my early days in practice, Saturday mornings were important and vital to the finances. It was a time when members of the public were able, without breaking time at work, to consult their solicitors. A pot pourri of matters were discussed in the office, it was not exactly a confessional but the opportunity to get things off their chest was afforded to potential or actual clients. Communities lived in one another's pockets then. Back-to-back terraced house occupants shared not only the party walls but the facilities; the outside toilet, the refuse area and the backstreet clothes line. Children played in the streets, balls were kicked, stones thrown, windows broken and other damage inflicted. So many causes for friction were compressed in a small area. I smile today when I hear the nostalgic recollection of elderly folk about those wonderful days gone by, when there was togetherness and spirit in the community and neighbourliness - if not related to cleanliness - was very close to godliness. Absolute nonsense. Turn the clocks back and come to my office on any Saturday morning and there could be seen startling evidence of anger, intolerance and wilful cussedness being displayed.

My fees and those of the average working solicitor in the same milieu were simple, cash in hand - half a guinea for advice and one guinea for advice plus a letter. The weekly take averaged six pounds and six shillings at least and, in those days, a dinner for two at a good restaurant was two pounds and seats at the Grand Theatre for a couple about a pound, so there was a temptation not to trouble the cashier with making an entry in the cash book; the consequential trousering of the money possibly being explained because the cashier did not work on Saturday. But on Monday morning she would confront you and demand an account for Saturday morning's enterprise as, invariably, there were no files kept.

One of the more bizarre complaints I heard was the claim that during the night raised voices coming from the upper floors caused a lady to conceive. Her explanation was that by being awoken by a noisy neighbour in the early hours, 'It was too late to get back to sleep and too early to get up' leading to an unplanned and totally unexpected pregnancy. The subject matters were inexhaustible but, above all, it was the failure to live and let live. Nevertheless, a solicitor's letter sent to the miscreant would end the dispute such was the confidence the public invested in their lawyers.

Sixty years on, that line of business has ended. Ineffective ASBO's have taken their place and society has been so fragmented that, more often than not, everyone including those in authority turn a deaf ear to complaints. The art of letter writing by solicitors seems to have been lost with good, persuasive and eloquent prose being replaced by staccato peremptory statements.

I divided solicitor's letters into categories; abrasive, aggressive, contumacious and caustic, though often unnecessarily verbose in an attempt to be persuasive. They were written from the heart not the head and one word of advice I gave to trainees was, after you've read your letter wait three hours before allowing it to go out of the office either by fax or in the post. That cooling off period permits essential changes to be made.

There were solicitors who would set your teeth on edge, others who would give you an excuse for kicking down your own door and some that provoked you into thoughts of physical retaliation. A sense of humour was a vital piece of armoury. Victor Zermansky, who was excitable but mainly exercised self control, would reduce his response to one word if he had not heard from his opponent in answer to a reasonable submission he had made in correspondence. He would write:

Dear Sir - Well?

Michael Lawrence, who was acidic until you knew him better, and could then be described as bittersweet would detail, with no punches held back, your errors and those of your clients in the most colourful language.

I treasure, above all the letters, the one sent out by a trainee.

Dear Mr. Thompson,
Mr Teeman will be on vacation during the first two weeks of August. Should you want to see us please contact Mr Jones who has the file and who will be pleased to see you in his loo.

I told her perhaps it would have been better to have said, 'at his convenience.'

There are occasions when the mouth of the advocate moves quicker than his brain and sadly this often occurs when the press benches are filled and the scribblers have their pencils sharpened at the ready. Sir Donald Kaberry BT was the serving Member of Parliament for North West Leeds and a previous chairman of the Conservative Party. For years he had been lampooned by satirists as 'the silent Knight' by way of holding a Parliamentary record for the length of time he did not speak in the House of Commons. He did, however, serve as a most diligent and attentive constituency representative. For a few years I sat alongside him on the board of governors of Leeds Grammar School and he was a man who did not waste words.

Donald entered Parliament on the same day as Prime Minister Edward Heath and many years later Mr Heath held a drinks party for all those who shared that anniversary with him. Kaberry was a guest and I suspect he found the party convivial and the host's generosity appealing and the hospitality irresistible. On his return journey he was stopped by the police, breathalysed, gave a sample of blood and was later charged with driving over the prescribed limit. Donald instructed David Napley, who sat on the Law Society Council with him, to represent him hoping for a low key trial. Napley, though, was a superb publicist and, in his only appearance in Leeds, deliberately parked his Rolls Royce in the front of the town hall so that it would come to no harm and at the same time attract the maximum amount of attention. Not surprisingly, the press swarmed to the court and Donald made headline news about being fortunate to escape prison. I did feel so sorry for him and his family and dropped him a line at once. It said:

Dear Sir Donald,
So sorry; I would like you to know, I don't think any worse of you today than I did yesterday.

Yours Sincerely,
Ronald Teeman

The reply promptly delivered was delicious.

Dear Ronald,
When I was awarded my Baronetcy, there were two vans
from the Royal Mail delivering congratulatory messages.
When my trouble in London was announced there were
two letters - one from you and the other from the vicar of
Leeds!

Kindest Regards,
Donald

The request, 'Can you keep it out of the papers', so often
asked by defendants of advocates was usually in vain. The
press has a vital role to play in the administration of justice
and a plea not to publish is generally doomed to failure.

6

*

International Notoriety

My horizons as a provincial city lawyer were somewhat, and rather spectacularly, widened in February 1959.

I had a small – one man, one girl – practice in the centre of Leeds, growing but causing no financial concern to the remainder of the city's legal profession as I dealt with the lower end of the trade. Petty crime, matrimonial disputes and affiliation cases - bastardies to give them the colloquial and more meaningful description - involving proceedings in the magistrates court to obtain maintenance from the father of the child. My income was augmented by a stipend from the faculty of law at the University of Leeds for lecturing on two half-day sessions a week as a consequence of my master's degree, which included a dissertation on the laws relating to gaming and wagering. I was the only 'staff member' with practical legal experience, which meant that if any current contemporary legal problems were addressed to the professor, he would field them but then pass then onto me. That, briefly, is the background as to how I became to be involved in the attempted assassination of President Nkrumah of Ghana.

The colonisation of Africa was coming to an end with a desire by politicians in the United Kingdom, allied to growing expressions for freedom from within, to grant independence. Ghana, formerly known as the Gold Coast, was one of the first. It gained independence in 1956 and their first head of state was Dr. Kwame Nkrumah. As the colonial administration came from here, an independent civil service had to be created almost overnight to serve the new regime. One of the key appointments was an attorney general, someone who could create, contain and administer a judicial system. The President's choice was Geoffrey Bing QC, a former Labour Member of Parliament but with no departmental experience in Westminster. Bing was a well-known left winger and his appointment gave him status that he did not have or was likely to achieve in this country.

Bing was not the only appointment from England for the new regime also had to quickly establish the equivalent of a Scotland Yard and MI5. They recruited from within the English police force for their senior ranks, welcoming on board with substantial financial packages those who were coming to the end of their careers. One of them was Superintendent Wells, who worked closely with Geoffrey Bing.

Leeds University had welcomed African students for very many years on numerous courses and, in 1959, the law department had one, Ken Osei-Bonsu. I later discovered he was a student of above average ability and who had settled into English life to the manor born. Early afternoon on 6th February, Professor Philip James phoned me. He had only been the head of the department for a few years having arrived from Exeter College, Oxford, which must have been something of a culture shock. James was a brilliant delegator and quite an artist in that art.

He told me of a situation that had arisen within the last 24 hours relating to Osei-Bonsu. According to James, there had been some trouble in Accra and the President of Ghana had uncovered a plot to assassinate him which involved Osei-Bonsu at Leeds University. The Ghanain police were on their way over here to see him he told me. He thought that we should, 'Keep a fatherly eye on him and have regard to his interests and wellbeing.'

'Would you see to it, Teeman?' he asked. I naturally accepted and agreed to see the student that day. Osei-Bonsu was a pleasant, well spoken young man in his early twenties. He was obviously worried by his predicament but told me a remarkable story. He was a member of a well-known family in Accra that had been politically active and it was fair to say were opponents of the Nkrumah regime. A plot had been discovered and the country alerted. For Nkrumah to re-establish his authority he had not only to deliver up those responsible but to put them behind bars so they could not cause further trouble to his regime. It would also be a disincentive to others.

I asked him how he was directly involved or implicated. 'Well,' he told me, 'a bank account had been discovered in London in my name with a large amount of money in it and out of it army uniforms were to be purchased'. I pressured him on this and enquired as to whether he had moved money to make any purchases or bought anything that could be possibly be used in a revolution or coup and he replied, 'Certainly not'. He told me that his uncle, Mr R.R. Amponsah was a leading member of the United Party, strong opponents of the Nkrumah regime. Together with a captain in the army, they had planned the coup and it was Amponsah who was trying to use the Osei-Bonsu account in England for the purchase of military apparel. He admitted to being worried, not only for himself but his family at home. What he wanted from me was to watch out for his interests and look after him at any forthcoming police interview. He said that a he had been told by the Leeds police alien's office that a high ranking officer had left Ghana to interview him. In simple terms all aliens, deemed as being citizens of foreign countries, had to register with the police in the location they intended to reside. They could not change their address without notifying the force first and had to report regularly to the alien's office during their stay. In Leeds at the time, the staff there comprised only of Sergeant Ben Wright plus one constable.

I phoned the immigration department they were a part of and spoke to Wright, who arranged to call and see me the following day. Osei-Bonsu was also present in my office. He was still very nervous but relaxed when I explained to him in simple terms what his rights were in this country. When Wright arrived he was accompanied by a burly man with a southern accent who was introduced to me as Mr Wells. His manner and tone was instantly aggressive. He explained that his brief was to fully investigate the plot and that he was mandated by the attorney general there to take Osei-Bonsu back to Ghana for further interviewing. I told Wells that he could forget about that. 'Osei-Bonsu is staying here and he will remain here and if the Ghanain government want to extradite him, they will have to go through established legal procedures' I said.

Wells seemed surprised at this outburst replying, 'I am acting on the specific orders of Geoffrey Bing. Scotland Yard are aware of my visit and its purpose and I have arranged for the assistance of Leeds city police.' He repeated what Osei-Bonsu had earlier told me but added that the uncle was now detained and that he had conclusive evidence that in June the previous year money had been withdrawn from the

Osei-Bonsu overseas study account in London by his relative. The meeting then became heated as my hackles had been raised by the inferences Wells made that he had English law on his side. I listened to outbursts and responded, 'I am telling you firmly and politely that Osei-Bonsu is firstly under no obligation to answer any of your questions and certainly has no requirement to return to his home with you or without you.'

Sergeant Wright at that stage intervened. 'Mr Teeman, I want to make it clear that the Leeds police role is purely out of courtesy to a visiting police and we are playing no part in these matters.' Wells said he would speak on the phone to Bing immediately and I allowed him to use mine. After a brief conversation, presumably with Bing, Wells said, 'I have to tell Osei-Bonsu that if he does not return voluntarily at once it will make things worse for his uncle.' I countered, 'Mr Wells, please do not threaten. This interview is at an end.' The two officers then left.

Osei-Bonsu was dreadfully upset and told me that he did not think that the Ghanain government would let things stand as they were and that other attempts would be made to get him back to Accra. I asked him, 'Ken, are you fearing force?' He nodded. I told him, 'Well the position is clear. We'll go to your flat and collect your belongings and you will stay at my house until things quieten down.' That is exactly what happened. We have a large modern house in a residential area in north Leeds which had an entire second floor that ran along the whole roof span. That became his hiding place for the next fortnight, after which he decided that it was safe to return to his student home. I heard later from Sergeant Wright that Wells had made his way back to Accra. I had the distinct impression he was not missing him.

Osei-Bonsu and his fiancé Justina, who was training to be a nurse in England, arranged for their wedding to take place at a Leeds city centre Methodist Chapel, with a lunch to follow at the Guildford Hotel. My wife and I were invited. I hired a morning suit and all the guests were similarly attired. The hotel management did not seem to be too happy when the large party of well dressed young black people assembled. I subsequently discovered that the bride and groom had arranged the affair via white friends for they believed that the hotel might not take a booking for a black party. It was obviously a shock to their system when over 100 black folk, the men wearing morning dress and the ladies attired in the most colourful and exotic African costumes dropped in on them that Saturday morning.

Osei-Bonsu was in the second of a three-year degree course when he was subjected to this ordeal and returned to Ghana in 1962, after being called to the Bar in London. He later wrote to me from Ghana:

'I cannot but recall your immense help to me during my second year at Leeds, when Superintendent Wells of Ghana Special Branch sought to bring me to Ghana with the help of Scotland Yard. But for your intervention I surely would not have been allowed to return to Leeds to complete my degree. Those were the days when the new Ghana government was jittery about the slightest rumour and saw evil in every little creature that squeaked. I am forever grateful to you.'

I tried to follow his fortunes thereafter. He became a minister in the military government after Nkrumah was overthrown in 1966, but resigned after a protest over control of the press which was under his brief. After a short interval he returned to politics in a civilian government as Minister of National Security. That government was overturned in 1972 and he was imprisoned for a year. Upon his release and his return to civilian life, he enjoyed a career in the private sector and served as chairman of Ghana Commercial Bank from 2001 to 2008.

Kwame Nkrumah's career was analysed, reviewed and reinterpreted in 2009, to commemorate the centenary of his birth. He was a visionary leader with a cruel streak and an obsession to rule a 'United Africa'. He imposed one party dictatorship on his countrymen and jailed his opponents although he never enriched himself and he died in penury. To his credit he did lead the country out of colonialism but several of his critics later questioned if Ghana had been wealthier prior to independence. Whenever I read of Ghana politically, economically or as a football nation, I think of my small service to Osei-Bonsu and reflect on the actions of dictators and the mercenaries who served them.

Nigeria is another oft-ignored, seemingly distant nation with a fractured past. In 1969/70 there was a raging civil war between the Ibos and the Biafirans. The country was torn apart and in January 1970 General Jack Gowon, the victorious leader of Nigeria – from the Ibos Tribe – promised help to the vanquished Biafirans, thousands of whom faced death from starvation.

The World's Relief Organisation was outraged at Gowon's apparent refusal to accept foreign aid and wanted to go it alone despite loud protests from the British Foreign Office. WRO had before it the unpalatable accusations of genocide. I got involved through acting for Edith Ike, a Nigerian student resident in Leeds taking a BSc Degree in Information Science. Edith was a Biafiran and the fiancée of Jack Gowon, although their engagement had broken up. She had a child who lived in Belgium who she wanted to be with her in England.

She was deeply and emotionally involved in the tragedy of her country and wanted to use any influence she still had with General Jack Gowon to persuade him to extend mercy to her kith and kin. She wanted to publicise her plea to help through the world's press so that Gowon could be influenced by global opinion. Others told me that he would find it an irritation and embarrassment to be reminded of his previous relationship with a Biafiran girl. With the aid of an excellent journalist, Frank Laws at the *Yorkshire Evening Post*, a campaign was organized and a cable was sent to Gowon from Edith. It read:

> Please allow mercy flights to leave England at once with food and medical supplies. The whole British people are anxious to see that your promise to the Bifiran people of friendship is carried out at once, and also by the provision of generous gifts of food and medical supplies to them. Knowing you as I do – I feel sure you will answer this appeal. Edith Ike

In addition to that plea, the head of Leeds CID was handed a bundle of her private and personal papers by me to take to the Foreign Office in the hope that they may be of assistance in their overtures to the Nigerian Government.

Whether it was anything to do with Edith's note or not I cannot say but within weeks it was evident that relief was getting through to the suffering people. Edith later returned to Nigeria and I did hear from her 15 years later when she came to London. Jack Gowon lost the leadership of his country and came to live in exile in the south of England.

7

*

Leeds Sporting Greats: Rugby

Lewis Jones arrived in Leeds from Wales in 1952 to play rugby league. Though a young man, he had already enjoyed a spectacular rugby union career becoming known as the 'Golden Boy.' By pure coincidence, as I was living in Guilford studying for my Law Society final examination, I saw what proved to be his final Welsh club game. I was also present when he made his debut for Leeds against Keighley before an excited crowd at Headingley. He became a client and remains a great friend.

Lewis received a £6,000 signing on fee from Leeds for becoming a professional player at a time when a newly qualified solicitor earned £450 a year and a large modern detached house in a good residential area of the city could be acquired for £3,500.

Rugby league had a history of luring top names 'up north'. They were terrific players, a great attraction through the turnstiles and Lewis was unquestionably the star of his generation. The payment he received was tax free and not treated as income but as a capital payment to compensate him for the loss of his amateur status which had a great value. Moreover, by taking the shilling, he had effectively cut his past ties and became 'persona non grata' in the union ranks. A Welsh doctor practicing in Leeds told me that Lewis had sold his birthright and his actions would never be forgiven by his countrymen. Such was the need for compensation or as David Oxley, the personable one time rugby league secretary general put it more quaintly, 'You can only lose your virginity once.' In addition to that capital sum, Lewis received match fees of £12 for a win, £8 a loss and special bonuses for cup ties.

He was also expected to have a day job as the sport was part-time and total professionalism prohibited. Players had to agree their match terms each year, if they did not they could not play. If he asked to leave and go elsewhere for better money, he was placed on the open to transfer list at a fee determined by the club. If no-one came forward, then the player could ask for the transfer fee to be reduced but it was very rarely granted when they had asked to go. There was no freedom of movement; a player could effectively be frozen out of the game. Nor was there a standard player's agreement setting out his duties and responsibilities and those of the club towards him. That was only remedied when I drafted one for the Rugby Football League in the 1990s.

From 1952 until 1964, Lewis served Leeds with distinction and was rewarded with a testimonial. Though granted by the club, it was the spectators who were expected to show their appreciation of his service and outstanding efforts with financial contributions. After that milestone, Lewis met up with me and we had a long conversation about his future. He was 32 at the time and in terms of the sport, an old man. I had, in the previous few years, developed a good connection with Australian rugby league clubs and sent several players over there. In fact, the first ever transfer of an English player down under was initiated by me when Derek Hallas, who was a colleague of Lewis' in Leeds' first-ever Championship winning team in 1961, joined Parramatta.

Lewis said that he fancied returning to Australia, having toured there with the Lions, and I was confident that one of the Sydney-based clubs would welcome him. Australian rugby league did not dominate the sport to the extent it does now but it was on the way up and crowds were large. I spoke to my colleague in Sydney, solicitor Jim Comyns, who was also an enthusiastic supporter and he said that the appetite of clubs there would be whetted by the thoughts of the Welsh wizard becoming available to them.

A week or so later Jim phoned me. 'Look, I'll be frank Ron,' he said. 'Short term it's not difficult to set Lou up with great money, but if its long term no-one will commit to a veteran for more than a year. If he does his stuff, though, they would continue to extend a deal.' That was undoubtedly disappointing news but something he dropped into the conversation did interest me. 'If Lewis wants to establish himself out here, he should look to either a country club or a second division one in the suburbs of Sydney – shall I discretely make enquiries?' He added.

I said that no harm would be done but under the caveat that I could not commit Lewis to playing in a lower division. I kept Lewis informed and a couple of days later Jim returned with a staggering offer which would guarantee an income for three years – the annual salary being equivalent to two years in England -with a house in a good area and a car. The club, Wentworthville, also agreed to be responsible for transporting him and his family to Sydney and Lewis stayed player/coaching them until 1972, regularly winning 'Wenty', the championship. Several of his contemporaries visited Lewis there, some as part of the 1968 Great Britain squad, and reported back that in the entire 80 minutes he was never once tackled and was hero worshipped by the fans.

His transfer was not, though, smooth. When Lewis spoke to the Leeds chairman Noel Stockdale (later to become Sir Noel for his services to the grocery industry) about his plans, he was told that the club required a fee of a few thousand pounds to grant his release and clearance. It came as shattering news and Lewis and I met and discussed the situation. I advised him that the Leeds position was totally unlawful, it being an unreasonable restraint of trade, and no court in the land would, in my view, declare that the club was acting reasonably. Furthermore, I said that as there was no formal contract, the Headingley outfit had nothing to sell.

My only reservations about taking legal action were the usual ones of how much it would cost and how long it would take. I advised Lewis that before going down that route and to protect ourselves as to recovering costs, we should give the club a further opportunity of remedying the position. With Lewis's permission I arranged to see Noel Stockdale, who I knew well, and the meeting took place at his company's office. I put the situation to him bluntly. He said that he had his club's interests at heart and that as all other English clubs has received a fee when established players went to down under, he could not see why Leeds should be treated differently. Indeed in support of this submission, he quoted that Keighley had received £3,000 from Parramatta for Hallas.

I suspected but was not sure that Noel had been briefed by William Fallowfield, the then Rugby League secretary, who liked to be in control of all matters relating to the sport. I countermanded that Lewis had given far longer service than Leeds had had a right to expect and that it had been distinguished, including attaining the one coveted honour the club had never had. I also reminded him that the club had contributed little to his testimonial, leaving that principally to the fans and that now was the opportunity for a grateful club to publically say to him, 'Go with our blessing and good memories. If and when you return, you will always be welcomed at Headingley.' As I was talking, Noel was nodding in agreement and I got the feeling that he was not the one who had put up the objection in the first place.

He said to me, 'The last thing I want to do is stand in the way and I'll tell you this, he can go with our blessing.' I asked him if he would confirm what he had said to the press in those very words and he agreed. I was delighted but at the same time disappointed that I had not been able to expose the system as being unjust and unfair. I did later, through the rugby league council chamber, manage to persuade the governing body that the rules should be changed to give players similar rights to other employees in the country.

Perhaps having realised the extent of their outlay but, nevertheless, keen to get their star man there as soon as possible, Wentworthville sent Lewis the air ticket but suggested that his wife Maureen, their two children and his mother-in-law should come over as assisted immigrants. The fee was £10, with the Australian government accepting responsibility for the balance. Not surprisingly, Maureen and the kids arrived at my office weeks later having not heard anything and asking if I could help. Lewis, being the laid-back type he displayed on the field, had been happy to let matters take their course but, knowing her husband's temperament, Maureen wanted some action. A few forceful words on the telephone to Sydney produced the necessary paperwork and soon the whole family were on their way.

When Lewis returned to Leeds years later he looked for a place to live and we found one on the southern boundary of the Headingley grounds. It was a bed and breakfast hotel of some size but could be managed by him and Maureen, with

A Lawyer for all Seasons

Lewis still being able to continue his teaching career at a girl's school. Sadly Maureen died far too young, leaving Lewis devastated. I can still vividly remember the day he telephoned me with the sad news. Maureen's mother, known to all as 'mamma', remained with Lewis until she passed away.

When I was elected President of the Rugby Football League in 1996, Lewis was my special guest at the presidential dinner. At the St Michael's Lane side of the ground, the Leeds club erected a superb new stand in 2005 and named a suite in it after him that will be a permanent tribute to the wonderful service and memories he gave in the famous blue and amber colours. Fittingly, it is hired out under the banner of 'Headingley Experience'. As a rugby league player he was probably to greatest I ever saw. His amazing change of pace would deceive defenders. His goose step kick, which allowed him to suddenly shoot off took all by surprise, and his ability to give a floating pass that put the recipient into space never failed to excite. Add to that his exceptional, record breaking kicking and points gathering and he was the complete artist.

Leeds also paid £6,000 to induce Wilf Rosenberg, the South Africa international rugby union centre, to leave Johannesburg in 1959 and change codes. Wilf took to his new dramatic career with alacrity, setting new records as their leading post-war try scorer.

I met Wilf shortly after his arrival. A fellow lawyer suggested I help him as a 'real mess' had been made of the negotiations for him to become a professional rugby player. When I examined the situation it was patently clear that a good experienced sport's lawyer should have been employed by the Rosenberg family before signing any contract and their failure to do so had cost Wilf dearly.

Wilf was the son of a rabbi and a medical student at Witswatersrand University in Johannesberg. Though he had been there for four years, his studies had been severely interrupted by his rugby union career. He had played for his country against the British Lions in 1955 and also France and had toured New Zealand. At the age of 25 he was engaged to Elinor, a nursery school teacher and they intended to marry. Rabbi Rosenberg had maintained his son while at school and university and during his 15-a-side career which was carried out with a higher intensity and demands than the professional environment here. The rabbi did not have a bottomless purse and money had to be found to see through Wilf's primary objective, a career in medicine.

Rugby Union was the major sport in South Africa and although the entire population worshipped their stars, it did not extend to financially maintaining them. They were genuine amateurs. When scouts from the north of England saw the talent and star quality of the Springbok backs, they made determined efforts to entice them to these shores. Winger Tom Van Vollenhoven was the first to be seduced by St Helens and became an overnight sensation. Wilf played inside him and became a target especially when the vulnerability of his financial circumstances became known.

Rabbi Rosenberg met with the chairman of Leeds, George Airey. He was flattered by him and deemed him to be a sincere businessman and thought that his son's future would be well looked after if he uprooted himself and his bride and honeymooned and studied in England. Leeds offered the signing fee tax free, fares to England, a place at Leeds medical school to continue his studies, match fees at the current rate and 'assistance with housing'.

What they did not say, however, was that though the length of the deal was three years, it would not be extended. But if Wilf stayed on, all he would receive would be match fees. Rugby league was a part time sport and no player could afford to live in England reasonably relying on such fees, never mind paying for university in addition. The housing assistance offered was restricted to a couple of weeks at a bed and breakfast hotel and an introduction to an estate agent nor could the club influence a place at the medical school which was dependant on the university Authorities.

Within days of his arrival and, following an interview, Wilf was offered a position on the course but told that credit would not be given for his long time studying medicine in Johannesburg and the exams passed there. If he was to go back to the beginning, that would constitute a very expensive six years. All such information could and should have been ascertained well before he arrived in Leeds. It was then that I met him and listened to his tale of woe. Anxious to be a success on the playing field, he was consumed with worries off it. He appreciated that he had been relaxed over his studies back home and his frequent absences for rugby reasons accounted for him missing some examinations. Although the fame he brought to the university was appreciated by them, it did not, quite rightly, extend to allowing him through on the nod. My experience was that faculties were their own masters and informal approaches I made, though sympathetic, convinced me that the medical school would be unbending. A career change was heralded and we moved quickly to dentistry. They said they would accept part of the curriculum Wilf had taken in South Africa and he interviewed well there and was admitted. It was not his first choice but in the circumstances the best course available and he became a prize winning student who qualified with honours quite easily.

On the field, his pace was remarkable but his strength in the centre was suspect in a game where the physical challenge was front on. Moved to the wing, he made try scoring look easy with his natural speed, swerve, change of pace and bravery. They became his hallmarks of crowd-pleasing displays week in week out. Having purchased a house and furnished it with his signing on fee, he struggled financially even though he had winning wages paid to him more often than not. He was quick to appreciate that if, at the end of his three year period at Leeds, there was nothing but 'pay as you play' his future was uncertain, especially with the risk of injury being ever present. Despite the club winning the title for the first time in its history and Wilf topping the try scoring list and being massively popular with the fans on the terraces, the new chairman was not prepared to renegotiate. To be fair to him he was consistent, adopting the same standards with all the players. Indeed when signing someone he would add money on the agreed transfer fee payable, so that the transferring club could make a termination payment to the player joining Leeds.

I advised Wilf that he made a request to leave and the club, appreciating that if he could not get funds he would be forced to return to South Africa, consented. Fortunately there was serious interest shown by Hull FC, they paid a fee that saw Leeds make a profit and entered into a service contract with Wilf from which tax was deducted. He had a successful stay in Hull, making his debut on one wing while Welshman Clive Sullivan, at the age of 18, made his on the other flank, and went on to become a legend in the sport and on both sides of the rugby-divided city. As Wilf said, 'You could not but enjoy playing in Hull, the fans were so knowledgeable and appreciative.' His sadness was that the once great Airlie Birds were going through a re-building process and he left the club before it was fulfilled.

I have seen Wilf on several occasions since he left Leeds, both back here at the invitation of the club and in his native South Africa. Sadly his wife died after a long illness in her late 40s and Wilf, now in his mid-70s, lives in a residential home in Israel. His dentistry career flourished until he had a stroke which caused loss of fine movement in his hand making it impossible for him to continue in the profession. His claim against his insurers under his critical illness policy sadly failed because he had not disclosed a brain injury suffered in his rugby league days – namely concussion - which is treated lightly by most players. Thereafter he pursued a career in journalism and became a professional boxing promoter. Team sport was no longer on his agenda but he turned to long distance running including a double marathon race known as the 'comrades', the 52 miles completed annually by the best and bravest of runners

A good friend indeed, but how I wish I had met him before he turned to rugby league. His dear father did his best and had his interests at heart but with the addition of specialised advice, a different outcome would have surely resulted. It is said that, back home, the rabbi was faced with an insuperable problem. 'Remember the Sabbath day and keep it holy' the Jewish scriptures beseeched. 'How come Rabbi, that you can allow your son to play rugby on the Sabbath day?' his congregation asked. Wilf's father was not fazed by this oft-repeated question. 'My friends,' he replied. 'If God has given my son such a wonderful gift to play, how can I be expected to argue him?'

My passionate interest in rugby league is matched by a similar devotion to rugby union of a very close friend, Ronnie Bidgood.

Ronnie was chairman of Roundhay, who subsequently merged with their traditional foes Headingley to become Leeds Tykes. He played for the club together with his brothers and, once his on field career was over, continued as an administrator. His duties ranged from cutting the grass to marking the pitch to cleaning the changing rooms. He had every right to be called 'Mr Roundhay.' When I was vice chairman of Bramley he would frequently slip unknown into McClaren Field, but I would openly visit Chandos Park.

Union players, in the days before open professionalism took hold of their game, often tried to boost their egos and self-esteem with tales that league clubs had made fantastic offers for them to switch codes. Because a number of those at Roundhay knew of my close friendship with Ronnie, they would try and get him going by hinting that I had made enquiries but, out of loyalty to him, they had spurned me. I would dismiss his suspicions with a laugh but I was never too sure that he was completely reassured. I remember one Saturday evening Ronnie coming round to my house. He had obviously had his ear bent by one of men because he warned me in the most serious of tones that I should not come into the clubhouse at Roundhay again. He relented later when he realised I had never poached any of his players. Ronnie genuinely and passionately believed that a true sportsman performed purely for his love of his sport and money never entered into it.

One of his heroes was Keith Smith, the club's star fly-half who was regularly selected by Yorkshire and eventually capped by England. That he should play for his country at Twickenham was a great tribute to the small suburban club that nurtured him as a youngster. Keith later donated his England cap and shirt to them and it had pride of place in the club's trophy cabinet. Keith was a working class lad with a rugby league background who lived modestly in a terraced house in East Leeds and worked at the shop floor level for the post office. He was certainly not a high earner and, having achieved all he set out to in union, offered his services to Wakefield Trinity – where he had a family connection – which were readily accepted. His career in the sport was relatively brief, although his class shone, and he retired with the same reticence that he moved from Roundhay, without fuss or fanfare.

During his time at Belle Vue, Ronnie kept in touch with him and called at his home regularly to enquire of his wellbeing. Ronnie hid his disappointment at Keith transferring but never lost his affection and respect for him. Keith slipped out the spotlight and it was rumoured he was coaching youngsters in his neighbourhood. One day I was reading a popular daily newspaper in the café where I had my morning coffee and spotted a headline which read, 'Rugby Union Star Leads Prison Team to Victory.' The gist of the article was that Keith Smith, a convicted felon and inmate in a prison in the south, who had previously enjoyed a distinguished career as an international with England, was both the captain and coach of a prison side. They had gone the whole season unbeaten and the governor paid fulsome tribute to his leadership.

I rang Ronnie who confessed that it was months since he had seen or heard of Keith and when I read him the piece he was both distressed and horrified and said he would call at his house on the way home from work that evening. Curiosity got the better of me and I wanted to do something quickly rather than wait for Ronnie to come back to me, so I rang Trevor Watson, the main rugby league writer for the *Yorkshire Evening Post* and asked him if he knew what had happened to Keith, who at the time would have been in his late thirties. His reply was, 'Oh, he just faded out of the game and I have never heard of him since he left Wakefield... but strangely enough there was an article in the morning paper saying he was in prison and that must be why.'

That evening Ronnie telephoned and said, 'I've caught up with Keith. He's alive and well and still working for the Royal Mail but hopping mad about the article. I am bringing him to see you in the morning.' Later that evening Ronnie phoned again, this time from the Roundhay clubhouse. 'The story is getting some momentum,' he said. 'I have had one of the committee come to the club angry that Keith has besmirched the name and he was going to propose that his jersey and cap be forthwith removed.'

The following day I saw Keith and he was not best pleased, especially as a relative who he had not seen for years had read the paper, believed the story and repeated it to another member of his family. I phoned the prison and spoke to someone in the governor's office and he confirmed that the newspaper story was true. I queried, 'What does this Smith look like?' He replied, 'Oh, he's a big fella - round about 40.' I asked him why he was serving a sentence and was told that he could not tell me as it was confidential information. I mused, 'Could it be for fraud?' and there was a silence which spoke volumes. It was abundantly clear that there were two Keith Smiths. I then formally wrote to the newspaper claiming that the one I represented had been defamed and asking for the withdrawal of the story, an apology, damages and costs. They acknowledged the letter saying that they would investigate my allegation and return to me.

A few days later there was a most apologetic voice on the phone from the paper. 'It's an error,' the man said and followed it up by asking, 'Can we talk?'. Talk we did. Eventually Keith received a cheque for a five-figure sum and an apology. The prisoner Smith was, as I thought, a conman. Positively, the episode brought Keith in from the wilderness. He continued to coach youngsters in the art and skills of rugby and met, from time to time, with Ronnie Bidgood and some of his old colleagues from Roundhay. Sadly, a cruel illness terminated his life, and his death at an early age was mourned by the very many friends made during his playing career and thereafter.

In rugby league terms, the city of Leeds is divided into two territories by the River Aire, creating and fermenting intense rivalry.

In the south, there was only one professional focus, Hunslet, occupying Parkside and wearing a shirt of myrtle and flame. They recruited from the local schools where every boy seemed to have a talent for playing the oval ball game. North of the river, Leeds RLFC had the wealth and a magnificent stadium at Headingley, their sole competitor for talent on their patch being homely Bramley to the west. In practical terms, it was the battle between Leeds and Hunslet that excited local passions and filled the grounds of each club when they met.

Hunslet certainly had the edge when it came to the talent pool. Each street corner bred youngsters steeped in the game, the best of them near-ready for the first team. At Headingley, however, junior recruitment was not so productive or proficient. Leeds had the financial clout to buy existing stars from rugby union or speculate on big name overseas players. They also dangled temptation in front of numerous Hunslet products over the years although, to some, moving up the road was seen as the equivalent of a sale of birthright.

Hunslet schoolboy prodigy Barry Seabourne, captain of Yorkshire schoolboys, quickly alerted scouts to his abilities and Leeds decided to start courting him. They tempted him with an immediate, substantial payment and the offer of additional incentive bonuses that would have breached the rather modest financial outlay policy that Hunslet maintained for their young prospects. As an additional incentive, Leeds offered a place on their backroom staff for his dad Ernest, who had great contacts within the game. Barry duly made his blue and amber debut when just over 16, becoming the youngest ever to do so at the club and added county and international caps before he was 24. He was small, round shouldered, stockily built and with a running action that resembled a badger but with amazing speed of over the first few yards. He could kick a ball superbly in open play with either foot and could pass a prodigious distance with accuracy. The impish number seven was easily identifiable.

At Odsal, when he joined Bradford Northern for the second glorious installment of his career, he added coaching qualifications to his high playing skills and had another crowd of supporters eating out of his hands. He was at Bradford when he made an appointment to see me. One of the daily tabloids had published a photograph of Barry – not an action shot – but a serious looking, studio portrait that could have been used in a passport. He was livid as he handed me the rag and the article that ran with his picture. It spoke of one of the most feared gangsters in the criminal history of this country, someone who had done plenty of time at the pleasure of Her Majesty and was a close associate of one of the most notorious gangsters known to the police. The name attached to Barry's mug-shot gloried in his criminal background and was always ready with an instant quote whenever an unsavoury crime had been committed. It was Frankie Fraser, whose moniker was never printed without the epithet of mad in front of it.

The newspaper had made a serious mix up. Spectators do not need an excuse to target stars in the opposition ranks and this clearly affronted Barry's standing and reputation. Moreover, he began receiving torrents of abuse and torment from the terraces, believing he would end his career known as 'Mad Frankie'. Barry realised the mistake was an error in the newspaper's picture library and, when I contacted them, they readily admitted their mistake, apologised profusely and agreed to make a payment to him to ease his feelings.

8

*

The Leeds Police Trial
and the Death of David Oluwale

There are some legal cases that, no matter what the outcome, nobody wins. The lingering feelings for all concerned are ones of intense sadness and despair.

At the beginning of the twenty-first century, literary critics hailed two northern writers, Kester Aspden and David Peace. The former, a doctor of history from Cambridge University and a lecturer in crime at the University of Leeds, wrote *The Hounding of David Oluwale*, the story of a seriously disturbed Nigerian immigrant pulled dead from the River Aire a few miles from the city centre having suffered abuse and torment from the Leeds police force over a fairly lengthy period of time.

The allegation was the Police had killed him and the book was followed by a play which had its premiere in Leeds and then toured the rest of the UK. Aspden was described by one reviewer as being the new David Peace while Peace himself endorsed the Oluwale book as being 'brave'.

I was one of the defence lawyers when the policemen

alleged to have killed Oluwale - and assaulted him on other occasions - stood trial. When Aspden commenced his research, before putting pen to paper he interviewed me at length. I was pleased to co-operate with him and read the resulting book with particular interest.

The other important link I had to this most high profile case was that if it had not been for the celebrated 'Leeds police trial' in 1970 – when four senior officers were charged with attempting to pervert the course of justice – which I was also a part of – there would have been no investigation into the death of Oluwale. The case, frankly, would have been as dead as poor David, buried in a pauper's grave at Killingbeck cemetery on the eastern outskirts of that city. Without examining the background of the Leeds police trial, when evidence was altered after an elderly widow was killed on Christmas Eve on Otley Road by a car driven by an off - duty superintendent, it is almost impossible to arrive at a considered view of the force; its controls, attitudes and behaviour.

The Leeds police trial lasted 25 days and was reported widely. Tongues wagged, not only in constabulary canteens but in offices, factories, pubs, clubs and legal circles. It centred on Superintendent Holmes, known to all as 'big red' and a man not averse to putting his extra large frame around. He was the driver concerned and was not even breathalysed at the scene. Even worse, and corroborated by the traffic officers who arrived quickly on the scene, word was put about that Minnie Wine, a lifelong teetotaller, had been drinking. The family of the poor lady were aghast, crushed by her tragic death, their anger increased at this smear put out by the police. The coroner who was to carry out the inquest was alerted to the disquiet of the relatives. Gossip had it that Holmes had been a guest at a party hosted by a well-known scrap metal merchant in south Leeds where the hospitality was fulsome, hence the rumours abounded about the reluctance to breathalyse.

The two 'bobbies' who arrived at the scene grew irate and complained to their superiors. The Assistant Chief Constable then instructed two senior men - Chief Superintendent Harry Royston, who had much experience of the traffic department and Inspector Thomas Dewar - to assist and commence an investigation into the constables' concerns. Armed with their initial written statements, the investigating officers decided to seek further clarification from their juniors. It may well have seemed more like the interrogation of witnesses rather than greater elucidation around the facts. Fortunately, Royston did not discard the original statements so it could be seen beyond any doubt where the alterations had been made.

If asked, I could have given evidence that in preparing cases for trial, witness statements are changed continually, corrections made, new insertions added and responses to further questions all set out, until a final statement to the satisfaction of the witness, of course, is produced. However, Assistant Chief Constable Haywood sent the entire file to the adjoining force in the county for evaluation, as was the procedure on matters involving one of their own. The final outcome of their enquiry and the report that was submitted to Haywood ensured that it was Royston and Dewer who became defendants in the Leeds police trial. They were charged with attempting to pervert the course of justice and Inspector Ellerker and Sergeant Nicholson faced a similar indictment by failing to act with propriety at the scene of the crime.

When the day arrived for the prosecution to present their evidence to the magistrate's court and show that the four defendants had a case to answer, there was a surprise presence in the public gallery. Assistant Chief Constable Austin Haywood, looking sombre and serious, knew the two constables who had complained to him well before any involvement of my clients Royston and Dewar in the enquiries. If he had his eye on them when they came to the stand, they would surely stick to the script and ensure that their present statements became the evidence that nailed the fate of the alleged conspirators. I could think of no other possible explanation and I thought that I needed to respond so as to preserve the integrity of my client's case. I walked down the corridor into the court office and issued a witness summons for Haywood to give evidence for the defence. I then dashed back into the courtroom having folded the document neatly and handed it to a surprised and unsuspecting Haywood, before resuming my place on the solicitor's bench as the clerk read the charges. I then rose and said to the clerk, 'Would you, sir, ask that all witnesses who are now in court should leave before evidence is called.' He replied, 'Of course I will,' and did so. As there was no movement at his announcement, I rose again and said, 'In the back of the court, Mr Austin Haywood is present. He is the Assistant Chief Constable and the defence has issued and served a witness summons upon him to give evidence on certain issues which related to his instructions to my clients. It is, therefore, my submission that he should leave the court.'

Haywood did not seem to be the least bit embarrassed. He rose to his feet and addressed the magistrates. 'But I am the Assistant Chief Constable of this city,' he began. The clerk interrupted him. 'Mr Haywood, that is not relevant. If you are a witness – or will be one – you must leave.' The gloves were off and he never came near that court or the assizes where the trial was held nor, to my knowledge, played any part in the procedures.

All the accused were committed for trial at the assizes. The defence team was formidable, Gilbert Gray, not yet a QC, leading Robert Smith, a very young barrister described then as highly promising, and who is now the most sought after QC in the north of England, representing Harry Royston. Peter Taylor QC, later to become a distinguished Lord Chief Justice, together with Brian Walsh, a future recorder of Leeds, as junior for Thomas Dewar. Frankly, it was a complete waste of talent to have such stellar performers appearing for Dewar for it was established in the defence team's conference before the hearing that as the prosecution had put Dewar in the margin, his cause could only be harmed by continual reference and focus. Taylor said he would not challenge any of the prosecution witnesses and so it transpired after each had given evidence. Indeed, I knew from almost day one, that the prosecution would not oppose a submission of 'no case to answer' at the conclusion of the evidence.

Taylor filled up his time well. An accomplished pianist of almost concert hall standing, he found the town hall instrument irresistible and an audience of cleaners and passing itinerants were treated to sonatas and preludes in abundance. The other two, Inspector Ellerker and Sergeant Nicholson were represented by Peter Fingret, who spent a great deal of his training period with me. He had briefed Mr Philip Owen QC, leading a very experienced junior, Arthur Myerson - later to become Judge Myerson. I confess that Philip Owen was unknown to me but he was a pleasant man who seemed to be struggling in the defence of Ellerker, although whether that was because of changes of directions or instructions from his client, I do not know.

Drama in the meantime was being conducted away from the town hall in total secrecy. Unbeknown to anyone participating in the trial a police cadet, Gary Galvin received some interesting information. Galvin, who later became an inspector and had beaten cancer once before finally succumbing to the disease when he was only 50, had heard something that perturbed him from a colleague. PC Topp, who probably was the tallest policeman in the Leeds ranks and at the time was part of Kitching's team at Millgarth in the city centre. He disliked Kitching and gossiped to Galvin of what he had been told about the violent methods employed by Kitching and Ellerker. Galvin did not know either but he had heard of Ellerker because he was standing in a highly publicised trial at that time. Galvin spoke to his inspector who reported it to Leeds CID who sent it quickly to Scotland Yard. With the force under such scrutiny, they moved into action immediately, interviewed Kitching and suspended him. Was it not for the publicity arising from the Leeds police trial, Galvin might not have come forward with his assertions.

Sadly, the Leeds force had endured a reputation for corrupt behaviour for several years. In 1955, officers had been dismissed for demanding and receiving weekly backhanders from the owners of betting shops for turning a blind eye to their then unlawful activities. There were two totally different reactions to the Leeds police trial and what it led on to. The public were generally hostile at what they thought was a clear case of protecting ones own from the consequences of breaking the law, while the ranks themselves had mixed views. Some believed that, like in sport when in the dressing room or on tour, what went on within the station should stay there and that colleagues who perpetuated and spread gossip were no better than informers. Such an attitude was brought home more forcefully to me during that trial by the comments of a retired army officer, then serving as the under sherrif of the county, who told me, 'A society that encourages and develops loyalty cannot complain if on occasion it is carried out to excess.' Indeed Mr Justice Mocatta, in sentencing Ellerker at the conclusion of the Leeds police trial, specifically said, 'You have ruined a very promising career by a misguided sense of loyalty to another officer.' Galvin, meanwhile – according to author Kester Aspden – was given a, 'hard time' by some fellow uniforms because of his actions. This was also to become a recurring theme in the Oluwale case. Time and time again the investigating officers came up against a blank wall. 'Heard nothing, saw nothing and am saying nowt,' seemed to be a common mantra adopted by all ranks. On viewing the transcripts of many of those questioned by Scotland Yard, their intransigence was as revealing as the limited amount they did put on record. There is a north-south divide to factor into that equation, irrational though it is with associated insecurities, prejudices and jealousies which led me to speculate as to whether the Yard were the right choice to carry out the questioning.

My two clients were acquitted at the Leeds police trial – Royston by the jury and Dewar by the judge's direction to them while the other two officers were sent to prison. Dewar was not fazed about returning to work but Harry Royston was bitter and angry as to how he had been treated. He was entitled to the services of a friend in the force to assist him as he faced disciplinary charges as well as the conspiracy allegations. Superintendent John Clark – a good friend of mine – accepted the role when I asked him. He was brilliant and was there when Royston was acquitted. We both recommended to Royston that the following day he put on his uniform and return to Austin Haywood's office. This he duly did to the latter's embarrassment, I understand. Finding a home for a Chief Superintendent who he thought was not returning must have been a shock to his system. He of course had to cancel the disciplinary charges. After weeks of taking temporary assignments, Royston secured a prestigious position with the local authority and resigned from the force. His new career was quickly on the rise to the extent that he was subsequently awarded an OBE. Sadly,

A Lawyer for all Seasons

Superintendent Clark was returned unfit having lost a leg because of cancer and died shortly afterwards. A truly brave man, when I visited him in hospital after the amputation he was lying on top of the bed and seeing me approach said, 'And if you've brought me a parrot you can go now.'

I had little respite from my efforts when the Leeds police trial concluded. I read later that Peter Fingret said that the two trials took over his life and that of his staff for two years and I shared his views entirely. The rest I thought I deserved was very short indeed and it ended abruptly.

One Saturday morning, my partner Leslie Gould had gone to our office in St Paul's Street to see one of his clients. Normally we did not open the office then and did not have any staff there. Leslie heard someone in the waiting room and, thinking it was the person he was expecting, looked in.

Sitting there, according to his description, was a very thin man with sharp features nervously playing with a trilby hat held in his hands. He asked for me and when told I was at home he enquired if Gould would kindly phone so that he could speak to me. I did speak to him. It was a conversation that to this day chills and excites me. In staccato tones it began, 'Mr Teeman, I am Sergeant Kitching stationed at Millgarth. I need you to represent me. I am about to be charged with murder.' I paused for a moment or two to let the news sink in and suggested that he stayed where he was and that I would join him in quarter of an hour.

When I arrived at the offices Kitching, who I recognised from seeing frequently in the court but did not know, was still agitated and he hurriedly told me of his predicament. The suggestion was being made that David Oluwale had been killed by officers from Millgarth and it was believed he was one of them. He went on that Inspector Ellerker was the

116

other and it immediately brought back to me the gossip I had heard around and since the ending of the police trial.

I had heard of Oluwale and had seen him. I was aware, as most people in the city centre who came to work early in the morning were, of his antics, his shouting and running up and down the street. Kitching told me that an officer from Scotland Yard had interviewed him but he was not represented at it. I said that I would revert to him when I knew more about it and whether I could find the time to prepare his defence. When he left I spoke to Leslie Gould and related to him the situation. I told him that if I was to take on this new case I would need some help. I had spent three months on the police trial, including 25 continuous days in court, and no sooner had I put away the file than another merry-go-round was starting. Leslie, who was a very competent advocate, said that he would look after the bread and butter stuff at the magistrate's court if I took on the defence of Kitching. From that moment I cleared the decks for action. Again the Leeds public were quick to voice their opinion and officers assisting at football matches, when hooliganism was at its peak, were subject to ribald chants from the crowd.

Ultimately, though, when the dust had settled, reviewing the murder trial of Ellerker and Kitching without emotion was not difficult. The Crown were unable to persuade the court that the two policemen were directly involved in the killing. The submission I had made before Mr John Randolph at the Leeds Magistrates was repeated point by point at the assizes, though Gilbert Gray expressed it more elegantly and eloquently. This time it found favour and Mr Justice Hinchcliffe threw out the charge leaving a jury only to adjudicate on matters of assault. Kitching admitted to that, although not as violent as the ones witnesses had described and he submitted that he had he only used force when under attack.

A Lawyer for all Seasons

The Leeds police force was 1,300 strong and it is my understanding that almost all were interviewed in the course of the investigations. The Scotland Yard Team were lead by Chief Superintendent Perkins and Detective Sergeant Basil Hadrell. It did not surprise me to learn much later that Perkins suffered a nervous breakdown shortly after the conclusion of the Oluwale trial, was discharged from the profession and died at the very early age of 51. He was intense, determined and focussed but all to excess.

The first of my dealings with him came when he brought some documents to my office which was in an area of Leeds where cloth merchants carried on their business. In my interview room there were two or three suit lengths. Perkins looked at them and made some quip and I replied, 'Many visitors from the south take back with them a piece of Yorkshire worsted - let me know if you want a length.' He gave me a look and said something to the effect that he hoped I was not trying to buy favour and I immediately dropped the topic.

At the committal proceedings before the stipendiary magistrate of Leeds, I had prepared a lengthy submission which I remember to this day without even referring to the notes. I recounted that firstly, there was no evidence that Oluwale was at the scene where his body was found; no evidence whatsoever of how he got into the river Aire nor as to where he went into it and there was a complete absence of evidence that anyone went into the river on that date, at that time and in that place. Peter Fingret, who represented Ellerker, agreed and adopted the submission for his man. The Crown was represented by Donald Herod and when he was called upon to respond, to put it crudely, he simply floundered. I was confident but as the time was 4.30pm or thereabouts, the magistrate announced that he would make his deliberations known the following morning and we all believed that it would most likely favour us. Herod had the look of a haunted man while Perkins was in the corridor pacing up and down beside himself with angst. I put it no higher than that. He did not seem to have any desire to talk with the prosecution team and silently left the building on his own. In my career I have met investigating officers and prosecuting counsel who believe that they have a mission to accomplish and that their task was supported by an outside power invested in them to bring that about. I thought Perkins was one of those men. That view was increased when I read the unused material that the prosecution sent me. Amongst a vast amount of paper there was a statement from a clairvoyant recording a conversation she held with Oluwale after his departure from this earth. It could not be said to be unused but more unusable material. Perhaps he found, that with the Leeds police closing ranks, he had to find other ways of discovering the truth.

Leaving the town hall that afternoon at the closure of the court, I had no doubt as to what the response of the stipendiary magistrate would be to my submission; I expected him to dismiss the case. Mr Randolph did not take long on his summation and he did not give any reasons. He merely told the defendants to stand and that he found there was a case to answer on the manslaughter charge and he committed both to trial. I found it hard to believe what I heard and struggled to restrain myself from reacting like a petulant footballer when a foul is called against him. The situation was not eased when weeks later, before the trial at the assizes had commenced, I met Randolph in the corridor of the town hall and he buttonholed me.

'Teeman,' he said. 'That was a very proper submission you made. I have no doubt that when it is repeated it will be upheld.' As I stood there open-mouthed he continued, 'This case, you know, has received such a tremendous amount of public interest and concern that I though it better that the assizes deal with it.'

There were some team changes for the trial. Ellerker dropped his leading counsel from the Leeds police trial and replaced him with a celebrated advocate from the Old Bailey, Basil Wigoder QC. I retained Gilbert Gray QC to lead for me and this time he had as his junior, Harry Ognal, later to become Mr Justice Ognal. It was more a bringing together of equals rather than a senior-junior combination and they shared the defence work, Ognal cross-examining some of the important prosecution witnesses. The trial was presided over by Mr Justice Hinchcliffe and the prosecution was, as previously, led by the straight-laced and predictable John Cobb QC, later to become Mr Justice Cobb. He was leading Donald Herod who had so nearly come unstuck in the magistrates court.

Though Cobb was an outstanding prosecutor, I never warmed to him. I regarded him as insular and distant. Extremely tall, he not only over-looked me but regularly through me although I admired his professionalism. His opening address to the jury was frequently type written and handed to defence counsel. It may have taken him three hours to outline his case to them in the Oluwale case but not a word was wasted or out of place. He knew the difficulties he faced in attempting to persuade that it was a viable charge but he set out the facts upon which he relied with clarity. The thrust of his submission was that on 18th April, 1969 the two policemen in the dock brought about the Nigerian's death by causing him to fall or jump into the River Aire, from which he never emerged save as a corpse some 16 days later. Quite fairly and properly, Cobb told the jury that the city of Leeds had during the previous year run riot with gossip and rumour and urged them to keep their minds open and forget anything that they may have heard before coming into court.

That opening gambit intrigued me but it was welcome for Cobb voiced the same serious concern that Gray and I had when we made an application in chambers to Mr Justice Hinchcliffe that the trial be moved from the Leeds area, which he refused.

I also have to say that Hinchcliffe conducted the trial admirably, but even he struggled to restrain his facial expressions which indicated that Oluwale's tendencies disgusted him. More particularly, when a prosecution witness was questioned by Ognal about the demeanour of Oluwale when arrested, Hinchcliffe intervened and though not reproaching Ognal, made sure that his own view came over to the jury saying that, 'Everyone knew that Oluwale was a dirty, filthy and violent vagrant.' Hinchcliffe was an establishment man and before he was promoted to the High Court he had been the recorder of Leeds. It had been his force and there was no doubting his discomfort during the trial when he heard about members of it and their confrontations with and attitude to the unfortunate Oluwale.

The main obstacle that the Crown had to overcome was the fact that so much of the wicked conduct meted out to Oluwale was not only known to other police officers stationed at Millgarth but had been actually witnessed by them. Not one complained to a higher ranking colleague or indeed offered their own rebuke to either Ellerker or Kitching. Nevertheless, Kitching's case was that those assaults were justified as no more than reasonable force being used in the most trying of circumstances.

The most challenging witness called by the prosecution was PC Keith Seager. He had been the driver of the police car on occasions when Kitching and Ellerker had taken in Oluwale in the city centre and then dumped him in either of two venues, Middleton Woods on the south side or to Bramhope, which was eight miles from the centre on the opposite boundary. He was also present on a great number of the occasions when the pair were said to be have beaten Oluwale. Seager was extremely uncomfortable when in the witness box. He was given a torrid time by, alternately, Grey and then Wigoder. As soon as one had finished tormenting him, the other would step up the verbal attacks and accusations.

He knew his script, however, and he had no excuse for memory lapses when one calculated the number of times he was interviewed during the course of the enquiry. It was not too difficult for him to describe the Kitching's kickings and the defence strategy was the only obvious one to adopt in these circumstances. We hammered home, ad nauseam, the obvious, 'If you are now telling the truth, PC Seager, why didn't you tell it earlier?' followed up with 'Are you not trying to save your own skin and keep out of the firing line?'

Then the question of camaraderie was raised, 'Kitching was always there for his men wasn't he?'. Seager replied, 'He was a Sergeant of the old school and old fashioned in his approach.' When put on the spot about driving the car that took Oluwale to the woods, Seager conceded that Kitching spoke to Oluwale in a kind voice asking about his home and parents and reminding him that the life he was leading in Leeds would not get him anywhere. That emboldened Gray to ask Seager, 'Did you ever think Kitching had killed Oluwale?' and Seager emphatically said, 'No, I did not.' He also conceded that after Oluwale's dead body had been recovered from the river, whenever his name was mentioned at Millgarth or elsewhere, Kitching did not behave as if he had a guilty conscience. Finally, PC Seager accepted that he was in a most difficult position for he was in contact with Oluwale just as frequently as others and had himself moved him on several times. In his quiet probing of Seager, Wigoder was most effective. He suggested that Seager was wriggling out of his culpability by heaping it on Ellerker, someone who had verbally lashed him on frequent occasions. It was put to him that Ellerker had seriously warned him for kicking Oluwale but Seager would have none of it. There was the falsification of his duty book entries and the failure to record the two visits to the woods and the abandonment there of Oluwale. He offered no explanation for the absences, allowing the defence to make its case that the rest of his evidence was equally as untrustworthy.

PC Woodhead, nicknamed by his colleagues 'chopper' was next to be called and he spoke of an incident when he was driving the station's Morris van in January 1969 and saw Oluwale sleeping outside a shop named John Peters. He contacted Kitching and when the officer arrived he told the vaigrant to move. The Nigerian became violent and excitable and tried to bite Kitching's thumb meaning he had to be subdued although only necessary force was used Woodhead declared. 'Chopper' was seen later at Millgarth half-carrying Oluwale to the charge desk and when released, his captive he fell to the floor and had to drag him to his feet by the policeman. Woodhead said that in his entire police service, he had never seen anyone display violence to Oluwale.

In contrast, a sickening contribution was made by PC Batty who told of his off-duty sighting of Kitching and Ellerker. He was in his car with his girlfriend when he came across the duo again in the area surrounding the John Peters shop. Ellerker was shining a torch in Oluwale's face, while Kitching was urinating on him. Kitching's instructions to his defence team were firm, that it was completely untrue and if such an incident had happened it did not involve him or Ellerker. Gray, therefore, forcibly challenged the assertion. 'Mr Batty,' he said, 'Not one blow on the horn of your car and not even a flash from your lights – is that correct?' 'Nothing' replied Batty. 'And not a report to the station when you returned to duty?' continued Gray. Once more Batty was defensive, 'I agree, there was nothing'. He did volunteer that he doubted a report of what he had seen would do any good as it would be his word against that of two more senior officers. Gray had concluded scornfully, 'No-one, Mr Batty, stands over a man who is known to bite and scratch and then proceeds to urinate on him - that's right isn't it?' There was no reply from the witness.

I looked forward, however, to PC Higgins giving evidence. He was well known in the force but few used his name, referring to him instead as 'glob'. A Humpty Dumpty figure of a man who had around 20 years service in the force, most of it at Millgarth, he had no teeth or dentures just a mouthful of gums. Rumour had it that the night shift was so fond of him that they had a collection and bought him a set of second hand teeth which were ceremonially presented to him, but he rarely adorned his mouth with them. Something must have come over him when he was alerted that he would be giving evidence at the town hall. He looked smart and when he took the oath it was noticeable that he had both upper and lower teeth. His evidence of the humiliating treatment Oluwale had metered out to him by both accused seemed convincing. Attempts by the defence team to paint him in less than a complimentary manner had, I think, the effect of establishing his honesty even further.

Throughout the proceedings the number one courtroom was always full. I recognised many former police officers in the public gallery along with a number of off-duty lawyers. I was asked one day to provide a ticket for one of my football clients who had been following the trial in the newspapers. Years later he would still vividly recall the day of his visit. It was the one when Sergeant Atkinson collapsed in the witness box while giving his evidence. 'To see a big man drop after appearing so solid a few moments earlier,' he said, 'made you appreciate the strain he was under and the impact it would have on the jury.'

Atkinson had been describing an occasion in January 1969 when Ellerker and Kitching came into Millgarth with a screaming Oluwale. He told of how they pushed Oluwale to the floor and, while he was down there, aimed a kick in the region of his private parts. He also spoke of another incident a month later when policemen again attacked their hapless prey. Wigoder met this new evidence face on. 'You are a liar, Sergeant Atkinson,' he shouted. 'Ellerker was not there on that time or that date, he was off duty, sick.' All eyes were focused on the sergeant in the box and the court went quiet. Atkinson's voice was weak and low as he muttered something about being unwell. The court usher poured some water from a flask and walked towards the witness who, by then, was staring into space before slumping backwards. The court had to adjourn as he left the witness box in a distressed state.

Overnight the defence determined to mount a counter-attack as quickly as possible. The following morning, when Atkinson took his place in the witness box, he had obviously recovered. Basil Wigoder faced him and quietly opined, 'You've invented all of this, haven't you?' Atkinson, looking more at ease, replied that he had not slept at all 'and laid awake thinking constantly about the evidence.' To his relief, Superintendent Leonard Barker, the boss at the station, had produced the duty roster for that day and it showed that Ellerker only went off sick at the completion of his shift and so would have been able to attack Oluwale as the sergeant had testified. What the jury made of Atkinson's evidence and 'performance' I do not know but, in my view, he was a completely unimpressive witness and reporters covering the trial confirmed that they shared that opinion.

Unusually for a defence lawyer, I had a great respect for the knowledge and analysis of the experienced members of the legal press rather than those journalists who only showed up for the celebrity show trials. In the north we were fortunate at the quality and accuracy of the court scribes despite their relatively limited space. Often after a day in court I would join them for a glass at the Town Hall Tavern. There I would receive a frank assessment of the state of play of the trial. The almost unanimous view was that the prosecution witnesses were not being frank, that they had something to hide and protect. Some appreciated how Oluwale's behaviour required a set of skills on restraint that most bobbies did not have especially when merely maintaining law and order in the city at the time was the main priority. Likewise, there was scepticism about the length of time it had taken for officers to now speak out.

Frequently in a long trial there is a change of climate that comes over the case. It can be evidence that negates the value of all that has been given earlier or something of such significance and inherent probity that it supports statements that had been previously challenged and open to argument. In the Oluwale trial it came from an unexpected source.

Two married police officers resigned from the force in December 1969. Phil Radcliffe, who had seen the appeal for witnesses, was persuaded by his wife not to come forward. They were, however, questioned extensively by the Scotland Yard team in the early months of 1971. Hazel Radcliffe had just given birth and she had seen the attack of Oluwale on 26th January 1969, which had occasioned the GBH charges against both defendants. She gave a vivid but factual account of what she saw, heard and did; leaving the interview office for another room at the time as she could not bear to watch. Despite a vigorous cross-examination and the suggestion that Oluwale was berserk and violent, she would have none of it. Her husband had seen Kitching in the Bridewell pushing Oluwale with a knee in his back. He described the

126

assailed as, 'A defeated man and broken.' Both had made no complaints at the time and expressed shame and fear as the reasons. Lawyers - and, I suspect, jurors in long trials - have a gut feeling when they are hearing the unvarnished truth told by people whose demeanour marks them out as genuine, with no motive otherwise. The Radcliffe's seemed to be in that category. There is an expression I used on some occasions that it was not what the witness said that caused me to believe, but the way it was said. Their recounting led me to believe them and, I'm almost certain, had a similar effect on the 12 men and women deciding the outcome.

At the conclusion of the evidence and before the summing up, there were three powerful speeches to the jury. Mr Cobb for the prosecution, referring to Kitching being described as an 'old fashioned bobbie' poured scorn on his conduct and pointed out how he had sought to denigrate a man who could not speak for himself and whose rights as a citizen had been diminished. I was surprised at the otherwise well reasoned argument put forward by Wigoder on behalf of Ellerker which criticised Cobb for describing Oluwale as a citizen, saying that his conduct had forfeited his right to be described in such terms. I am doubtful that this proposition would have found a seconder in the jury box.

The jury had been bombarded by witnesses, the defence counsel and even the judge with a catalogue of the nasty traits possessed by Oluwale but it was going too far to suggest that he was not a citizen. Gray, as was his norm, had prepared his summation speech well. More factual than emotional, he rightly contrasted the lifestyle and habits of Oluwale and, while conceding that he was without friends, postulated that there was little he did that encouraged friendship. He took the jury down the road that the 'copper in the city centre' had to tread and his responsibilities to the wider community to establish good order and conduct and the pressure they were under to control those whose actions threatened it. The judge's directions were balanced and accurate, he reinforced his assessment of Oluwale and the serious responsibility that the police had in, 'enabling us to sleep well at night.'

The jury were away for over four hours and returned to the court having reaching verdicts of guilty against both accused except for the charge of 'Assault Occasioning Actual Bodily Harm' at John Peters on 18th April, which was the last sighting of the victim alive. The length of time they were deliberating caused me to say to Gilbert Gray that the defence were in with a chance – but it was not to be. Mr Justice Hinchcliffe, in what I thought was a skillful and well prepared sentencing exercise, sent Ellerker to prison for three years and Kitching to serve 27 months. Looking back at the evidence, I could not quarrel with the jury's verdict. My last ever talk with Kitching was when I went to see him after sentencing in the cells below the court. He rose to his feet as I entered and shook my hand vigorously 'Thank you, thank you, Mr Teeman,' he said. 'You'll never know how grateful I am to you and Mr Gray'. I left the small room, collected my papers and, with the assistance of a clerk, returned them to the office. I never heard of Kitching again. He seemed a lonely man.

David Oluwale was not created by the Leeds city police force. They neither placed him on the streets nor did they have powers other than the temporary solution of continual arrests to alleviate the situations his conduct created. Officers on the beat never had any specialist training to help them cope with those who had fallen off society's ladder, unwashed, uncouth and unwanted. In 1968, there were many drop-outs who slept rough on park benches and under railway bridges out of sight and sound of the general public. The few hostels who admitted the unfortunates were

Above: Three budding lawyers. The writer, *left*, with Stanley Berwin and Barrie Black - later to become His Honour Judge Barrington Black - fighting election battle at Wakefield in 1950 for the Liberal Party

Above: As President of the Rugby Football League, talking with Sir Lawrence Byford, former Chief Constable of Lincolnshire, HM Inspector of Constabulary, Chairman of Yorkshire County Cricket Club and one of Ronnie's law students at Leeds University

Ronnie Teeman, footballer's agent, accompanies Joe Jordan on his arrival in Italy to sign for AC Milan

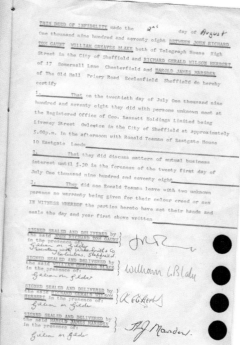

THIS DEED OF INFIDELITY made the 2nd day of August One thousand nine hundred and seventy eight BETWEEN JOHN RICHARD TOM GAUNT WILLIAM GREAVES BLAKE both of Telegraph House High Street in the City of Sheffield and RICHARD GERALD WILSON HERBERT of 17 Somersall Lane Chesterfield and HAROLD JAMES MARSDEN of The Old Hall Priory Road Ecclesfield Sheffield do hereby certify

1. That on the twentieth day of July One thousand nine hundred and seventy eight they did with persons unknown meet at the Registered Office of Geo. Bassett Holdings Limited being Livesey Street Owleston in the City of Sheffield at approximately 5.00p.m. in the afternoon with Ronald Teeman of Eastgate House 10 Eastgate Leeds

2. That they did discuss matters of mutual business interest until 3.30 in the forenoon of the twenty first day of July One thousand nine hundred and seventy eight

3. They did see Ronald Teeman leave with two unknown persons no warranty being given for their colour creed or sex IN WITNESS WHEREOF the parties hereto have set their hands and seals the day and year first above written

SIGNED SEALED AND DELIVERED by }
the said JOHN RICHARD TOM GAUNT
in the presence of:

SIGNED SEALED AND DELIVERED by }
the said WILLIAM GREAVES BLAKE
in the presence of:

SIGNED SEALED AND DELIVERED by }
the said RICHARD GERALD WILSON
HERBERT in the presence of:

SIGNED SEALED AND DELIVERED by }
the said HAROLD JAMES MARSDEN
in the presence of:

Above and right: The 'famous' Deed of Fidelity prepared by colleagues to convince Ronnie's wife that he was working right through the night

Left: Former Leeds United midfielder Johnny Giles, with whom Ronnie Teeman has enjoyed a close working relationship

His signature made R.L. history

A DEAL that made Rugby League history was completed in Leeds. Derek Hallas, the Keighley centre, is seen here signing for the Australian club, Parramatta, to become the first R.L. player to be transferred from England to Australia.

Watching him are Mr. Ronald Teeman, of Leeds (left), who acted for Parramatta and handed over a £3,000 cheque to Keighley's representative, director Mr. Geoff Beadnall (right).

HALLAS SIG FOR AUSSIES

KEIGHLEY centre Derek Hallas is pictured here signing for Australian club Parramatta in Leeds this afternoon after a £3,000 cheque had arrived from Sydney to clinch his transfer.

He has made history by becoming the first R.L. player to be transferred between England and Australia.

Watching Hallas sign are Mr. Ronald Teeman (left), the Leeds solicitor, acting for Parramatta, who handed the cheque to Mr. Geoff Beadnall (right), a director of the Keighley club.

Above: Ronnie Teeman has had a lengthy and illustrious influence on the sport of rugby league, including taking a hand in the first transfer from the UK to Australia

Left: Ronnie and Shirley Teeman beneath the twin towers on RL Challenge Cup final day at the old Wembley Stadium

RIPPON BROS
for
ROLLS-ROYCE · BENTLEY
* * *
Huddersfield · Bradford · Leeds · Sheffield

TUESDAY
FEBRUARY 10, 1959

No. 21,280

Tel. LEEDS 32701

THE YORKSHIRE

EVENING POST

COVERS THE COUNTY

Ghana plot-probe chief dashes to Leeds for interview with student

By ALLEN ROWLEY

A SECOND-YEAR law student at Leeds University has been interviewed by the Chief of Ghana's Special Security Police, who flew to Britain at the specific request of Mr. Geoffrey Bing, Q.C., Ghana's Attorney-General.

The security man—Chief-supt. Wells—was checking on the ownership of a banking account in the name of the student, 25-year-old Mr. K. G. Osei-Bonsu, who is the nephew and ward of Mr. R. Amponsah, a Ghana M.P. and General Secretary of the Ghana Opposition party, now detained under Ghana's Preventive Detention Act.

At an inquiry now going on in Accra, allegations have been made of a proposed coup d'état and a plot to kill Dr Nkrumah, Prime Minister of Ghana. At the inquiry it was alleged that Mr. Amponsah visited London to buy uniforms and military equipment, in connection with the proposed coup d'état.

MR. OSEI-BONSU TELLS HIS STORY

The dramatic story of the highly-secret interview—which led the visitor of a ...

insisted that no political matters be discussed at the interview and this was agreed.

"It is a fact that there is an account of that name in London, but my only connection is that I can have money from that transferred to my own bank account as and when required.

MY ONLY INTEREST IS STUDYING

"I have no knowledge of any other withdrawals from the Bonsu Overseas Study Account.

"My only interest is in pursuing my studies in law at Leeds University. I am quite worried —and have been for some time —about what is happening back home. But I have no intention of returning there at the moment. Mr. Teeman has agreed that he will go and investigate for me in Ghana if his business allows.

"I certainly have no knowledge of money being spent for uniforms or any other political matters. I do not wish to become involved in political matters."

MR. K. G. OSEI-BONSU and Mr. R. Teeman, pictured today.   On the right is Dr. Nkrumah.

SECURITY MAN SEES STUDENT

Detained Ghana MP's nephew and bank account

'I KNOW NOTHING'

By a Yorkshire Post reporter

FLYING back to Ghana with the details of a secret interview he had with a student of the University of Leeds is the chief of Ghana's Special Security Police, Chief Superintendent Wells. He made the visit to Leeds at the specific request of Mr. Geoffrey Bing, QC, Attorney-General of Ghana, to whom he will report on his return.

The student, 25-year-old Mr. K. G. Osei-Bonsu, is the nephew and ward of Mr. R. Amponsah, a Ghana MP and general secretary of the Ghana Opposition party, who has been detained under Ghana's Preventive Detention Act.

In Accra allegations have been made of a proposed coup d'état and a plot to kill Dr Nkrumah, the

Prime Minister. At an inquiry going on there it has been alleged that Mr. Amponsah went to London to purchase uniforms and military equipment for the proposed coup d'état.

Mr. Ronald Teeman, a Leeds solicitor, who represents Mr. Osei-Bonsu, gave details of the visit of Chief Superintendent Wells. It was made, he said, with the full knowledge of Scotland Yard, who got in touch with Leeds City Police on the matter.

Consulted the Dean

When Mr. Osei-Bonsu heard of the visit, he approached the Dean of the Faculty at the University of Leeds Law School, where he is a second-year student. The Dean suggested that if there was to be an interview the student should be accompanied by a solicitor. Mr. Teeman, who lectures at the University, agreed to represent him, and a Leeds CID man sat in at the interview.

Chief Superintendent Wells said he was making inquiries on behalf of Mr. Bing about an alleged plot to kill Dr Nkrumah. Pointing out that Mr. Amponsah had been detained, he said he was investigating the matter of a London bank account in the name of the Bonsu Overseas Study Account. Money had been drawn from this account last June, when Mr. Amponsah was in this country, he said.

At this stage Mr. Osei-Bonsu agreed to make a statement, to be witnessed by a Notary Public, who was, in fact, called out late at night to attend the interview.

Mr. Osei-Bonsu told me: "It is a fact that there is an account in that name in London, but my only connection is that I can have money from that transferred to my own bank account as and when required.

"I have no knowledge of any other withdrawals from the Bonsu Overseas Study Account.

"I insisted that no political matters be discussed at the interview, and this was agreed. My only interest is in pursuing my studies in law at the University of Leeds. I am quite worried, and have been for some time about what is happening at home. But I have no intention of returning there at the moment. Mr. Teeman has agreed that he will go and investigate for me in Ghana if his business allows.

"I certainly have no knowledge of money being spent for uniforms, or any other political matters. I do not wish to become involved in political matters."

Mr K. G. Osei-Bonsu

Newspaper clippings: One of Ronnie Teeman's most high-profile cases concerned the attempted assassination of Dr Nkrumah, Prime Minister of Ghana (*pictured far right in Evening Post story above*).

Leeds law student, 25-year-old K.G. Osei-Bonsu, is pictured *above* with Ronnie and *right*, alone

International rescue: Ronnie Teeman made front page news with Miss Edith Ike when the former fiancee of Major General Jack Gowon, the federal leader of Nigeria, hit the headlines during the Biafran troubles of 1970

Left: The unfortunate David Oluwale, whose sad demise threw the entire Leeds city police force into complete disarray

Above: Ronnie's great dual-code rugby hero Lewis Jones, pictured at Headingley Carnegie Stadium recently

Above: The legendary BBC commentator Eddie Waring, a close friend of Ronnie's

Above: Ronnie Teeman in his role of President of the Rugby Football League

selective and the obstructive and disruptive like Oluwale could not find a place to stay. It was only after his death that the St Anne's Day Centre for the homeless was opened. How poignant it was to discover that, when he signed a receipt for monetary benefit, Oluwale gave his home address as the doorway of a well known shop in the city centre.

Digging deeper, I examined the organisation that Oluwale had more other contact with than any other. Menston was the asylum where ten years of his young life were spent between 1953 and 1969. He was committed there within four years of his arrival in the United Kingdom, was released and sectioned again in 1965. The policy seemed to be one of out of sight, out of mind. In Oluwale's case this was especially true as he did not receive even one visitor. As to keeping the patient quiet, if that required liberal doses of calming medicine, so be it. I looked in vain for any programme that would prepare patients like him to live in the community but in Oluwale's time there was none.

The policy of Care in the Community was only put forward by the government in 1961 and within a month he had been discharged from Menston, although how he could be said to be fit to re-integrate, I do not know. The homeless shelter founded by the Reverend Don Robins at St George's Crypt at Leeds was not to his liking and he resorted to living rough. Clearly his mental and behavioural problems remained and may well have increased. In 1962 he was arrested on Woodhouse Moor and sentenced to six months imprisonment for maliciously wounding an elderly park ranger by breaking his finger. A few years later there are reports of increased social abuse to both people and property all, seemingly, without cause and necessitating increasingly scarce police resources to restrain it.

Lawyers have responsibilities for coming to the aid of unfortunates who are alleged to have broken the law and be their voices, but what could they do for the Nigerian? Kester Aspden's research took him to Judge Black among others who, at the time, was a Leeds solicitor who defended Oluwale when he was convicted of assault and sent to prison. Aspden wrote - and presumably he was quoting Black's views - 'Defending such a man against charges of assault on the police was hopeless. To suggest that the police were themselves the violent aggressor was a non-starter.' Black was an experienced criminal lawyer with an excellent reputation and I would concur with him, especially given my experience with the 'prosecutor's friend' John Randolph who would never accept that the police displayed violence and may well have increased the sentence for suggesting possible impropriety by a serving officer.

When I sat down with Aspden to revisit the tragic case of the mentally ill Nigerian whose body was taken from the river Aire and buried in a pauper's grave, I surprised myself at being able to speak of events so many years ago with ease and clarity although I found the experience disturbing. Lawyers become blasé. They finish a case and march on to the next, forgetting the one just closed believing, quite rightly, that there is nothing more that can be done. The Oluwale case was different and I still had in my mind two troubling issues.

The first was the undoubted bad behaviour of the police force to the victim and secondly, a gut feeling that the constabulary had more respect and concern for one another than they did for the public they purported to serve. I never contemplated, either before, during or in the years after the trial, that Oluwale was the victim of racism by the force. For me, colour played no part in the dreadful story, despite this being an issue that, because of my heritage where persecution and prejudice loom large, I am particularly sensitive to. He was a deranged stranger who few, if any, appeared to deal kindly with and it was the whole of society that failed him, the colour of his skin being irrelevant.

Society could not find a place for him and to see him around was a constant reminder of its failure. So its agents tried to hide him in a wood hoping, as at Menston, that out of sight would mean out of mind.

After my first long session with Kester Aspden I tried to re-evaluate who could have been expected to help him and it is a catalogue of missed opportunities starting with the mental hospital who released him unfit to cope with the world. The probation department would have seen him regularly, on sentence by the court, in prison and when being released but could not provide much assistance, apart from a few pounds to help him. The courts must take some of the blame for sentencing a man to custody who was clearly an antisocial misfit, their line being that he could be of no harm to the public while locked up rather than to identify and deal with the underlying causes.

But I repeat, in my view, there was no evidence that the colour and race of Oluwale singled him out for the disgraceful treatment he suffered at the hands and feet of the police. For me, the real issue is the true meaning of justice and how best to administer the law.

9

*

Leeds Sporting Greats: Football

A s the old footballing adage goes, goalkeepers are somewhat different, eccentric even. David Harvey was certainly the former, possibly the latter but definitely non-conformist.

The Scot by adoption but Englishman by birth with a city boy upbringing was at-heart a country lad. Signed as a schoolboy by Leeds United, his local team, he served a long apprenticeship before achieving first team status ahead of Welsh international Gary Sprake who could be brilliant but at the same time unpredictable. To this day I wear an Omega watch given to me by David in March 1980, engraved, 'With grateful thanks for everything.' Believe me 'everything' included a lot. The true tale of him missing the European Cup Final in 1975, in Paris, against Bayern Munich has not been recounted - but if it happened today it would be front page news in all the tabloids.

The story actually started with the postponement of a match between Leeds and Derby because of the weather and the effect it had on County's notorious Baseball Ground. The Leeds team had returned to Elland Road and dispersed. David and fellow Scots Gordon McQueen and Frankie Gray decided to go to a pub in Morley, a stone's throw from the ground. McQueen had transport handy and drove there but they did not stay long, David had a couple of pints. On the return journey, a vehicle travelling at speed on the wrong side of the road caused Gordon to swerve, his car leaving the road and ending up in a ditch. The only person hurt was David who complained that his leg was 'killing him' and he could not move. It was David's suggestion that they phone John Giles, the United midfield maestro who was unflappable in all situations and calmed them down saying, 'Stay where you are and I'll get help.'

John was concerned that if the story reached the ears of the press it would be national news in minutes, so he phoned me. I was having a winter break in Bournemouth and my daughter gave him the hotel's number. During his short resumé of events I advised that he contact my own doctor Gerald Bickler and I would, in the meantime, put him in the picture. Gerald agreed to go to the scene and when he did so, after a cursory examination of the damaged leg, he took the view that a fracture was a distinct possibility. Knowing his way around the hospitals, Gerald took David to the local infirmary and an X-ray confirmed his diagnosis. Gordon was distressed at the thought of his friend missing the highlight of his club career, the European Cup Final. I spoke to Gordon and urged him at once to report the matter to the police and to give them his account. A sensible lad, he accepted my advice and gave them a full and frank statement which took about an hour or so.

When John Giles reported the incident to me he said that it was proving difficult to contact the gaffer, Jimmy Armfield, who lived in Blackpool. He said, 'I have to smile because if

DR [Don Revie] was around he would have been in action within minutes.' There was little press comment. The chance of David making a recovery for Paris was negligible and he was philosophical about his bad luck. Instead, another fellow Scot, David Stewart, had his moment of glory. Leeds United lost however and the fans, incensed by the performance of the referee, rioted. The football authorities acted swiftly and imposed a heavy ban on the club and Revie's original dream vanished.

By missing the match David had, relatively speaking, lost a considerable amount of money. I advised him to claim from Gordon explaining that his insurers would have to cover him. I thought that before I sent the 'letter before action' with details of the claim, I would do the decent thing and speak to Gordon as I did not want there to be any conflict of interest. I rang and wished I hadn't. He was furious that he would lose his no claims bonus. I assured him that by claiming from his insurers for the cost of the very extensive repairs to his car he had eliminated it anyway. Gordon saw the sense of the situation and told me to go ahead and write and act for David.

David settled down, if that is the correct description for a man who spent much of his spare time at night roaming the countryside with his gun in pursuit of game and whose car back seat often carried a dead rabbit, hare or pheasant. He knew that Armfield, like his predecessor Brian Clough, was willing and anxious to transfer him elsewhere. Clough had supposedly lined up England custodian Peter Shilton but David carried on regardless while the storm surrounding him and then Clough blew out. In my opinion, he made a serious and diplomatic error in wearing spectacles. I cannot recall any other keeper of repute revealing a sight deficiency to the public and his playing colleagues, although all told me that his eyesight had never contributed to a goal being scored against him. The appearance of Jimmy Armfield did not, at first, improve the situation. Jimmy was a thinker but struggled to implement, prompting the famous statement from Duncan McKenzie, 'the indecision of the manager is final.'

In a frank confrontation, David eventually asked his boss if he was wanted and was reassured to discover that he was but, within a few weeks, received a phone call from Jimmy telling him that the club had received an enquiry from Gordon Lee, the manger at Everton, and he recommended that it would be good to meet him. When David told me of this I said, 'It seems to me he wants you out.' David replied that when he asked that question he was told by Jimmy, 'I'd personally like you to stay but I must give you the opportunity of hearing what is on offer.'

Given my experience of the workings of football clubs, the word personally disturbed me. I saw it as an indication that his hand was most likely being forced by the board who were under pressure to liquidate some assets. David went to the meeting with an open mind, first reminding Jimmy Armfield that he was sitting on a secure contract with a good time unexpired and that the terms would have to be exceptional if he was to move. He added that I would be accompanying him and Jimmy, who knew me well, raised no objection.

The meeting was arranged for a Wednesday evening in January and Jimmy said he would come with us as he was going to watch a game at Bolton. He arranged for Gordon to meet us there and suggested we drove into Lancashire via the scenic route rather than on the motorway. Jimmy is a very pleasant man and talkative, as one would expect from someone who is a most illuminating summariser on the radio and knowledgeable on a variety of topics. Being a former manager at Bolton, he was instantly recognised and feted on his arrival. He made the introductions with Gordon and headed for the match while we drove on to a motel to begin discussions. After half an hour of listening to Lee's proposition David said, 'I'd like to thank you for the interest but as I am a Leeds lad I prefer to remain in the area.' The following day David told Jimmy of the outcome and he seemed pleased enough.

The only other occasion on which David required my assistance came when John Giles was the successful manager of Vancouver Whitecaps, playing in the North American soccer league, and he told me they had a vacancy for a senior keeper. The job was David's if he was interested. I carried out negotiations with the general manager of the Canadian outfit and a deal was structured which was an improvement on his earnings in the UK. David went out and was successful until he broke a bone in his neck which signalled the end of his career. Working his way from the schoolboy ranks to play for Leeds United and then in the World Cup for Scotland in 1974 - where he was described as the best keeper in the competition - was no mean achievement but it did not adequately compensate him for his yearning for the outdoor life. So it was no surprise when he moved to the Orkney Islands which gave him the freedom to roam and where he now happily resides.

I doubt if anyone can find a footballer who was as universally admired and acclaimed as David's tartan and club colleague Peter Lorimer.

No matter club loyalties, even ardent Leeds detractors held an admiration for the man known as 'hot shot' on account of his ability to fire the ball accurately at tremendous speed. I acted for Peter or, as he was known to his team mates, 'lash'. He was always mister charming and it was not feigned. It was no surprise that when Ken Bates acquired the club, which was in a very sorry state, he appointed Peter to a director-ambassador role which he continues to perform with dignity and expertise. Fans hope that their sporting idols share their love and loyalty but so often these days the players are, more often than not, hired guns or short term mercenaries. With Peter it is the exact opposite. He has never ceased to be a fan of the club whose white number seven shirt he wore for so many years with distinction.

I accompanied him to Canada on two occasions; the first when he was recruited for the emerging North American soccer league by Toronto Blizzard, and then to Vancouver where he became player and assistant coach to his life-long friend John Giles. Peter can be very witty. Once, when we arrived at an airport in North America, we were asked by a burly security guard in an abrupt manner, 'Are you two guys together?' Quick as a flash Peter fired a verbal volley as ferocious as one of his shots at goal in his pomp. 'No sir, we are just good friends.' Similarly, on our first visit to Toronto, Peter was faced with a barrage of questioning from a bureaucratic government official. 'Sir, have you brought with you any raw meat, raw chicken, offal and any cooked meat, chicken or offal?' he said. 'No sir,' said Lorimer. The bureaucrat continued, 'Have you brought any fish or seafood, whether cooked or not?' Again, 'No sir,' was the reply. He went on, 'Have you brought any flour, wheat, corn, other grains or rice?' Once again Lorimer replied in the negative. The final question was, 'Have you any fruit or vegetables?' By now the football star was becoming weary. 'If I had known of such shortages I would have asked my mam to send over regular food parcels,' he ventured and even the stern po-face of his inquisitor managed a smile.

Our paths crossed again when he contemplated an offer to play in Israel. Peter, at the time, was working as the manager of a sports centre in Leeds when he received a telephone call from a gentleman called Yoram, a representative of Hapoel Haifa, a club associated with the trade union movement. The offer was to both play and assist with the coaching and would have been generous for a then star. For a veteran out of the game, it was quite fantastic. Peter and I discussed the possibilities and, having evaluated the pros and cons, came to the conclusion that it was too good an offer to ignore at that stage of his career.

The first practical problem to overcome was that the rules then of the Israeli Football Association only permitted a club to play Israeli citizens. It followed that to be eligible Peter would have to quickly become one.

When the State was established in 1948, the 'law of return' was enacted whereby a Jew from anywhere in the world could return to the land of his forefathers and be entitled to citizenship. There followed the need to define who a Jew was and it was decided that there would be two classifications, those born of a Jewish mother – which ruled him out – and ones who converted to the faith. Yoram was resourceful and suggested that I took Peter to a rabbi in Leeds to be rushed through the process and obtain the necessary certification. I had to tell him that although it was not unknown, the normal course of instruction took around two years of formal study, would end with an examination in front of a rabbinical panel and, in the case of a male, would involve a ritual circumcision. Even to suggest overnight conversion would have brought scorn and ridicule. Yoram was unfazed by my response and I am sure he thought that I was just placing obstacles in his path. He returned to me a few days later and said, triumphantly, that he had found the answer. Peter would go to New York and stay with a 'progressive' rabbi, have a quick course, receive his certificate and that would do the trick in Israel.

Peter, being tolerant, compliant and co-operative,

travelled to New York and duly received the relevant paperwork from the pliable rabbi after a couple of weeks and flew into Israel to be regally received by the club and its fans. The Israeli Football Association however did not join in the rapture and they declared that the conversion certificate was invalid and he was not eligible to play. Ever the optimist, Yoram declared, 'Don't worry, we will appeal to the courts and in the meantime you will be the coach for the team.' So Peter did, never kicking a ball in anger but enjoying his tutorial role and the young players responding well. Legal processes are slow all over the world and Israel is no exception and it was only after his return to the UK that permission was granted.

I visited Peter in Haifa, he was treated well by the fans but, as in England, the clubs had financial problems and wages were not often paid on time. Peter had an unusual way of dealing with the problem. He would drive to the bank but stay in the car and give two blasts on the horn. A clerk would come to the window and if the wages were in the account he would give a thumbs up and if not, he would signal no goal. At the end of his time there the fans made a handsome presentation to him as a memento of his stay. Peter told me that Israeli supporters could be very volatile and excitable and explained to me that on one occasion at an opponent's ground his team were unable to leave the dressing room because of the fear of physical attack and had to wait there for a couple of hours while fanatics were demonstrating outside. I said to him, 'It must be unusual for home fans to stay so long to abuse the visitors,' to which he replied, 'Ron, you've read the script wrong - it was our fans outside that were baying for our blood.' As to whether his conversion and all it – quite literally – entailed was in vain, I do not know as I never asked him about it or saw him in a synagogue.

'I recognise the face but don't remember the name,' was often overheard in the presence of Leeds-born actor Graham Luty.

Though his skills were many, he made his name because he was ugly. His unforgettable face looked as though it was hewn out of Yorkshire stone with all the rough edges left on, while his torso was an assortment of seemingly hastily assembled spare parts. His instantly recognisable look – along with that of great friend and former rugby league player Ted Carroll, famed for his flattened nose - was a boon to advertising agencies and he became a regular presence in commercials in particular. He took the stage name Paul.

I first met Graham at a rugby league match. He was an enthusiast who said his career was shortened because of his chronic inability to play the game, which his former team mates readily agreed with. His main job enabled him to pursue his other major interests, predominantly sleeping during the day time and out socialising at night until the early hours. He gained additional work as a door supervisor at the premier dance halls in the city. Live bands were the norm and among the 800 or so dancers at the Mecca or Majestic there were invariably the sports stars of the day, whom he befriended.

Graham's engaging personality allied to his ability to get admittance for his friends without them troubling the ballroom ticket office gained him not only allies but also complimentary tickets for Leeds United, Leeds rugby and Hunslet. Colin Welland, then a talented actor of *Z Cars* fame, was a regular at Elland Road during the glory days there and the pair's friendship was cemented by Colin offering Graham small speaking roles in his plays. When in London for a civil trial at the Law Courts, Graham gave me a ticket for *Kisses for Grandma,* in which he was appearing in the West

End. 'I just play myself,' he told me, 'and I don't then have any problems. He also had the good fortune to secure the role of Nobby Garside, a barman in the comedy TV series *Love Thy Neighbour*, which had magnificent viewing figures and led to numerous other cameo roles. He had very many female friends but none could persuade him to enter into a permanent relationship. He was a thrifty man when in Leeds living with his aged parents on a council estate.

He phoned up to make an appointment with me and said he thought the time had arrived for him to make a will; he would have been in his late thirties. I jokingly said, 'What's brought this on?' and he replied, 'Nothing, I've got views on what I would like to happen with my money when I have gone.' I asked him how much he was worth and he pondered that, with his life insurance policies and building society monies probably between £25-30,000. As he was a confirmed batchelor I asked shyly about his dependants and he said there were none but he wanted to leave everything he had to charities devoted to medical research with particular reference to cancer. The will was duly executed and placed in the safe.

A few months later I bumped into him, the theatrical work had dried up but rather than 'rest' as most of his fellow thespians did, he had taken a job as a scene shifter at the Yorkshire television studios. 'The money's not great but the graft is easy and I don't have to dip into savings,' he said. Not long after, I had a telephone call at home from Peter Gunby, who was a member of the coaching staff at Elland Road. 'I have some sad news Ron,' he told me, clearly shocked. 'We have just lost a good pal, Graham, who's died suddenly from a heart attack.' I told Peter how saddened I was and that as executor under his will, if there was any assistance he required in the funeral arrangements that he should not hesitate to contact me. No sooner had I replaced the receiver than a strange bizarre thought ran through me and put me into a cold sweat. I remembered our discussion about medical research and, for some reason, I confused myself into thinking that he had stipulated to leave his body for medical research. In a panic and I pride myself in never becoming shocked, surprised or astonished by anything said, seen or done, I got a taxi to my city centre office, planning on the journey what to do if my prognostication was correct. A quick read of the will confirmed, however, that it was the charities who were to benefit.

The following day Peter contacted me. I explained to him that Graham had left all his monies for medical research after payment of his debts and funeral expenses. Peter Gunby proved to be a great friend to his mate in death as he was in life. He was not surprised by the terms of the will but what he told me caused me further surprise. Apparently Yorkshire TV was dominated by the trade unions and had negotiated for its members not only a pension scheme but a 'death in service benefit' and he had told the YTV administrators to make contact with me which they eventually did. When it came, the staggering news was that with the contribution from them, the estate was now a sum approaching six figures. Peter then gave me some news which distressed me; Graham's elderly parents were obviously devastated by the death of their son but shaken that there was no mention in the testament of them.

When I had taken instructions from him he satisfied me that he had no dependants and I could only think that he had not betrayed any filial duty by his submission but had considered that, in the normal course of events, they would pre-decease him. I suggested to Peter that he should tell the parents that I would look into the position and come back to them. There then followed correspondence and dialogue with the charities, culminating in a most generous gesture on their part. They proposed to invest the money and ensure that the income went to the elderly parents whilst they were alive. As a consequence I re-visited my office practice when taking instructions from testators and was able to pass a word of advice to the trainees.

Graham's funeral was massive by Leeds standards and his local church was not able to accommodate all the mourners. So many 'luvvies' and sporting stars assembled as a generous tribute to a man who was a friend to all. As we entered the church I was standing at the side of Jack Charlton. I said, 'We've lost a good friend' and he replied, 'And I've lost a hundred quid, which I only loaned to him a few weeks ago.'

That humorous remark would have tickled Graham for it was said in jest, among all who knew him, that Jack liked to live up to his frugal image which, in fact, was not true. Even so, he did have a passion for cadging cigarettes, even from strangers. Even now, I always refer to my former client and good friend as Graham, his real name. But to his theatrical colleagues and television audience, he will always be remembered as Paul or mister ugly.

10

*

The Seedier Side

y father told me before government interfered, firstly by extending licensing hours and then introducing all day drinking, that if a man had not drunk enough by ten o'clock, then he should stop drinking.

That was the historic closing time in most cities. The breathalyser had an effect on the drinking habits of drivers but, alas, there are on average more young drunks today than ever before. Sadly many lawyers took to the bottle and paid the penalty. Frequently after a Bar mess or a Law Society dinner there were a few casualties and even serving judges had their wings clipped when found to be over the limit.

My good friend, the late Judge Raymond Dean was a proficient drinker all his career and afterwards, and when the court had finished its business for the day he would retire to the pub. He was caught and convicted for drink driving and the Lord Chancellor was not amused, his punishment being to send him from Leeds to London to sit, forcing Raymond to bear his own travelling and accommodation expenditure.

It is the regular, unconventional drunks that trouble the lower courts. They tend to live rough, sleep out, eat little food and drink much cheap wine, meths and anything else upon which they can quench their thirst. Socially they are drop-outs, more to be pitied than blamed. Asked to move on by the police, the only friendships they have are those with fellow sufferers. The offences they commit are predominantly either being drunk and disorderly or drunk and incapable and apart from a small fine - which is likely to go unpaid - there is little that a court can do for them. Voluntary organisations do their best but these unfortunates still return to the courts. Merely hearing their name called by the usher is enough to know the offence.

Patrick McCarthy was one of our regulars, in his early fifties and of Irish decent. He lived in St George's Crypt at night time but spent the remainder of the day pursuing drink wherever he could find it. At lunchtime he would wait outside the Cathedral hoping that some attender at Mass would hand over a few coins. I'm sure that though he had pages of drink convictions listed, there would have been more if he had been booked every time he had been spotted rolling about on the pavement or staggering between motor cars on the road.

One particular afternoon hearing - and I always thought it was a tactical error to schedule their cases for after lunch when the likelihood was that they would stumble in the worse for wear - there was no answer when Patrick's name was called. The usher opened the door again and shouted his name more loudly in the corridor and, after a couple of minutes, McCarthy came in.

'Is your name Patrick McCarthy?' asked the clerk.

'No,' he replied.

So it continued. 'I'll ask you again, is your name Patrick McCarthy?'.

'I've told you once, no.'

The court officer tried again, appearing exasperated, as if he could explode any minute. 'Well, what is your name?' he demanded.

'Jesus Christ,' was the defiant response.

'Well, was it once Patrick McCarthy?'

'Yes,' said the Irishman. 'That's right but I changed my name by deed poll to Jesus Christ.'

The clerk seemed nonplussed. 'Oh, well, I see,' but Patrick interrupted, 'Don't say 'well' to me. I insist you address me as Jesus Christ.'

Increasingly agitated, the clerk continued through clenched teeth. 'Alright, alright Mr Jesus Christ, what is the date of your birth?'

'Call yourself a court clerk and you don't know Jesus Christ was born on the 25th of December?' came the reply, at which point both the prosecutor and the court official threw down their pens.

The only client who asked for my services after a heavy night out was John Morgan, a horse racing correspondent and tipster, author of *Morgan's Tales* and a renowned after dinner speaker who was always in demand at charity functions. It was a Friday night and I was in bed. I reached for the phone when it rang. 'Sorry to disturb you Mr Teeman but this is Pudsey police station,' said the voice on the other end. 'We have your client Mr Morgan. It's an allegation of drunkenness and he wants you to come over.'

I agreed and as a non-driver whose wife was unwilling at that time of night to chauffeur me, I rang for a taxi and arrived there about three quarters of an hour later. Standing on the duty sergeant's desk was a very happy John Morgan giving a passable impression of Fred Astaire singing and dancing to the tune of Tiptoe through the Tulips. He looked at me and coyly remarked, 'See Mr Teeman,' as he did a twirl and stage whispered to me in confidential tones, 'And they think I'm drunk.' I replied, 'Say no more'. Mr Morgan became a client in 1955 and had a unique arrangement with my practice. 'You only get paid if you win,' he said. In the 55 years of our association, I have to declare, he has never paid me one penny.

The Divorce Commissioner charged with the duty of handing our decrees frequently rattled a few sabres and caused the odd heart to miss a beat merely to assert that the role was much more than a rubber stamp. As a good number of petitions were based on the respondent's adultery, enquiry agents were instructed by solicitors to obtain the essential evidence.

It was usually a confession statement with a small addendum that the agent had been the accommodation where the suspected guilty parties were cohabiting. More often than not, the paid enquirer did not have to pry but was made welcome and often appeared by appointment. One of the agents I used was George Duffield Mackereth, at least 25 stone in weight and 6ft 3', he was a former policeman, not very nimble but as straightforward as you could find. On one occasion when giving his evidence, he was startled when the judge commented, 'What if I do not believe what this man and women told you of their life together. What if they were lying, what would your response be to that Mr Mackereth?' He thought for a second or two, wiped his brow and responded, 'Short of asking them to perform in front of me I can offer no other suggestion my Lord.'

The procedures on divorce have altered dramatically. First, the monopoly of barristers ended and solicitors were allowed to appear. Then the divorce division was abolished and the county court became the forum. 'My Lord' reverted to being 'your Honour' and, finally, appearances by any lawyer were rendered unnecessary. Pieces of paper sufficed. All of that was done within a generation, which just shows that the law can move with devastating effect when it has the will to do so. As a consequence, Mr and Mrs Public were saved hundreds of pounds in fees, the humiliation of appearing in court reciting episodes of a life they would dearly wish to forget to a judge who was not really interested, and having to admit sexual acts committed in privacy which caused no harm to society.

I practised in the divorce courts well before changes were made and, with retrospect, I now shake my head at how we stood for the nonsense accepted for generations. If a marriage broke down it was because one party had behaved badly and the possibility of a couple falling out of love never entered into the equation; the court had to find someone guilty of a matrimonial offence. Committing adultery, even on an isolated occasion, was quite sufficient, although it had to be proved beyond reasonable doubt, just like murder. Cruelty to your spouse was similarly indictable and staying away for a continuous period of three years without an excuse completed the triumvirate of accepted matrimonial crimes. When divorce cases were defended, it was invariably because of money.

We are now more civilised and there is no stigma of guilty behaviour attaching to a divorce. We talk of a marriage having broken down and we do not allocate blame. Couples are becoming less interested in formal ceremonies but more concerned with forming partnerships, recognising that it would be great if they endured forever but acknowledging that they could be fragile and break up. Medieval mysticism was an apt description of matrimonial law until the end of the twentieth century, a relic of the ball and chain approach the church held over the lives of citizens regardless of whether they were believers or not. Even though their one-time monopoly dwindled, the church did not see fit to remove its clenched fists from the termination process.

I think of Ellen, a tiny lady who was the attendant in the ladies rest rooms situated below ground level in Briggate, Leeds. She married a soldier on leave from the battle of the Somme in 1917 on impulse, knowing nothing of him or his background and when he left for the battlefield he kissed her goodbye, literally and metaphorically. Apart from the fact that he was discharged from the army after the end of hostilities in 1919, she did not know whether he remained alive or dead.

Thirty-seven years later she was happy, having met her mister right some 30 years earlier and settled down with him. Though the association was childless it was successful. The man in her life was approaching 64 and due to retire and that made Ellen open her eyes for the first time to reality. I asked her why she had waited so long and she told me, 'I was frightened that the neighbours might find out that I was not married to Herbert and I had been living 'in sin' so we kept off the subject.' George Bernard Shaw spoke of middle class morality but this was the working class existing – and barely living – in poverty, worried about the attitudes of their peers towards them.

It was the opening of the Legal Aid purse that empowered her to seek advice and I explained the position as I saw it. She produced a crumpled piece of paper from her handbag that was a cutting from a Tuesday edition of the *Yorkshire Evening Post,* with a list of *decrees nisi* granted the previous day and with the grounds for the divorce shown, that was what troubled her. I told her that the press had the right to publish but she should not worry, the name used would be the surname given to her by the missing husband and not the name she had adopted when living with Herbert and the neighbours would not recognise it. She had to remove her spectacles to dry her eyes with a handkerchief. After she regained her composure she gave a startled cry. 'Oh Mr Teeman, what will you think of me,' she said. 'I can't even remember his name'. We discovered her marriage certificate and obtained leave of the court to dispense with serving the petition on the husband personally by advertising it in a newspaper and, after a long wait to see if the missing 'husband' came forward, a *decree nisi* was granted and six months later made absolute. Mind you, she had signed a discretion statement admitting her 'adultery' with Herbert .

Similarly, one seriously abused wife petitioner who left her spouse to live with a more loving partner confessed to me that when enjoying a night of passion with her new love, she paused every now and then to reflect upon her good fortune and to consider whether the commissioner of divorces would exercise his discretion.

For many, the entire divorce process started with a Legal Aid application which insisted that the client had to place in a sealed envelope a statement saying whether or not adultery had taken place during the marriage. Solicitors were counselled to explain what adultery meant and consisted of. I have met those who believe it can only be done in the open air and others who thought that it entailed drinking with the opposite sex in public houses but behind the divorce court lurked the shadow of the Queen's Proctor. I knew neither his or her name, address or telephone number. I did not comprehend of their precise authority and to whom they answered but I did know they were a busybody, a voyeur and, on occasion, an agent provocateur. I had an image of them hiding in wardrobes, peering through bedroom keyholes and listening to conversations in solicitor's offices. Their prey was either or both of the parties who sought relief via the divorce division. They would make a random search to ensure that the court was not being deceived by connivance. At worst they could intervene and at best unnecessarily increase the work load of a solicitor.

It was hardly the greatest of footings to get off on with a new client by asking if adultery had been committed. The question frequently produced a verbal riposte but I have heard of more aggressive reactions. Nevertheless, feathers have to be ruffled, apologies made and duties explained. A female relative once called me at home. Her solicitor she said was 'sex mad'. Every time she saw him about her divorce, which was contested, he asked whether she had had sex since their last meeting. She was indignant that he had, perhaps, formed a moral view of her which was very far from the truth. To be honest, she could hardly be described as the best bloom in the flowerbed. She wanted me to call and tell him that I would now act for her. I quickly informed her that being a relative would embarrass me and her husband and that I would have to decline but she still asked me to have a word with her representative. I was trapped but agreed so to do. The lawyer in question was Dennis Lythe, the doyen of the matrimonial solicitors in the city who had plenty of experience and was an acknowledged authority on divorce as he did no other legal work.

I knew him well and I was sure his questions were not merely prurient. Indeed, his legal executive was his wife, Myrtle, who always referred to him as Mr Lythe. To the amusement of many in the profession, when they left the office on an evening en route to the railway station, she would always walk a few paces behind him. Dennis laughed at first when I eventually contacted him and told me his question was for self preservation motivated by a nasty experience some years earlier. He was acting for a lady past the first blush of youth but could pass for middle aged in a crowd. She petitioned for divorce and they had difficulty in finding the husband to serve him with the papers and eventually sought and obtained leave of the court to dispense with the need. All that took time and it was, perhaps, a year from the date he first took instructions for the case to be listed. On the hearing date, Mrs Lythe took the lady to the court to meet the barrister and when she was called to the witness box she confirmed on oath that the respondent had left her over four years before and she had not seen or heard from him since. The judge looked up from his papers and stared at her and said, quite gently, 'Are you with child, madam?' It was obvious to all that she was coming to the end of her pregnancy. She confirmed, 'I am expecting in a month, Sir.' 'Oh,' said the judge to her counsel sharply. 'There is no discretion statement here,' and without an explanation the judge turned to the lady and declared, 'I am standing your case down'. She looked up into the rafters of the court, promptly collapsed and was carried away, seemingly lifeless.

The judge said that he would adjourn the case for the solicitor to appear before him with an explanation. Dennis Lythe told me that the incident had a profound influence on him. He explained, 'She signed a discretion statement saying she had not committed adultery before the Legal Aid certificate was issued. I prepared the petition and because of the problems of service did not see her until months later.' He went on, 'Frankly, I did not notice any bump and had no reason to believe that she was pregnant. In any event,' he protested, 'eyes can deceive'. A couple of weeks before the hearing she came into the office, it was a bitterly cold day, she was wearing a heavy coat, and again nothing was said. Then the judge looked at her and bingo I have the indignity of being ordered to appear before him.' All ended well, however, and she got her decree, the judge exercising discretion as her adultery was with a man she met months after instituting proceedings. But the Queen's Proctor became involved and, from that moment on, Dennis Lythe said, 'I no longer trust my eyes or my intuition – I ask each time when they sign as I am not going to go through that experience again.' He went on with a smile, 'and you will find it amazing how many women ask if a snogging session after the pub counts?'

There was only one such occasion when I had a nervous twinge in the stomach and that was after I heard that a lady petitioner I acted for had not asked for discretion and given birth barely two months after the *decree nisi* had been granted and before it had been made absolute. My quandary was whether I should file a retrospective discretion statement and the Law Society's phone helplines were of no assistance. The three local divorce lawyers that I referred the dilemma to had not experienced the situation so there was nothing for it, I decided to be better safe than sorry. I telephoned the Lord Chancellor's department and was shunted through various hands before, eventually, a male authoritative voice listened and answered, 'Oh forget about it, dear boy, they all do it don't they?' He then went on to say, 'We have not the time, the staff or the inclination and frankly the finance to get involved. Do have a nice weekend, sir.' Replacing the phone I realised that no-one, at any stage, had asked my name or that of my firm. Often, the preparation of the statement was often the only interesting, exciting, and skilful part of the entire divorce process.

In my early days colleagues frequently used to ask me if I continued to work a nightshift. The answer, regrettably, was yes. The one-man band played much better tunes at night when all around was tranquil. I was quite a night owl, preferring to return to my office after supper rather than work at home.

I liked to be surrounded by files and books, they were my

companions. My other companion was a well-fed budgerigar, the sole occupant of a gilded cage in the waiting room. The phone ringing used to set her off chattering and it was only when a cover was thrown over the cage that she would become silent. Working late hours went with the territory for if I was in the magistrate's court most of the day there was office work awaiting my return as well as the following day's files to be worked on.

Years later when I left the firm of Teeman, Gould and Ake to pursue a career in commercial law, abandoning the criminal courts and public funded work, it was a test of my patience waiting for instructions to arrive. One Thursday evening I took a telephone call, at home on this occasion, from Robin Peters a chartered accountant and a partner in the local branch of a national firm. He asked, 'Could I find the time to act for two of his clients who were selling their business to a public quoted company for a princely sum?' The potential rubbing of hands was tempered by the declaration that the job had to be completed in seven to ten days as the buyer wanted to incorporate the new business profits into his own balance sheets before their financial year end. I had to ask the obvious question, 'What was wrong with approaching the client's own solicitors, and inviting them to act?' The answer was they had done so but that there was not one partner in the firm available to see them for a further fortnight. To me it was a godsend that could make my financial year. I put on one side that I would have to postpone other work for a short time and, rubbing my hands with much anticipation, welcomed and accepted the challenge.

I met the vendors immediately and was told the buying company were the liquorice allsorts manufacturers Bassetts, based in Sheffield. The solicitors acting for them were Wake Smith & Co. a solid old-established, multi disciplined legal practice in South Yorkshire. We quickly made contact, my clients being Adam Imports Ltd whose balance sheet was healthy and, being cash rich, of considerable interest to a public limited company. The meeting was convened to take place at Bassett's factory in Sheffield and I can still, all these years later, recall the sweet, sugary smell that permeated those premises.

Robin Peters and the clients had briefed me thoroughly, the purchase price was agreed and Chris Ryecroft who with his business partner James Kenyon had started the business only a few years earlier importing electronic games from the far east, was to remain after the sell out as managing director. His co-founder took the money and moved on to pastures new, which I believe took him overseas. I arrived at the purchaser's factory with Robin and my clients at about 2.30pm and we worked continuously until 5.30 the following morning. It was then that the deal was finally put to bed. I was relatively unknown in the field, the solicitors on Bassett's side readily admitting they had never heard of me, I have to say that I was not such a greenhorn as they might have believed. I had been both lecturer and examiner in company law at the University of Leeds for some years but it was my lack of practical experience that, probably, slowed the process.

Over the long hours there was much scratching of heads, many queries to resolve and numerous debates on the substance of the minutiae contained in the draft documents. Just before midnight, when everyone was tired and perhaps irritable, we came to a sticking point on one particular clause. The purchasers would not give way and I probably out of sheer cussedness resisted their overtures. To ease the situation which was causing a stand off, I leaned back and suggested a vote be taken by a show of hands. The five members of the purchaser's team proceeded to put up their hands in unison and I was the only vote cast for the vendors. Immediately I said, 'Gentlemen the vote is not binding as you are all biased and have an interest.' The ice was broken and eventually a satisfactory compromise reached amid much laughter.

As we were finally putting away our files I said to my hosts, 'Gentlemen, my wife will simply not believe firstly that I was working continuously until 5.30 in the morning and, secondly, that I have been in a jelly baby factory all of that time.' I pleaded with them. 'I must show her some proof.' The senior partner of Wake Smith said, 'What you need, Ron, is a Deed of Fidelity.' He duly drafted one which was signed and sealed by each member of the purchaser's team. That document is a precedent which I have regarded as both unique and original over the years that have passed. It remains a cherished part of my practice memorabilia.

At 6.30am having been driven back to Leeds by my clients, I crawled into bed. My good lady was deep in sleep so I put the deed on her bedside table. I obviously was still slumbering when she awoke and I cannot recall her reaction but certainly there was not the cross-examination that I usually had to face of 'where have you been and who have you seen', when I came in with the milk.

Street walkers will exist forever. The oldest profession is not governed by the Law Society, the General Medical Council or even the TUC, it is the essence of free bargaining.

Thankfully, today prostitutes are very rarely sent to prison, but it was not always so. I represented a regular client of mixed race, her face topped with long blonde hair. At the age of 31 her record was several pages long and if you read the last 12 convictions you would be covering only two years of her life. To be fair, she always left the courtroom to go directly to the fines office to discharge her obligations. One particular day, after assessing the monetary penalty, the chair announced, 'Financial penalties do not act as a deterrent to you. If I see you in court again you will not be given an opportunity to pay a fine, you will be straight down the stairs and will be leaving in a van. Do you understand me?' She nodded her head accordingly.

It was at least six months before I saw her again. There she was a charge sheet in her hand as she told me of the date of her latest hearing. I agreed to meet her at the door of the courtroom on the appointed day. I rescued her last three files from our storage system but, if necessary, I could have given her mitigation in the middle of the night without reference to any documents. It was a well worn litany; she had resolved to pack it in, she's got a day job as a waitress in a café, sadly her youngest child was taken ill, she had to give up the job to look after the child, the man she was living with went off with another woman leaving her bills for furniture, clothing and falling into arrears with the rent. She reacted to the pressure and the need for money by returning to the streets in the evening and was only on the streets for a few days when she was arrested. I could not claim copyright for that mitigation which, with only a slight amendment, would fit the bill for virtually any 'working girl' appearing before a magistrate.

I met her outside court as agreed. She was, I thought, unusually fidgety and we had no more than three minutes conversation in the crowded corridor where she confirmed what I had to tell the court was correct. Just then the usher appeared and shouted out her name. I opened the court door for her to enter, I was possibly the only man who ever treated her as a lady. I followed in when she stopped suddenly. 'I can't,' she exclaimed, 'it's him.' I said, 'What are you trying to tell me?' She retorted, 'The guy sitting in the middle is the one who said he would send me down.' It all came back to me and I understood her anxiety and why she had real concern for her liberty. I have always maintained that the advocate's greatest gift is the ability to think on their feet and I realised that our only course of action was to get my client out of there as expeditiously as possible.

I had to say something to the court and began, 'Your Worship, there are reasons why I make this application, which is to transfer this case to another court.' I was interrupted by the clerk, Mr Lillyman, a very nervous man who always seemed wary when I was around that something would go seriously wrong. 'Now come on Mr Teeman,' he said. 'We cannot transfer cases without good or sufficient reason. You know that surely' he continued rather angrily.

I was in a quandary. The golden rule is that a lawyer must not deceive the court and in the few seconds at my disposal I had to come up with a plausible reason. 'Your Worships,' I declared. 'Your learned clerk is quite right. It falls upon me to give a sufficiently weighty reason why this case should go before another court. The gravaman of my submission is that justice could be better served if this court recused itself. You see,' and I paused for dramatic effect, 'the defendant knows one of the magistrates sitting here today.'

There were audible gasps and intakes of breath but my conscience was clear. I had not told a lie even though the assumption of those around that the recognition was carnal rather than legal. The transfer was duly granted. That court listened to my mitigation and fined the defendant £20 which, in customary fashion, she duly paid on the spot. But the story does not end there. That night each of the magistrates in turn and unbeknown to each other phoned me at home. Their words were not identical but the purport of the conversation was the same, 'Tell me Ronnie, who was it she knew?'

These unfortunate ladies and, alas, many were not so

young, had a dangerous lifestyle. For some it cost them their lives while others were injured when attacked by their punters. It may have deterred them for a short time but their inexorable return to the streets followed and one thing was noticeable, they looked after the other.

One 'working girl' told me, 'We only have one another to turn to.' The drug problem, particularly cocaine, was always there in the background as was the presence of a pimp. The most saddening spectacle was to see a girl very heavily pregnant stand in court and admit soliciting and learn that she was only a teenager, yet all the freshness and vitality of youth had disappeared. Mary was one of them and as the prosecution read out the police observations that led to her arrest followed by a lengthy list of previous convictions, the kindly chairman of the bench said, 'Don't get up – tell us what you want us to know – seated.' The young girl, well spoken and articulate hinting at a good education then recounted, 'You can see my condition, sir. I cannot work now and I am determined that I will be a stay-at-home mother in a few weeks time and this court will not see me again.' She was about to continue when the magistrate flagged her down, 'Say no more my dear, you may need help.' Looking at the solicitors present he ruminated, 'I wonder if one of you gentlemen could speak to her and come back with some more information that could help her and ourselves in how we can best deal with this case.' There was no rush of volunteers from those seated on the solicitor's bench who seemed more content in studying their files so the chairman went on, 'Mr Phipps, will you help me?' Of course he could not refuse and he left the court followed by the girl.

About half an hour later they both returned. The chairman immediately adjourned the case he was then considering and invited the solicitor to speak. It is worthy of note that an experienced practitioner can gain an inordinate amount of relevant material in a short time where others can take hours and still be short of facts. Mr Phipps gave a potted biography of this client which was sad but familiar. The chairman now revelling in his role as the kind do-gooder announced that she would be bound over to be of good behaviour for 12 months and preceded to give her not only a homily of what leading a virtuous existence would bring but finished with the peroration, 'I tell you in concluding that I pass on my way home the street where you stood and if I ever see you there I will stop my car and put you over my knee and smack your behind, do you understand?'

Before she could reply, the genial Mr Phipps rose and said, 'You know Mr Chairman, you have given her a sharp reminder, because that is exactly what most of her clients did.'

11

*

My Love Affair with Italy

I had a long and happy association with AC Milan. Certainly, I was on their Christmas card list. In fact, their generosity extended to much more munificent gifts ranging from vintage wine to paintings. In the summer of 1984 they engaged me to act for them as they wanted to acquire Mark Hateley from Portsmouth Football Club. I frankly knew little of Hateley other than that he was playing for a club outside of the top division.

We met in a very fine Italian restaurant, the chairman of Pompey, Mr John Deakin and his wife, who were accompanied by Ron Noades who was the chairman of Crystal Palace, who Mr Deakin told me was advising him. The Italians were represented by their commercial manager who I knew well and, on entering, I saw that Alan Ball, the wonderful engine of the 1966 World Cup winning team and who was the manager at Frattan Park was also present. He did not join us at the dinner table but waited in the bar. After the meal we adjourned to the home of a Mr Santine, who I understood to be a restaurateur, although I could not define his role in the negotiations. Hateley was represented by Dennis Roach, a well-known agent, who vigorously explained that the offer on the table made to his man was, 'Too low by far.' He quickly added that his client was aware that other English players in Italy were receiving much more than he was being offered.

I did not consider that to be a fair point in the negotiations. I replied with some acerbity, 'I am sorry I have to say this but I must point out that the players who are in Italy now from England are of a much higher standard and reputation than Mr Hateley – indeed Wilkins and Brady are world class players – and he is nowhere near that at this stage of his career.' There was an adjournment so my clients could consider their position. They had made their valuation and were not prepared to increase it. After a short time we spoke to Roach alone. We told him that Milan's offer for a player from a lower division team in England who had a basic wage of £350 a week was most generous and could not be increased. Roach was not pleased and, quite frankly, we could understand his position. If the proposed deal collapsed, Portsmouth would not get a transfer fee and Roach would not get his agents cut. Milan's bidders gently suggested that if the player accepted their offer, albeit reluctantly, they would ensure that no deductions were made from it for agent's fees which Milan would pay to Roach. He saw the logic of that and Hateley signed the appropriate forms. The transfer fee was £1,000,000, I did not advise on it but that was a huge amount in 1984. Ray Wilkins was already at the San Siro when Hateley joined and I knew that he was very happy with the treatment he received from the club.

Paulo Mantovani, the president of Sampdoria FC, based in Genoa, was living in Switzerland when I first met him to negotiate the acquisition of Liam Brady from Juventus. He explained that due to a disagreement and confrontation with the fiscal authorities in Italy, it was in his own interests to remain in the neutral country until matters were cleared up. He had much to be thankful for in 1984. In the previous year he had brought to his club top line overseas players Liam Brady and Trevor Francis, raising the profile and standard considerably. His self-imposed exile ceased and he was able to return to running the club from its home base. Sadly I had to tell him that Brady, after two years with him, had decided to move on and that it was not a question of money but purely he wished to join to a bigger club with greater opportunities for success in his final term in Italy. Mantovani was deeply saddened by the news but appreciated being told early of Brady's decisions and not having read of it as an 'exclusive' in a newspaper as was often the case. He said he wanted a quality replacement and mentioned several names. I generally hate shopping lists, inevitably what you are shown is overpriced and soiled having been in the market place far too long and handled by many. I suggested to Paulo that he let me put out some discreet enquiries without disclosing his club's interests.

A few days later I heard some gossip that Liverpool star Graeme Souness was planning to make the forthcoming European Cup Final, which would hopefully complete a treble, his last appearance for the Reds. I told Mantovani and suggested we made some discrete enquiries. My information was that Souness' father in law had sold his business for a princely sum and, to circumvent capital gains tax, was planning to move abroad and take the family with him, ideally including his daughter. There was the perfect incentive for Souness to continue his playing career in Europe if he wanted to do so. I emphasised to Mantovani that a leak would be unfortunate and cause anger at Liverpool so I spoke to the club's secretary, Peter Robinson.

A Lawyer for all Seasons

He did not seem surprised at the approach but advised that as the club had just returned from a tour of Israel and was planning for the European Cup decider on the Wednesday that I should be patient and he would note my position and come back to me after that game. Realising the situation was delicate, I again urged caution to Mantovani. Five days before the final I wrote formally to Robinson – a power broker at the Football League incidentally – telling him of my instructions to act on behalf of Sampdoria and asking bluntly whether they would be prepared to negotiate for the transfer of Souness. Speed and bravado was of the essence as the transfer and registration of players to Italy had to be completed by the end of June as there was set to be a moratorium on them for two years. I then added, 'This matter is treated by our client's with the utmost confidence and we trust that you respect that confidence and will make no disclosure of their interest contained in this letter.' I emphasized to reassure them that, 'There will be no approach to the player until such time as you have decided whether you wish to negotiate a transfer or not, and the negotiations have been concluded between yourselves and our client.'

Paulo Mantovani went to Rome for the European Cup final and kept his mouth firmly shut. His interest in Souness was further increased by the midfielder's devastating display and leadership which contributed to Liverpool's success. After that game, the team went on tour to Swaziland and, on 1st June, I fielded a call from Peter Robinson. He described himself as a reluctant seller and confirmed the rumour I had heard earlier about Souness' wife being an heiress and the desire to 'go into exile'. He was saddened at the thought of releasing a player who was only 31 and had another two years to run on his contract. Robinson would not quote an exact fee that Liverpool required and suggested that we make an offer of over £600,000. There then followed the most polite and reasonable negotiations and, on the 8th June, I met him and his chairman John Smith at Anfield and agreed a transfer valued at £675,000 spread over the following year. John Smith, who I had never met before, was very down to earth. He was a brewer who once had responsibility for the leading manufacturer in Leeds, Tetley's. He was quite witty and invited me to use his phone to speak to Mantovani and offered to leave the room, which I said was not necessary. The call lasted three of four minutes, and I had to shout because the connection was not the best. When I had finished Smith said to me, 'Do you realise Teeman that you were speaking to your Italian contact in broken English?'

We were aware of interest from two other clubs and one agent who had been phoning Sampdoria about various players included Souness in his shopping list. He claimed to have an agreement by association with Liverpool to arrange Souness's possible transfer and warned the Italian club, 'If you are going to approach Liverpool, I would be automatically involved'. Mantovani firmly told the imposter that they did not work in such a way. Peter Robinson confirmed that he had spoken to Souness in Durban and the player then phoned me. I gave him the up-to-date information and he said that he didn't have an agent nor did he intend to be represented by anyone other than his father-in-law. We then arranged for a party to travel to Genoa to complete the deal, Peter Robinson and David Ensor, a Liverpool solicitor, myself and the Souness clan.

Mantovani, in telling me of the travel arrangements said, 'I will be at the airport but I will not be alone – at least 5,000 fans will be there'. He was not wrong, when the plane touched down we were greeted on the tarmac by the Sampdoria official and two large cars. We were driven out of the airport, past where the crowds had gathered, and a barrage of sound greeted us as we moved to the city. I cannot recall going though passport control or customs. As is traditional in Italy, the club's offices were situated in the centre and, when we arrived, Trevor Francis was leaning against a wall in the background of the reception area. He had been the largest purchase made by Manchester City under the chairmanship of Peter Swales. Bought from Nottingham Forest, where he had enjoyed success in the European Cup, I was told that City's eyes had been 'bigger than their belly' to coin a well known phrase and that the fee paid for Trevor was weighing heavily on them. Mantovani when told said, 'Go ahead Ron and sort it out.' I never had contact with Swales or City's manager John Bond but deal directly with earthy club secretary Bernard Halford. He checked out my credentials with his equivalent at Arsenal Ken Friar and I must have been given a good reference for quickly we were in business at Maine Road. A deal was set up and agreed except for one missing ingredient, Trevor Francis, who was somewhere in Europe at the time. Nevertheless, all parties eventually came together and Trevor became a Sampdoria player sharing the same luxurious villa with the 'Brady bunch'.

Souness went into the president's office and it was not long before the negotiations were concluded and, to his utter embarrassment, he made an appearance on the balcony and waved to the cheering masses down below. More hysteria was to follow as Souness, this time wearing the club scarf, walked through the streets with the Sampdoria president. The crowds were chanting and shouting, 'Grazie Presidente – Grazie.' On 12th June, the formal agreement between the two clubs was executed.

Tony Ensor – later to become Judge Ensor – certainly enjoyed his break from the normal legal routine and was fascinated by the coverage in the media, particular the two papers published each day devoted entirely to sport. Everything down to the minutest detail was fully chronicled. He was bemused by one paper referring to me as *L'avoccato* and himself as *Legale*. I paused for a moment before posing the thought, '*Legale* is like a law clerk, whilst *L'avoccato* is the finished article.' He could quickly see by the twinkle in my eye that I was having him on. Souness and family moved to the flat in the mansion previously occupied by Liam Brady in the delightful sea side town of Nervi and chalked up another successful chapter in a great career.

Football agents are now legitimate traders having to hold a license granted by the Sports Registered body and their influence and power – and more often than not criticism of them – has spiralled in the last 30 years. Until 'freedom of contract' was established there was nothing for them to negotiate about with a limit imposed on the amount a player could receive as his share of a transfer fee. Agents truly arrived on the scene when the advertising world began to appreciate that a player's endorsement of a product was of real value. The first to exploit the changing landscape were Dennis Compton – the original Brylcream Boy – and Stanley Matthews, whose boots were made in Leeds. They, though, were the exceptions.

The top football agent in the early days was Gigi Peronace, a tubby little Italian whose hands were as demonstrative as his voice. He was more than an agent, he would bring parties together and create a deal from which everyone benefited including himself. The gregarious Italian's first appearance in England was quite sensational. He called at Leeds United who had on their books arguably their greatest ever star, Welshman John Charles, equally as effective and dominating as either a centre half or goal scorer. Peronace knew that money was scarce at Elland Road and sought the permission of the Leeds Board to transfer him to

A Lawyer for all Seasons

Juventus, the Turin club supported and financed by the Agnelli family of Fiat fame. Leeds received a transfer fee far higher than the English market would have paid and Charles was content. For him the move was akin to winning the lottery as his weekly wage in England was less than £25 a week. John was a sensational success in Italy and is still spoken of in Turin in hallowed tones, eventually ending his career in Rome after another, less successful, stint back at Leeds.

Gigi, after such a coup, was unable to repeat his success, the likes of Jimmy Greaves and Joe Baker not finding the same mark and Italian clubs then lessening their interest in British players. He worked as the London representative of the Italian Football Association and being in a close relationship with one of the wealthiest families in Italy did him no harm. He lived in a stylish house in Twickenham with his family, furnished in true Italian style with an abundance of marble. Although he never lost his Italian accent, in many respects he was an Anglophile, shopping in Harrods and Fortrum & Mason, attending Arsenal matches and English International games as a guest of his friend, Football Association secretary Dennis Fellows.

When he heard that I was advising Liam Brady of Arsenal, he suggested we meet up. Gigi had style, lunch at his house was an occasion. He suggested we worked closely together, he would provide the expertise of the Italian scene and if a deal was done he would be paid by the Italians. What followed was fascinating. I would receive calls from the Italian press authenticated or originated by him and visits from many of their clubs. I told him on one occasion after I had met a representative from a club in the south of the country that it was an area that Liam would prefer not to live in. 'Ron, I know' he said, 'but it's only fair for my own reputation and good name to allow all those who show an interest to be given an opportunity of putting themselves forward.' In the end, Juventus was the successful bidder and Gigi accompanied me to Turin to conclude the deal at the home of their president Bonaperti, himself an outstanding International player in the John Charles era. Gigi and I had a great relationship. I would visit him in London and, in return, he would stay with me when coming north. Before we could finalise another major transaction, he died suddenly in Italy in a hotel while staying with the national Team. He brought to the table a deep knowledge of Italian soccer, its personalities and that of the clubs, their strengths and weaknesses. He earned universal respect, especially back home, from all with whom he dealt.

As Gigi appreciated, the football world was shrinking and living over here not only expanded his horizons but made him value the idea of being a European. He was fascinated when I discussed the UEFA Regulations for compensating clubs when a player left at the end of a contract which I'd made something of a specialist subject. I recall an incident that had a profound effect on me and caused me to give serious thought as to whether I wished to continue down the road I seemed to be stumbling rather than walking. AC Milan were interested in acquiring England International Ray Wilkins from Manchester United. United at that time were managed by Ron Atkinson and the Italians wanted me to represent them in the negotiations. Accompanied by a young solicitor from my office, Simon Minton, we met at one of the Airport hotels on a Saturday morning. United were playing at Everton on that particular day. AC Milan had their commercial manager with them who had a working knowledge of English as well as the club president who was a sullen man more prone to a grunt than a speech.

It emerged before the meeting started that the parties had

been in communication for some weeks. It seemed that the Italian's initial target had been Bryan Robson but then switched to Wilkins as their surveillance continued. United started off as reluctant suitors but later allowed themselves to be seduced into parting with their midfield star. We went into a meeting room; Martin Edwards, United's chairman introduced himself and the man on his right – Dennis Roach – describing him as, 'Wilkins' agent.' I knew Edwards well. He was an influential power broker, succeeding his father Louis who had acquired control over the club with the help of their distinguished manager at the time, Matt Busby. Gigi, incidentally, was also close to Louis Edwards although he always referred to him as Luigi.

The AC Milan file that I saw prior to the meeting showed there had been contact with Ron Atkinson but no mention of a price for Wilkins. I could understand why the player was not at the meeting, obviously being required at Everton but the on-going table talk merely skirted around the remaining live issue, namely, how much was the fee? The Milan chairman became agitated, he could not understand what was going on and summoned his team to leave the room and we all dutifully trooped out. He was given a thumbnail sketch of what had taken place and I put in my two-penneth worth. I told him that my sources had informed that Manchester United had already arranged for a replacement for Wilkins in negotiating the transfer of Scottish International Gordon Strachan and they were committed to that deal so Wilkins had to go. The Chairman's instructions to me in broken English tell Manchester United, 'This is the offer – if it is accepted - say so – and we must then speak to the player – if it is not to your liking – say so – we will shake hands and go back to Italy.' He laid it on the line and the United team retired including Wilkins' apparent appointee Roach.

They returned and Edwards said that the offer fell short of their requirements but we were near to the asking price. Eventually and as I anticipated, the Italians holding firm, the deal was done with a sweetener of Manchester United playing a pre-season match at the San Siro Stadium and Milan making a return trip to Old Trafford the following year. For the first time, the Italian chairman let a smile of satisfaction cross his lips. He returned to his old self however when told he could now negotiate with Wilkins via Mr Roach. 'No, no' he shouted. 'I want to see Wilkins.' Martin Edwards could see the merit in that suggestion and said he would send a message to Everton asking Wilkins to come straight to the hotel after the game. We passed the time in small talk but eventually the man in question appeared and Edwards introduced everyone to Wilkins including me. Before he could add anything Wilkins spotted Roach for the first time and queried politely, 'What's he doing here? He has nothing to do with me.' Turning to face Roach he added quite sharply, 'You do not represent me and I do not want you to – I have my own representative.' I waited for some reaction from Roach but none was forthcoming. Wilkins, however, assured the Italians that subject to the terms being acceptable he would love to play in Italy and particularly for AC Milan.

The meeting broke up with Wilkins agreeing to go over to Italy with his solicitor, London based Michael Kennedy. The Italians had not wasted their journey and as they prepared to leave they insisted that I also travelled there to see the deal through. To this day I have wondered why Roach should appear as Wilkins agent, Edwards should hold him out as such, Wilkins was so adamant in his refusal to be represented by him and why there was no protest. The whole scene to my mind was totally unsatisfactory and for the first time in dealing with professional football at the highest level, I thought I was in a world which was as surprising as it was unreal. I travelled from Manchester to Milan and at the Airport before my departure, saw Strachan arrive from Scotland proving by information to be correct. I met up with Ray Wilkins and Michael Kennedy and full and proper negotiations took place. Kennedy was both thorough and skilful, asking me about usual practice in Italy concerning accommodation, cars, return air travel tickets and other pre-requisites. I was able to give him the benefit of my experience which allowed him to properly advise his client. Some time later, a second trip to Milan for me was caused by UEFA banning English clubs from competing against European teams as a consequence of the Heysel disaster. I flew with Martin Edwards and his co-director and solicitor Maurice Watkins to try and reach an accommodation on those issues.

In 2003, Tom Bower an investigative journalist and biographer produced a well acclaimed and fascinating book *Broken Dreams* which was compulsive reading for all those interested in the national game. Bower commanded attention having earlier produced authoritative, well researched tomes on such diverse characters as Richard Branson, Mohammed Al-Fayed, Robert Maxwell and Labour politician and donor Geoffery Robinson. When Bower turned his intuitions to soccer, he showed how people without scruples exploited the sport to enrich themselves at the expense of others.

Dennis Roach was one of his targets, describing him as a, 'Former minor football player who had fashioned an art of inserting himself into the trade of players between clubs.' Bower did not shrink from criticism of certain agents and reading his book confirmed the view that I took after the Wilkins escapade to discretely bow out and limit my activities. I thought it improper then, and still do now, for solicitors to take commission for acting as an agent. I charged professional fees based on the time involved, responsibility, expertise and value to the client.

I noted that excluded from the characters in Bower's explosive exposure were the names of two reputable and responsible men that I had met. The reputation of Michael Kennedy remains solid and he successfully represented many other international stars including David O'Leary and Roy Keane. The other was Jonathan Holmes who it was always a pleasure to have dealings with because he was so professional in outlook and, like the best in the profession, put his client's interests first. We met when he was representing Luther Blisset, a Watford striker with goal scoring prowess that did not extend to his short stay in Italy. John was negotiating with an Italian club and confessed to me that he was short of local knowledge and wanted help on terms that were relevant and realistic for an English player out there. I went over to meet him and was pleased to assist. At his request I sent him a bill for services rendered and he sent his cheque with a gracious letter of appreciation. It was no surprise to learn several years later that Jonathan was regarded as one of the best exponents of his branch of the trade.

12

*

Fighting for Justice

I seldom took umbrage at the frequent references by friend or foe alike to my lack of height, the diminutive lawyer from Leeds being a frequent description of me. Indeed, on many occasions I turned it to my advantage responding, 'Yes, I am frequently overlooked but very seldom ignored.'

I always sought solace and consolation from ruminating on the many men, small of stature but large in influence, who have had influential roles in society or, as my father often told me sarcastically, started wars. It is, however, the determination to succeed or, as I prefer to call it the refusal to be put down, that is a motivating force.

If there was one type of case that aggravated and annoyed me more than any other it was those involving bribery and corruption, a form of dishonesty that corrodes public and commercial life. It is a facet of society that we can well do without, with decisions being made solely for personal greed and benefit to the detriment of the common, greater good and wider responsibility. Notwithstanding my personal views, one particular case angered me to the extent that, I decided to do something about it. Recently, in an old file, I found a cutting from the *Daily Express* of June 1973 which reminded me of the widespread corruption in local authorities at the time. It centred primarily on building concerns showering their wealth on lower income council officials who had the power to award multi million pound contracts. Even more depressingly when such revelations were eventually brought to light, shocking as they were, the general response was not one of either surprise or horror but a shrug of the shoulders and a general acceptance or resignation that it had become almost accepted practice.

For a while it seemed that the corruption 'industry' was dominated by Pontefract architect John Poulson and Newcastle City Council leader T. Dan Smith, with willing aids such as Andrew Cunningham and Scottish civil servant Pottinger. Although they were big players there were very many other small town bosses who welcomed their palms being greased. I can tell you from my own experience that discovering that a civic project for the benefit of the community at large had been born out of monies passed to local councillors and inveigling officials is sickening.

In the summer of 1967, I was present as a recently elected city councillor at the opening of the Leeds International Pool, a swimming venue of note, designed by John Poulson. The building had many defects but was extravagant in design. It only lasted forty years before being demolished and in its place now is an open space. Whether to have a centrally located prestigious international pool or several smaller ones dotted around the city was a controversial political issue but the ruling party went ahead with the grandiose scheme. Unfortunately for them, the electorate decide, only weeks before the official opening, to remove them from office. Indeed, an opulent reception and unveiling ceremony at a cost of thousands had been scheduled, only to be scrapped by the incoming Tory leader Frank Marshall who replaced it with a more modest cup of tea and a bun. I was there and architect Poulson presented a trophy in his name. I remember remarking to a colleague that it was not a very substantial gesture for a high value contract. Years later, when in his bankruptcy and subsequent criminal trial the extent of his corruption of others was revealed, those words of mine alluding to his meanness were thrown back at me.

Later I was to see a list of the names of those in my own city who had important roles in civic life and were on Poulson's pay roll. I was shattered at the huge sums that were paid over for showing favour to him. Before Poulson and his academic Scottish co-accused Pottinger were exposed, a trial had taken place in Leeds of four men employed by Carlton Contractors Ltd charged with taking bribes from sub-contractors. That company was a subsidiary of the Trafalgar House Investment Group, the directors of which were from the City of London. It was not a subtle or sophisticated scam operated by the directors of Carlton who mainly worked in the North East of England. They had two experienced builders at the head with the added advantage of a man who had, when very young, been the mayor of the borough of Pontefract. He was well known in the Labour movement in the region and his main task was to introduce sources of work, primarily councils, from his contacts for the benefit of Carlton and he was very successful. Carlton specialised in design and build contracts for local authorities. The latter would submit a brief of their requirements, for example a leisure centre, with a proposed budget expenditure and statement of the facilities they required. The contractor would return with a plan and an all inclusive price which made it near impossible to obtain a comparative tender as it was so specific. It was a far less costly and time consuming modus operandi for the builder and, often, the decision on whether to accept the plan was left to an individual who could be 'influenced'. To be successful with design and build, firms needed a good PR man with a significant entertainment budget and pound notes in his hand to ease the passage.

I represented two of the accused and the defence was that as a subsidiary company they were answerable to trading practices instituted at headquarters and there was much documentary evidence to support this. It was even suggested that to recover any 'outlay', subcontractors would be invited to pay for the privilege of being awarded a contract or, as it was so quaintly and delicately phrased, 'having their name prominently displayed on the board at the site'. I have no doubt that the actions of the elderly silver-haired managing director of Carlton, Cyril Rance were known to his senior colleagues. He was not in the dock but spoke of passing on £750 in fivers wrapped in a heavily sealed brown paper parcel to a north eastern Councillor at a lunchtime meeting in the sophisticated rooms of the London Carlton Club renowned as a watering and resting place of many of the country's leaders.

I held the view when my client had been convicted that he had been unfairly treated by the judge. It seemed to me that he was holding my client as being the principal perpetrator of the corrupt practices when it was clear, firstly, that his superiors knew of what was going on, secondly, they actively encouraged it and, thirdly, they actively participated in it. The corrupt practices were planned, directed and controlled, there were few other reasons for a councillor from the North East meeting in somewhere as salubrious as the Carlton Club and £750 was approaching a decent annual salary. To be fair, at the end of the trial the judge ordered that the Director of Public Prosecutions be informed of allegations of local government corruption given in evidence. At the end of the trial, counsel for Trafalgar House sought leave to make a statement and in it said that they emphatically denied that the company or any of the directors had known of illegal payments. I would like to know, out of pure curiosity, how the payment of £750 in 'fivers' was recorded. All in all I thought that my convicted client – the other was acquitted – had been treated as the author of the crime instead of a participant. He had been an unsuspecting pawn and there was no evidence whatsoever that he had personally benefitted. Cyril Rance was prosecuted and convicted some years later but I am unaware of any action taken against the corrupt councillors. Though I detected hostility towards my client throughout the trial by Mr Justice Waller, I could not give reason for it. Waller I found to be a straightforward commonsense judge. As a QC with an extensive mixed practice in the North East I had, on several occasions, the pleasure of briefing him - with some success I might add. It may be that he disliked the demeanour of the accused who was relatively young and demonstrably confident.

The whole case, on reflection, was a mere appetiser for what was to follow and I felt that the prosecution was firing its bullets at my clients and skillfully avoiding more important targets. I had hoped that the days of putting forward sacrificial lambs to atone for the sins of the establishment had long ended and that the hackneyed expression, 'all men are equal before the law' meant exactly what it said. Nothing said to me or read by me will rid me of the bitter taste one gets when something foul gets into your mouth, but I cannot define what it was. All I knew was that I felt discomfort for a considerable time and the passing years had not removed that feeling entirely. The danger for a lawyer who has doubts is that it is a distraction and can cause lack of objectivity leading to them becoming a fighter for a cause instead of a fighter of a case. I leave the account of this troublesome case with the memorable words of Gilbert Gray who I had briefed for the defence. He was remarkable wordsmith and when referring to the activities of the PR intermediary said, 'He made PR mean, instead of public relations - private receipts.'

When the small legal firm of Ronald Teeman merged with the equally diminutive legal practice of Leslie Gould, an entity was created with insufficient strength to challenge the long established practices in the city.

We each had experience in different disciplines and it extended the service we could provide for our respective clients but, moreover, it gave the two of us a modicum of comfort in that there was an ear to bend when a problem arose. We were two difference personalities. I was gregarious and outgoing while Leslie had an urbane manner and a diffident, modest approach to other professionals and indeed to our clientele. He looked the part. If he had been selected to appear on the once popular programme *What's My Line*, I think he would have been identified as a lawyer without having to provide many clues. Leslie was humorous and although not spontaneous, had the ability to craft words into sentences whose deadpan recital of them and made you laugh.

We acted for a young married women blessed with good looks and money. She was of Mediterranean appearance and her friends said if she could sing she would have been ideal to play the part of the flower girl in Bizet's *Carmen*. She had a roving eye and was seen often in the cafes of Leeds with a young man also blessed with good looks and employed in a family business that did not pressurize him. He had been married for a few years to a well educated lady who was home loving. The woman who was to become our client made an appointment to see me. She produced a letter from a local firm of solicitors well known to us and was agitated, saying that she was, 'Afraid of what my husband will say if he read the contents.' The letter read:

> Acting on behalf of Mrs T whose marriage has been unhappy for some time, our client was suspicious that her husband had formed an association with another woman which caused us to instruct a private enquiry agent to carry out observations on her. We have before us his report which stated on Thursday evening the 3rd instant at 7.19pm a man knocked on the door of 33 Ellestree Avenue – your home. You were seen to open the front door and after a short conversation admit him to the home. He was seen talking to you in the front room, - the curtains being open. The curtains were then closed and 33 minutes later the male visitor was seen to leave by the front door, walk down the drive and enter his car which was parked in the roadway. The circumstances indicate that adultery had taken place beyond doubt.
>
> In order to save time and expense we would request you to give a statement under caution to an enquiry agent admitting your adultery to enable our client to present a petition for divorce without delay. We would suggest that you attend upon your legal advisor with this letter and invite him to discuss the matter with us.

I told her that I would revert to her after I had spoken to the wife's solicitors. It occurred to me that the roaming husband would probably be receiving a similar letter but she assured me that he had not contacted her. I was not looking forward to my contact with the 'other side' but I made the call and, after the usual pleasantries, he said that the husband was just as anxious for the wife to end the marriage and had admitted adultery but refused to give details of the same and more particularly identify the lady. He advised me that because of this it was his duty to check out the party concerned. I told him bluntly, 'She is not going to make any statement except deny the allegation, and you will have to rely on the enquiry agent's evidence of his observation for what they are worth.' He then became hot under the collar. 'What explanation has she for the facts that the enquiry agent noted?' I thought I would tease him a little. 'Come off it,' I exploded, 'If you think back what significance did the third of this month have?' He retorted, 'It is no significance to me.' 'Think again,' I continued, 'It was three days before the general election.' 'What on earth has that got to do with my allegation of adultery?' he shouted over the phone. I was in full flow by now, 'Keep cool,' I ventured, 'Could it not be that your client's husband was canvassing for the Labour candidate? My client was a floating voter and he asked if she could spare a few minutes to listen to the manifesto's case and she agreed and invited him in where he did his best to convince her.' He became even more angry, 'Rubbish, rubbish,' he shouted. 'No-one will believe that rubbish.' I continued, 'I told you she is under no obligation to explain herself – she denies the allegation.' The phone went dead so I replaced the receiver at my end thinking that when he examined what I had said he would realise firstly that my explanation, though fanciful, was possible.

Within an hour I had hand delivered to me a letter from the solicitor placing on record that, *Your client admitted that at her home was my client's husband who was engaged in political activity that evening.* I sent a reply back but by ordinary post. *You have accurately summarised what I have said to you but have omitted to confirm that I told you firstly that our client denied adultery, secondly would not make any statement and thirdly was under no obligation to give any explanation of an action that to the pure is innocent. I feel you should now write to each political party advising them of the dangers of entering houses to discuss political matters at night. It is not my intention to progress this matter further. You must follow your client's wishes.* I later saw among the list of divorce cases printed in the local paper that the wife had been granted a decree nisi on the grounds of her husband's adultery with a woman unknown. My client's honour had been protected and even I felt virtuous.

Frank Dawson, otherwise known as 'Dolly', was certainly not a look-alike for the Shirley Temple. He was a rough, tough and fearless former rugby league forward with his gnarled features a testament to his former profession. After a distinguished playing career he took up coaching. Hunslet, Leeds and Halifax availed themselves of his services and he was very successful. Very few can recall him putting on a tracksuit, but most remembered the sound of his voice. His teams were fashioned in his image, uncompromising forwards had to master their opponents and then the backs were permitted to have the ball and finish them off. Dolly had a word for everyone and he loved a chat with supporters whether they followed his team or not. In the summer he liked his cricket and nothing better than watching it at Headingley. My father was one of his mates. Dad being a great listener made a good companion for Dolly who was a good talker and both were great walkers, memory lane being their favourite route. One day at Headingley, Dolly asked my dad if I could help a friend of his and what it would cost for her to see me. When the request was relayed to me, my response was, 'Tell Dolly I will see her for free and if there is anything I can do for her only then I will charge.'

Dolly made an appointment to see me and arrived with a middle aged lady wearing dark glasses and displaying a white stick. He explained that she had been the passenger in a car involved in an accident and had been injured quite severely. She added that the police report of the accident showed that the driver was responsible and she continued that she had been to solicitors who told her that it was an 'open and shut case' and she would get 'thousands'. I ascertained some facts, that the accident had taken place five years before and that she had sought legal advice about two years afterwards. She confirmed that she had had no correspondence from them but when she phoned enquiring as to progress she was only ever told, 'We will be writing you soon'. It just didn't ring true.

In a personal injury claim, a writ has to be issued within three years of the accident and no solicitor worth their salt would sit back and do nothing. I confess to a feeling that the lady may herself have been too late in taking legal advice. I have always said that it is not for the lawyer to doubt his client at a first meeting and I therefore agreed to investigate and report back to her. My first port of call was the solicitors. Although she could remember the firm she could not identify the man who was supposedly advising her. I knew the firm well, they were diligent and reputable. When I telephoned the receptionist she did not recall the name of the client but promised to ring me back the next day when she had made enquiries. True to her word, she phoned and said the senior partner would like to see me and made an appointment for that afternoon. I walked round and found him in a relatively agitated state.

'I'll be blunt,' he said. 'I've expected this call for some time. Not from your client, because I cannot trace a file yet but because I have a common law clerk who is brilliant but eccentric and sooner or later I knew one of his 'bloomers' would surface.' He confided that the man in question was away suffering from stress and when I enquired about his return date he said that, as far as he could tell, it would not be in the foreseeable future. I asked, 'Can you confirm your firm accepted instructions from her?' He rather sheepishly responding, 'Not at the moment but I cannot dispute what she had told you.' I returned to my client and remembering that she was blind, asked her how she could identify the clerk, reporting what the senior partner had told me. She said, 'As you will have guessed Mr Teeman, I would not have gone to the solicitors unaccompanied. My Niece came with me.' I contacted her and she said she had retained a piece of paper with the firm's name and phone number on it. 'Eureka,' I shouted, when she came back to the phone after a few minutes and read me the details, fortunately it was the firm that I had been speaking to. She then said, 'I've been back with her at least three times, Mr Teeman, possibly four'. I asked her who they saw and she was under the impression that it was the boss. When I asked her to describe him she recalled, 'He was in his thirties, a little scruffy and chain smoked.' That was not the senior partner for sure. I returned to him and passed over the information I had gleaned and was told, 'That's my clerk, the description fits him accurately, give me two or three weeks to sort it out.'

Returning to the office, I dictated a letter setting out the facts as I understood them and alleging that his firm had been negligent in not issuing proceedings. When it was placed before me for signature I had second thoughts as once I sent it he would have to forward it to his insurers and would then be precluded from communicating with me orally or in writing. I waited a little while until he returned to me as promised. 'Number one,' he said, 'I have found the instruction sheet. It is dated and it reads 'told client she has good case.' I regret I have nothing else after that except three entries in our call book when she came to the office.' He went on, 'You know Teeman, I've had my suspicions this fellow had lost the plot with other clients and when a case took a turn so did he and ignored it. I've got plenty of complaints to answer.' I genuinely sympathised with him. It is difficult to look over an employee's shoulder at all times. He then said, 'I'll spell it out and this is not for quotation. He missed the date for issuing writs and allowed the file to disappear, hoping the client would adopt the same course.' He further declared, 'I've had nightmares over this man and his 'breakdown'. I've never known when the lights are to go out or the curtain fall.'

Sympathy for him did not affect my duties to my client who had suffered dreadful injuries and receiving no compensation. I was worried whether his insurers would repudiate liability on the grounds that we had not shown his firm had been formally instructed to actually commence proceedings. This time it was me who asked for a couple of week's grace. I wrote to the driver of the car alleging negligence and saying that the previous correspondence had not brought 'any satisfactory response' and would he pass it immediately to his insurers. It worked for within the week the well known insurance company phoned and their representative was quick to disabuse me. A letter had been sent to the solicitors saying they would enquire into the circumstances but they had heard nothing for a number of years. When further correspondence arrived from the lawyers, they were politely told that the time for making a claim had expired. Very kindly they forwarded copies of the exchange which I delivered by hand to the practice in question. I swear I could hear a sigh of relief over the phone when I spoke to the senior partner. He could now claim indemnity from his insurers and I knew that my client would get what was her due as recompense for their negligence.

Sometimes, but not very often, lawyers are involved in cases of the unexpected. So it was regarding the wife of a journalist. Her father who lived in the south of England had died and in his will left the majority of his estate to his housekeeper who had cared for him. The daughter brought with her a building society pass book with over £10,000 on deposit. She said that her father had sent it to her after he went into hospital a few weeks before he died. She did not begrudge the beneficiary of her inheritance saying she deserved it but wanted to be assured that any duty accruing on the account would not fall on her. To the lady's total surprise I told her that the money in the Building Society belonged to her and the gift in the will to the housekeeper did not affect it. It was her property and a *donatio mortis causa*, which I last heard of as a student half a century before – a gift conditional only on the donor's death. I tested all the young legal eagles in the office on this teaser and found them wanting.

If a dress code for entry said neat and tidy, my client and good friend Ron Black would have been refused. Ron was a skilled sheet metal worker running his own business with an abundance of work from engineering companies in the city. When I first met him he was 50, liked a drink and an evening in the pub but put work first on his agenda. If Harry H. Corbett had been unable to play the role of Steptoe's son, Ron would have walked into the part. Everyone was his friend and he valued and respected that. He lived and worked in Middleton in South Leeds, a predominantly industrial area. His premises were quite extensive and were the target of thieves who would get over the wall and steal his metal. To be frank, he and the police had an unsteady relationship, Ron complaining regularly when his premises were attacked and the constabulary just as regularly shrugging their collective shoulders at their inability to bring the miscreants to justice.

They were known to be local youths, fuelled by drink and the lure of easy money from scrap dealers. An Inspector gave

A Lawyer for all Seasons

Ron what he thought was sound advice in getting a practical deterrent. 'Get yourself a dog,' he said, and a few days later produced an animal that looked like a German Shepherd but without the documents to support its breeding. As Ron said, 'One look from that animal would 'freeten you to death.'

The premises were sufficiently large to enable the animal with a long lead to patrol at its leisure all parts of the compound and the innovative solution seemed to work. The dog had a growl and a ferocious disposition, and for weeks there were no intruders. However, the peace did not last and one evening or early morning, an intruder went over the wall into the premises. The animal growled and grabbed and the upshot was that the miscreant was severely bitten and lost his right testicle. Ron was quite thrilled that the dog was earning its keep but his joy was short-lived. A few weeks later he received a letter from a local solicitor advising him of the injuries and that a claim was to be made for damages. Ron saw me with the letter and gave me a full account of the position. He could not believe it when I told him that in English law, even though the intruder was a trespasser, the owner of the premises could be liable for the actions of the dog which was clearly dangerous.

The situation was aggravated when the writ was issued, the defendant was on Legal Aid and so the proceedings would cost him nothing but the unfortunate Ron had no insurance policy that covered the acts of his dog. I had to tell him what his liability and the costs could be if the matter went to trial. Ron instructed me to defend and to keep him informed of all steps taken by the injured party and do my best to mitigate his loss. The plaintiff's solicitors proceeded on the usual lines and supplied me with a copy of the medical report from a leading surgeon which confirmed the loss of the testicle and the effect that it would have on the assailed's life. It dramatized things to a certain extent and said that it had affected his ability to work and estimated that the trauma he had suffered would lengthen the period of recuperation. The damages claimed would be considerable and the plaintiff's solicitor said that, 'At the present time he was on statutory benefits but prior to the accident he worked as a painter and decorator earning in the range of £80 a week.'

I invited Ron to see me to discuss the situation. I had placed an evaluation on the claim for general damages that took into account the pain and suffering and the consequential loss and then I made some calculations for the loss of earnings and we were talking of quite a considerable amount. Ron knew when he walked into my interview room that he was not to be the recipient of good news which somehow softened the blow but he could not get out of his head that a wrongdoer caught in the act could get compensation from the party that he had tried to violate. His eyes lit up when I told him that the plaintiff was not working and that he was entitled to his loss of wages. 'Rubbish, rubbish,' he cried. 'That bastard is working, I know he is and what's more I can prove it.' I told him that if he could, that would very much change matters.Ron returned a week later with a list of households in the Middleton area which the plaintiff had painted. The list included dates and an amount was typed alongside. Even though every week of his absence from work could not be accounted for, there were sufficient to show that it was probable that in the blank weeks he had also been up and working.

I telephoned the litigation clerk of his solicitors to say that there was a live issue on special damages and that we could show the defendant was not absent from working the entire period he was claiming for. What is more, he had been claiming statutory benefits for weeks we had definite proof that he had worked. Furthermore, I asked if his Legal Aid

191

certificate had been amended because of his return to work as we had not received notification. I said that we would be writing and establishing our submissions and requesting more information from them. He said, 'Don't do that, do not write at the moment, give me a week. I'll have him in and I'll come back to you.' I could understand their concern and anxiety at receiving a letter setting out their client's falsehood which would compromise them and so I agreed. A week later he contacted me and said that his client had decided not to proceed, 'I'll serve you with a notice of discontinuance,' he announced. My articled clerk endorsed the file 'plaintiff did not have the balls to continue.'

Even the most squeamish are fascinated by a murder and the interest is heightened when there are multiple killings and the methods are brutal or salacious.

Several decades have passed since the 'Ripper' caused havoc in the West Riding of Yorkshire and gained mythological status. I would not be surprised if a copycat appears some time to revive his horrendous deeds. Dr Harold Shipman did not look anything other than a gentle hardworking general practitioner but he sent many of his patients to their graves.

How remarkable it is that when a body is found there is a huge wave of concern for the victim and his or her family but after an arrest and conviction of the perpetrator, some sympathy resides with the offender. That was especially so when we had the death penalty. For most of my legal career there was no such sentence available and the public executioner made redundant. Nevertheless, the debate continued about whether it acted as a deterrent or whether such a sentence could ever be justified, particularly in the light of wrongful convictions. Thankfully I never defended when the accused faced the ultimate sanction but one of my earlier cases was a reminder of the, often intolerable, burden faced in such circumstances.

One of my most enjoyable murder cases, and I make no apologies for using such a seemingly inappropriate adjective, was the Woodhouse Moor killings. The area is a large open space on either side of Otley Road which proceeds from the city in the direction of Headingley and onwards to the Dales. It is not a beauty spot and, to be frank, even today appears to be in need of some tender love and attention. One side was uglier than the other. It was used for the circus when in town and the fair or feast as the locals described the miscellany of rides, roundabouts and side shows for children and adults. For most of the year it was an unattended car park on the edge of the centre or for the nearby university and its busiest time was when there was a Test Match at Headingley and motorists were encouraged to leave their cars there and ride to the famous ground on specially chartered buses. Across the dual carriageway on the better tended part there was some grass and trees, an abundance of bushes, gravel tennis courts and a block of toilets. That part of the Moor was flanked by generous-sized terraced houses with gardens at the front that had been the homes of the wealthy gentry of the city in the nineteenth century but over the years had become multi-occupied.

In 1961, The Leeds Magistrates Court assigned me to represent Stanley Kennedy, a labourer from Sunderland who had been charged with the murder of a shop manager. The accused was 25 years of age and the victim, a few years older, a local resident. The scene of the crime was near the toilet block on Woodhouse Moor and, in those days, bringing such a prosecution to trial was convoluted and cumbersome. The defendant, who because of the serious nature of the charge was in custody in Armley Jail, was produced from time to time until a date was fixed for his committal proceedings.

A Lawyer for all Seasons

The Director of Public Prosecutions sent his barrister to show that the defendant initially had a case to answer and to persuade the magistrates such. My poor client at the committal proceeding before Ralph Cleworth QC who was then the stipendiary magistrate for the city, made the headlines for a different reason. Cleworth listened to the prosecution's evidence, heard my cross-examinations and submission that there was no case to answer on the charge of murder and when I was overruled, the man in the dock completely broke down, wept uncontrollably and was carried out of the court and returned to the cells where he was attended by the police surgeon Dr ASR Sinton. The court was in limbo, he had collapsed before the formalities had been completed. When he returned from the cells he looked decidedly unwell but I was assured by Dr. Sinton that it was safe to proceed and he was remanded in custody to take his trial at Leeds assizes. Though disappointed that my submission had been rejected, I recognised why the magistrate had made such a ruling.

After court, I had a coffee in the canteen with DS Dennis Hoban who had the conduct of the police investigation. Hoban later became head of the CID and I admitted to him that I was baffled by the medical evidence that showed on the face of the deceased marks which matched, according to the pathologist, the nails in the sole of the boots of the accused. That supported the Crown's assertion that the accused had stamped on the face of the deceased whilst he was on the ground.

I told Hoban that the defendant had given me an account that matched entirely the prosecution evidence, before he had even seen it but he denied 'putting the boot in'. What was common ground between prosecution and defence was that Stanley Kennedy had been to the toilet to urinate having been drinking beer in a nearby pub and was on his way to his lodgings after closing time. Coming out of the public convenience, he was accosted by the deceased who propositioned him. He told the man he was not interested and walked away but the stranger persisted and followed him. The accused saw a police officer on patrol and stopped him. He made a complaint that he was being followed and pointed out the deceased who could be seen a distance away. Kennedy said to the constable, 'If he starts on me I'll clip him one.' The officer told him not to do anything foolish and to get away quickly but, unfortunately, did not approach the soon-to-be victim. The deceased did not give up on chase of his quarry and closed on Kennedy who, believing that he was about to be the subject of a homosexual attack, grappled with him and they fell to the floor. Kennedy said he probably did hit him with a couple of blows before the fall but strenuously denied that he either kicked him or stamped on him. He said that those allegations were offensive and were something that he just did not do and would not do. He also volunteered that he realised that the defendant was severely hurt and he made two telephone calls for the ambulance and the police. There was no response to the first and he tried them again soon after but noted, 'It seemed ages before help arrived.'

Hoban said, 'The only help I can give is to advise you to visit the scene and examine the ground.' I went to the Moor and tramped over the area for several minutes at the exact spot where the fight took place and saw much loose gravel. It was not in any regular pattern, in some parts of the patch there was a great deal of whitish small stones and in others there were very little. I went again to this section of the Moor but this time was accompanied by a photographer and he produced several shots of the area, some in close up. Unfortunately, the deceased's body had been disposed of after the post mortem examination and all I could see were photographs of it. I obtained the services of another pathologist and he examined the photographs and sampled the gravel on the boots of the accused and gave the opinion that the marks on the deceased's face were more appropriate and consistent with a rolling around on the ground than an attack with the boot. He said that if there had been either kicking or stamping, the pathologist in the course of his examination would have seen bruises to the face but in his report he had not commented on any being present.

My career incidentally coincided with the establishment of Dennis Hoban as a 'top cop' with a solid reputation as a great thief catcher, in particular. He was an officer conscious of the value of proven facts being produced to ascertain guilt rather than verbal admissions made by the accused when arrested. Indeed, although on many occasions we differed, as one would expect, I believe that we never lost respect for one another and I regard it as a compliment when he asked me to take his young son who was leaving school into the office during the summer to get some work experience. I was a little taken aback when at the conclusion of this work Dennis expressed his gratitude to me but tainted it by saying, 'It only took the lad six weeks, Ron, to copy your files.' Dennis, sadly, died in harness. He had been a sufferer from diabetes all his adult life and that illness finally took him away from his family, friends and the Leeds City police force, too young.

For Kennedy's trial, I briefed Rudolph Lyons QC, later to become Sir Rudolph Lyons on his appointment as Recorder of Liverpool and Gilbert Gray as his junior. He was found not guilty of murder but guilty of manslaughter. Mr Lyons made the point in mitigation that in sentencing, credit must be given to him firstly for not running away from the scene, secondly for summoning assistance to come to the aid of the deceased on two occasions and thirdly, the fact that had medical assistance been available more speedily it was possible that death would not have been the outcome as the injuries were not life threatening. The judge, Mr Justice Nield, in passing sentence said that while he agreed with the jury's verdict, the attack was, 'A very serious one' which resulted in death and justified a sentence of three years imprisonment. I thought then – as I do now, that he was heavy handed and the mitigation cogent and persuasive. I was concerned and took the advice of my leader, Mr Lyons, who counselled against an appeal. When I saw Kennedy in the cells after sentencing he expressed his gratitude to all the defence team for our efforts to have him acquitted of the charge of murder. I rather fancy that in 2011, the agreed facts would have indicated a much lower sentence.

It is rare for a person charged with murder to use his own solicitor's office as a confession box but it happened to me. One day, after a session in the magistrate's, my clerk had come into court to tell me that a client wished to see me urgently at 2pm. I okayed the appointment and hurried my lunch break. Waiting for me was a man in his thirties sitting next to a much older lady. I asked him to come in and he did so followed by the lady who he introduced as his mother. He said, 'Is it alright, Mr Teeman, that my Mam sits in just in case I miss anything out she will be able to help?' I said that it was his decision but that it was alright by me. He started his story. He told me his name and reminded me, 'I came to see you a couple of years ago about a divorce.' I vaguely remembered him and he continued. 'It's not about the divorce today – although I am at fault because I have not replied to your letters asking me what was happening – well the truth is....' he paused and looked at his mother, 'There is no need for a divorce, Mr Teeman, she is dead.' I was not startled initially as death often intervened in the assortment of situations that a law firm deals with. But I did become excited when he went on. 'You see, Mr Teeman, I killed her and buried her in the cellar.' The grimace on my face must have made him appreciate that I was taken aback by his disclosure. His mother then took over, 'He wants to give himself up and get it all over as it's been on his mind for some time now,' she said. 'Hang on,' I replied. 'I'll ring for my secretary,' and on the intercom asked Susan to bring her notebook in.

Susan Robinson had been with me since she left secretarial college about six years earlier and she was quiet and accurate in her transcription of her shorthand notes onto paper. She never showed reaction to what she typed and never seemed shocked or amazed. I said to her, 'This man has just told me that he has killed his wife. Would you make the following note and bring it back to me for signature. I dictated, *Dear Mr Teeman. I authorise you to inform the Leeds Police force that I have killed my wife and that I am willing to provide all details, explanation and assistance to them. Yours faithfully......*She left the room and I thought it better that nothing be said until she returned with the note typed. In her absence, mother and son sat completely silent, looking ahead and not at each other, he mostly staring at his shoes and she not giving him even a glance. Susan returned with the note, I read it and passed it on to the confessor. He looked at it and nodded. I passed over a pen and he signed it. I gave it to Susan saying, 'Put the original in a new file marked 'wife's death' and let me have a copy. When you've done that, retrieve the old divorce file and put it on my desk.'

I explained to them that I would now phone the C.I.D and I expected they would come round immediately. I would give them the note and they would arrest him, take him away and question him under caution and, if the facts warranted it, charge him with the killing of his wife. I further explained that he would have to tell the police what happened to the body and undoubtedly he would remain in custody until his court appearance if he was charged with murder. I got on the phone but Dennis Hoban had not returned from his lunch break. I asked them if they would contact him on his walkie-talkie to ask him to call at my office urgently as I had a client who wished to advise him that he had killed his wife. It was not long before Hoban and a colleague arrived and they were shown into my room. I made the introductions and handed over the note. Hoban said, 'It is a very serious matter to waste police time and if that is what you are doing you could be arrested and charged. Do you understand that?' The man informed him that he understood the situation and Hoban turned to me and said, 'What's the spiel?' I told him that my client had instructed me a couple of years ago to commence divorce proceedings on the grounds of her cruelty. I lost contact with him until today when he came in and gave me the new information. Hoban said to him, 'If that is all true, what did you do with the body?' The reply was, 'I dug a grave in the cellar and buried her there and later covered the grave up with concrete.' Hoban got the address which was in downtown Leeds in an area at one time thickly populated but then the subject to slum clearance. 'Okay,' said Hoban, 'Let's go' and as he took the 'murderer' with him, the other officer said to me, 'I will ring you when I have seen what I expect to see.' The mother stayed and I explained to her what the procedure was from here.

When I next spoke to Hoban it was to hear him confirm that an area in the now unoccupied house had fresh concrete in the cellar and he was waiting for a forensic team to arrive. Before the close of play that night he confirmed to me that there was a body of a female buried in a shallow grave that had been concealed by a concrete topping and that he was preparing to caution and Interview the suspect. At the interview my client was clearly anxious to tell the whole story and did not require much prompting or questioning by

Hoban, he just poured it out. It appeared that his wife was partly of far eastern origin. It had been a strong relationship but she was highly strung and argumentative and if she could not get her own way, would fly into a rage, becoming demented and flailing at him at him with her long nails and scratching at his face and arms. She would also bite. The rage came over her quickly and could not be seen coming in advance. From time to time after an attack she would run away from the house and it was often several days before she would return. At first she appeared to be making an effort to control herself but she would then revert to her old self and was violent in speech and action. He had come to see me and completed a Legal Aid application form to enable him to issue a divorce petition. When he returned home she asked for forgiveness and promised that there would be no more trouble but within days she reverted to type and on that particular evening she was more violent than usual, scratching and biting but this time had a pair of scissors and went to stab him with them. He defended himself as well as he could but eventually to restrain her he grabbed her by the neck and she became limp in his arms and he realised that she was dead. He said that he had no intention to kill her or even inflict harm on her, he just wanted to restrain her from doing harm to him. He then decided to bury her in the cellar and stayed in the house for a few weeks before leaving to live with his mother.

When charged with murder, he argued that it was both self defence and provocation but a verdict of manslaughter was brought in and he was sentenced to three years imprisonment. Between arrest and trial, Hoban arranged to see me. He said, 'I am going to surprise you, Ron. At the police station there is a record of a call by a male who did not leave his name saying he had killed his wife and buried her in the cellar of his home, the address of which he gave us.' I found this hard to believe but Hoban continued, 'I believe the caller must have been him but I am going to further surprise you that our records show that an inspector from the division went round to the house which was unoccupied and down into the cellar and could find no evidence to corroborate that a body had been buried there.' That was staggering and it took some time to sink in. 'Well Dennis,' I said, 'What's your theory?' Hoban replied, 'I am convinced the phone call came from him. I believe he knew that the property was to be demolished and the body might be found and traced to him. He did not want anyone to conclude that he must have killed her deliberately and concealed the body to conceal his guilt. The clever lad, by coming to you to confess, gave himself the opportunity of preparing his answer in advance and to make it more believable.'

In 1995 the most gripping criminal case fell into my hands and one of the three men charged with a scam on the Customs & Excise department involving up to £3 million was Mick Martin.

A former Republic of Ireland star who had a glittering career at Manchester United, West Bromwich Albion and Newcastle United, when advancing years brought his playing days to an end he joined Celtic as a coach. Mick came from a famous soccer family, his dad Con appearing for both Northern Ireland and the Republic and who eventually arrived in England after the end of the Second World War to play for Leeds United and subsequently Aston Villa.

I can find no other player who represented his country as a goalkeeper and a central defender. When John Giles was the manager of West Brom, one of his first acquisitions was Mick and he played a leading role in the Baggies side that gained promotion to the first division in his first year. During Liam Brady's managerial baptism at Celtic, Mick joined him.

The going was tough and results patchy. The inevitable happened and Mick lost his job and for the first time in his life was seeking work. He did have local radio involvement in Newcastle but there were too many quiet interludes in his daily routine and collecting state benefits was something he hated. He told me that life on the dole was debilitating.

Fortunately he was well liked in the Newcastle area and had a large circle of friends who were not all from the soccer scene and he was engaged as a long distance lorry driver on an 'as and when' basis delivering spirits from a bonded warehouse in England to Dublin and returning with an empty lorry to base. The usual route was to take the Stranraer ferry into Larne in Northern Ireland and then drive onto Dublin. On the last occasion – when the vehicle was stopped by customs officials – the route was Hollyhead to Dun Laoghaire in the Republic. The prosecution said that two of Mick's friends David Carr, a property owning developer as well as a garage proprietor of substantial means and Heinz Deinhoffer, a wine and spirits merchant, had with Mick's assistance conspired to defraud the Customs & Excise of duties by a 'clever dodge' which they had successfully used on several occasions.

The supposed plot was simple. The idea was to export spirits from England to another EEC country where the duty levied was lower. All you needed was a document identifying the consignee at the receiving end, many of whom were fictitious. It lead to cheap booze flooding the market and raised suspicion. The arrest of the three men, particularly one with a sporting reputation was national news fuelled by the crowing tax authorities.

Mick's instructions to me were clear. 'Yes, I was the driver. Yes, I did take a wagon several times containing spirits to Dublin. Yes, I did deliver it to the address I was given which was a warehouse and when the load had been taken from me I returned to Newcastle. At no time did I have any idea whatsoever that duty was being fiddled or that that there was anything dishonest about the transactions. Indeed being a well-known face, whenever I moved through a custom's point I was recognised by the official who would greet me 'Hi, how you doing Mick?'

The case was sent to the Newcastle Crown Court for trial. I briefed Michael Harrison QC and I indeed was fortunate to get him, he was much in demand for both criminal and civil cases that required analytical skills. As junior I called upon my daughter Miriam.

She had much experience as a solicitor in the Fraud and Insolvency department of a leading firm and was familiar with the ways and means of government revenue departments and had a gift, which I did not share with her, of patience in the preparation of submission in writing and of spread sheets. I sensed, however, that there was something unusual going on. In court, conversations with the prosecution's representatives, which are normal in trials were vague and not material to any issue.

Indeed something was afoot and it was the lugubrious Mr Cripps, in charge of the Crown's case, who announced that he was to see the judge alone on matters of, 'public interest immunity.' There are circumstances that may arise in the course of criminal proceedings in which material held by the prosecution and tending to undermine them or assist the defence cannot be disclosed to the defendant fully, or even at all, without some prejudice to an important public interest.

Most regularly it entails the use of informers or undercover agents using surveillance techniques which cannot be disclosed without exposing individuals to the risk of personal injury or jeopardizing the success of future operations. It is for the court to decide and not the prosecution whether the material should be disclosed and all we could do was wait around for hours outside the court and play no part in the discussions behind closed doors.

Cripps told us merely what he had been instructed to divulge and the following day he returned to the legal battleground and announced that he had occasion to withdraw the allegations the prosecution had made against each of the accused as they were not prepared to comply with any order to disclose. All the defendants left the court obviously delighted with the outcome but as bemused as their advocates.

We still, to this day, do not know what was so sacred that it could not be revealed in open court. What constitutes public interest is another, increasingly nebulous legal minefield as seen by the current vogue for and debate about super-injunctions, many surrounding sport's stars.

13

*

And they Play, All the Way
for Leeds United

Defamation, and particularly libel in a newspaper, can be hard to prove. The defendant can escape the action if they can prove the statement was true or justified, fair comment or published on an occasion that was privileged. Acting for the plaintiff, I had to prove that such statements injured feelings and harmed reputations. As far as the papers are concerned, particularly the tabloids, there is nothing like a juicy story about someone in the public eye to increase circulation.

In February 1982, Billy Bremner hit the defamation jackpot and I received acclaim and applause from Leeds United supporters. The High court in London awarded record damages in a libel case of £100,000 against the *Sunday People* for a front page 'exclusive' which explicitly said that Bremner had offered bribes to fix matches. The verdict and award was made by a jury of seven men and five women. Looking back, it is fair to say that it was not only Billy Bremner who was on trial but Leeds United in general and their former manager Don Revie in particular. Revie, imagined to be a svengali, was the greatest factor in the emergence of Leeds United from being an average second division team in the Football League to mixing it with the cream of European football.

Bremner, his skipper, and Dubliner Johnny Giles were the midfield stars who were the heart and brains of the United performances. Bremner was fiery and as one would expect of a small compact body topped with bright red hair, was aggressive and confident in not only his own ability but that of his mates to succeed. He always gave full value to his club and his never say die attitude and up and at 'em leadership style was contagious. Heart alone, though, is not enough for a professional footballer. Billy had skills in abundance. He was an accurate passer of the ball and frequently popped up to score vital goals in big games. He was captain courageous, worshipped by the supporters and taken to his bosom by the manager who referred to him as 'Billy son'. John Giles was a small, slightly built player who was far more worldly-wise than Billy. The Irishman was meticulous in his training, diet, and sleep patterns while Billy accepted the arduous training but was not an enthusiast. Billy scorned food and when staying in hotels with the team it was easy to spot his room as the breakfast tray would be left outside often untouched. Billy smoked and boozed, Giles did neither except for enjoying a Bacardi and Coke at the weekend. Billy played cards, Giles read a good book. Billy was impulsive, Giles was studious and shrewd. Giles had been at the top before arriving at Leeds from Manchester United and already held a Cup winner's medal. Going down into the second division was not going to be a last resting place but a jumping off platform, he still had a lot to prove and did so.

The pair, for well over ten years, epitomised what Leeds stood for. Aggression allied to enthusiasm and skill with a high work ethic, were the ingredients for success. They were hard to beat, their methods were often not pretty and the image of the 'beautiful game' may not have been enhanced but they clawed their way from near oblivion and, to everyone's surprise, found life in the first division enervating. Quickly they became a side to be feared and even their detractors grudgingly respected them. Their foibles - and there were many - did not disguise the skills they possessed. In that era, to be successful meant survival first, to have the ability to intimidate opponents and, as a coup de gras, to then enchant and entertain the spectators.

Revie had a fine reputation as being a skilful player but as a manager and discoverer of young talent, he had few peers. His nickname, 'the Don' more than adequately described him and his attitude. Like a Mafia boss, he surrounded himself with people who accepted what he said with blind obedience and were prepared to follow and support him without question. His devotion to them was only matched by theirs to him. To this day, his flock say nothing to detract from his management talents and indeed his humanity, save perhaps that he did not make allowance for his players maturing with experience and developing fertile and independent minds. There were, however, those who despised him and his methods and wanted to belittle the achievements of his team. Waiting for him to fall was an enthusiastic pastime of some eminent football journalists and if he was stumbling, they were prepared to give him a push. While his contemporaries, Sir Matt Busby, Bill Shankly and Bill Nicholson were spoken of with reverence and affection, Revie - though conceded to be in their league - was excluded from the paeans written about and goodwill showered upon them.

Football fans often forget that in the glory days of United, the game was more physical and violent, tackles from behind had not been outlawed and, furthermore grounds were uneven, muddy and poorly maintained. It must have been akin to playing snooker on a torn and shredded tablecloth. Rugby had the catchphrase, 'get your retaliation in first' while soccer, like boxing, had the command, 'protect yourself at all times'. There were plenty who rejoiced in a reputation for clogging and Leeds' players quickly learned how to take evasive action and meter out their own. They developed two sides to their game, they could outplay or outmuscle whatever seemed appropriate and often within the same 90 minutes. Norman Hunter, Jack Charlton, Paul Reaney, John Giles and Allan Clarke to name but a few could fight with the best and no one welcomed an encounter with United at their Elland Road fortress, in particular. Whereas it was said that some folk, wherever they went, made friends that was not the case with Don Revie. He collected enemies and not for short periods. Some were in powerful places, like Alan Hardaker the Football League Secretary based in the most of unlikely sporting citadels, St Annes on Sea, on the Fylde Coast in Lancashire. In the East Riding of Yorkshire, the Hardaker family was well known, his brother Ernest the long serving chairman of Hull rugby league club. Ernest was well liked in the city and in his sport but Alan never coveted popularity. It was said that Alan woke early in the morning so that he could hate Revie for longer. He made no secret of his dislike, although loathing was perhaps a more appropriate description.

The 1971/2 season was arguably the most exciting, successful and dramatic in the Leeds' history. At Elland Road, they consistently entertained their passionate fans and in the first 17 league games there, dropped only two points. On their travels they had similar success, and at the business end of the season were candidates to win both the Championship and the FA Cup. It meant, however, an arduous run in. The possible double came down to the final league fixture which, in view of their appearance in the cup final was due to be played two days after Wembley. Alan Hardaker was asked, not unreasonably, if it could be altered but he showed no sympathy and detailed that the defining match at Wolverhampton would go ahead as planned. It was hard to fathom then but would be unthinkable now and highlighted a power struggle between the Football Association and Football League as to who ran or had the most influence in the sport. It also gave the indefatigable Hardaker an opportunity to put one over his detested rival. Leeds duly won the centenary FA Cup for the first and, so far, only time in their history, deservedly beating Arsenal 1-0 at Wembley. There were no celebrations that evening because of the match to come and, although the traditional banquet was held, the players were missing, the parade through the city of and traditional civic reception postponed until the following Thursday. The squad was taken, almost at once, from north London to a hotel in the Midlands in readiness for the Monday night match against Wolves. Revie was targeted in many newspapers and there were many hints that attempts would be made to 'influence' the match at Molyneux. The manager of the host club, Bill McGarry was supposed to have given a warning to his players that approaches might be made to them to deflect them from their responsibilities to their club and to the game.

The match was an anticlimax for Leeds. They lost by two goals to one and the Derby County players, managed by a certain Brian Clough, on holiday in Majorca celebrated their success as championship winners. Contemporary reports seemed to agree that Leeds were harshly done by and were denied penalties by the match officials. Significantly for what subsequently occurred was the fact that because of troublesome injuries in the squad, Billy Bremner played at centre forward. The failure hurt United badly but inspired them to rise from the ashes. Revies' belief that the world was against him and his team increased his bitterness against the football establishment but away from the Leeds area, the football world rejoiced in their downfall, 'they got what they deserved' was a universal theme of their legions of haters.

The story of that final game which shattered the dream of the double did not go away. It was revisited some years later by *The People* newspaper, with a wide circulation and a readership ever hungry for scandals and shaming particularly of people in the public eye. The front page headline was startling. 'Bremner tried to bribe me -give me a pen and I'll give you a grand'. The informant was Danny Hegan, a Scottish player in the Wolves side on that day. What he was claiming was that a shameful, deceitful dishonest act had been committed by the Leeds skipper.

Sunday morning in the Teeman household is devoted completely to relaxation; a sleep-in, a leisurely read of the papers, lunch and normally a rugby league match in the afternoon. The calm was punctuated by a phone call before 9.30. It was Billy Bremner. 'Sorry, to disturb you Ron, but have you seen *The People*?' he asked. That paper was not on my reading list and when I asked him to read it out to me, he recited in a halting voice the entire article. I said, 'Bill, I've got to ask you this - I just have to, so don't misunderstand me - is there any truth in the article? And to be blunt, Bill, did you make any attempt to bribe Hegan, that night?' His answer was loud, forthright and unequivocal, 'No effing chance. It's a load of bollocks and shite.' There and then I made an appointment to see him next morning. I left him with a warning, 'Bill, you're going to be pressurised by the national press either on the phone or on the doorstep, just say, 'the allegations are totally untrue, I've already placed the matter in the hands of my solicitor and on his advice I'm saying nothing further'.' What I forgot to say was have you spoken to Mr Revie? and I later found that he had not. Revie had been long since departed from Leeds, been England manager and then decamped in somewhat acrimonious circumstances to take over the United Arab Emirates. The humiliated Football Association, a bastion of establishment figures, imposed a ten year ban from the game in England on him. That imposed exile and general bad odour surrounding the name of Revie was seen as the start for his enemies to revile his name with stories of match fixing and character assassination. Bob Stokoe, the former Sunderland manager who led them to an unexpected cup final victory over Leeds in 1973, was in for the kill. He said that Revie had offered him £500 when he was manager of Bury to throw one of the games played during the Easter holiday. The Daily Mirror alleged that Revie tried to fix a match at Newcastle in that same season which they won 3-0 and was vital to their survival in the second division.

In November 1979, Revie having resumed residence in the United Kingdom, took the FA to the High Court to fight his ban. He was not only loyal to his players but also to his lawyers. He had always used a firm of solicitors in Leeds respected for their general work but not renowned for their litigious practice. There was no way he would hurt their feelings by using someone else in their place to conduct the litigation, no matter how important. He spoke to me, I agreed to help him and I then spoke to John Brodwell, the solicitor having conduct of the case, who was aware of my general football knowledge. John, on my suggestions, instructed Gilbert Gray QC - my oldest colleague in the law - to present Revie's case. Whilst Gray might not have possessed the most brilliant legal mind of his generation, few were at his level as an advocate and I thought that his consummate skill in cross-examination of the FA hierarchy would be decisive and so it proved. I also suggested that two club managers of repute be invited to give evidence, to point out that the Revie situation with England was intolerable. The media howled for his blood and there was no evidence of support coming from the Football Association. It meant that his departure from the post was inevitable and imminent thus, leaving him the option of waiting to be sacked or beating them to the game and making away sharply of his own accord. Laurie McMenemy, an awesome figure in the game and a successful manager at Southampton and John Giles, then an international manager with the Republic of Ireland, both agreed to give evidence. Both owed a great deal to the assistance Revie had given them in their careers. The outcome of the case was that Revie succeeded and the ban was removed. Sadly, Mr. Justice Cantley, who had presided over a murder case at Leeds Assizes in which I was engaged, savagely attacked and reviled the character and reputation of Revie saying he was, 'Disloyal, discourteous and selfish,' which took away all the gloss of victory. Cantley did not try to sweeten the pill, for he poured a further measure of opprobrium on Revie by disallowing him the costs that otherwise a successful plaintiff could expect to receive from the defendants. I doubted whether Revie would ever live down the emasculation of his character and suffice to say, he never had another job in English football. The vilification in the press continued and, though far removed from the scene of his alleged crimes, living in retirement in Scotland, he succumbed to motor neuron disease in 1989, at an age when he had not yet received his state pension.

It was natural for a lawyer with knowledge of the entire background to the libel in *The People* to have an abundance of material to sort through. The first act was to explain to Billy the nature and cost of libel proceedings against a national newspaper with unlimited funds and resources at their disposal. We also warned him that the proceedings would be many months ahead and the anxiety as to the outcome would make great call on his acknowledged mental stamina. We added that he would need the assistance of a great many people to rebut the allegations and, though it was the responsibility in law for the newspaper to prove that what Hegan said was true and that there was justification for publishing - a difficult task indeed - witnesses as to Hegan's behaviour at the time and subsequently would be of importance. Bremner said in a very frank plea, 'I'll go to the end of my days protesting that what Hegan said is a pack of fucking lies and whatever it costs me will be nothing to protect the good honest name I have as a pro.' I introduced him to my assistant solicitor, later to become my partner, Peter Levine who I explained would have the day to day responsibility for the conduct of the case but that I was there to ensure that the case was driven along the correct lines.

Peter Levine had only recently qualified at that time but in my view was developing into an outstanding lawyer, showing maturity far beyond his years. He was an Oxford graduate and in his twenties who, in his time with me, had an appetite for work which could best be described as voracious. He was thoughtful and decisive, deliberative and considerate. If there was any matter that caused him doubts before resolving the position, he would throw it at me. He would listen and argue, put his points succinctly with clarity and resolve any lingering doubts he had in his mind. He was patient, and while aggressive by temperament, was conciliatory in speech. He knew that the many approaches for evidence would dissolve into a few and we should determine not to be frustrated if certain avenues travelled in our investigations lead to dead ends. He was a detailed planner by nature and, above all, though being devoted to the file, he never lost the objectivity that a good lawyer should possess. On our many discussions on this case, I recall saying to him, 'Peter, think about it - and then think what your opponent is thinking.' That message was heeded as was my assertion, 'Your opponents are represented by lawyers at the head of the profession, with far greater resources than we can call upon but whereas this case is one of many to them, it is the only one of its type in our office.' The firm Bindmans, who acted for the newspaper, had a great reputation for representing the lowly and it surprised many in the profession that *The People* chose not been represented by a more fashionable firm of libel lawyers. Peter Levine, cut his teeth on the Bremner file and I maintain that it gave him the impetus to reach the top of the legal profession and eventually in commerce, where he exercises his skills and talents today. Few lawyers achieve fame in industry but Peter did. I discerned a weakness in his make up in the very early days, which took time to correct. He would bristle with anger and show annoyance to criticism and those who challenged him. I had an expression that he eventually took on board, 'Peter, don't bite and rise, that's what they're trying to make you do.' He remains as one of the most outstanding lawyers I've met in a long career.

The record award in libel damages was a tribute to Peter's skill and tenacity. We both agreed that it was essential that we knew more of Danny Hegan, who had startled the football world with his allegations, than his own mother. His time at Wolverhampton, his subsequent career and what happened to him after he was unable to dribble a ball, were on our agenda. 'We must find out,' I demanded, 'Who did he tell of the offer to bribe him? Did he go to his skipper, his manager or trainer? Did any other member of his team hear Bremner make the offer or learn of it post match? Why did he wait so long before spewing it out to a journalist? Was it money that made him talk?' Peter took all this on board. In the Wolves team that night was veteran centre forward Derek

Dougan, a Northern Irish international who was in the papers more often than fish and chips. A tall, handsome man with a fashionable hairstyle, he epitomised the glamour that publicity hungry footballers attracted. He stood tall and in addition to his football skills and showmanship, was a key member of the Professional Footballer's Association and at the time of his assistance to us, was its chairman. That Association served its members well. It found a loud voice in the inexhaustible, voluble Jimmy Hill who led them to 'freedom of contract' and he had a great successor in 'the Doog' as he was fondly known in the game. Peter saw Derek and he agreed to help. To be blunt he was angry at the allegation that Hegan had made and offended and suspicious of its timing. He was as sure as anyone could be that Hegan was telling lies. He gave evidence that he'd never witnessed any member of the Leeds team offer bribes to Wolves players, and neither Hegan nor anyone else had mentioned attempts by Bremner to bribe him.

Frank Monroe was the Wolves skipper that night. He told the Court that Bremner had offered him £500 to give away a penalty. Mr Monroe was a late arrival at the scene and no one had heard of his allegation prior to the date of the trial as he was living in Australia. Under cross examination he told the jury, that *The People* had paid £4,000 to bring him and his entire family back to this country and was giving evidence in 1982 of a bribe offered to him in May 1972, having done nothing at all about this unusual occurrence in the meantime. In their defence, which was undertaken by a specialised libel barrister, the newspaper raised what we called in our office, the 'Revie defence'. In alleging that Billy was the willing tool of his manager, they claimed that he took a leading role in his manager's corrupt and nefarious activities.The newspaper had interviewed Gary Sprake, Leeds' regular goalkeeper until displaced by David Harvey. Sprake had received a five figure sum at a time when he was going through personal difficulties for spilling the beans on Don Revie and in his confession referred to three incidents to show that his manager was 'bent' and that his captain was at his side. He was a key defence witness. Peter Levine had made the decision to investigate fully all the incidents related by Sprake.

The goalkeeper told of a pre-match team meeting held at the Mansion Hotel in Roundhay Park, which was a regular game day venue for the side. They were due to play Nottingham Forest at Elland Road that afternoon. Leeds were going well at the time and Forest were not the best of travellers. Sprake said that Revie told the players not to worry about the game, 'Billy will go into the dressing room, speak to the Scottish lads and the right result will be achieved.' This verbal volley of a compromising nature seems strange behaviour and out of character for a manager who was both cautious in his approach and meticulous in his preparation. It seemed unthinkable that an experienced practitioner of his art would, at the very least, be so misguided and stupid as to provide evidence of deceit to at least a dozen players who would be able to hold it over him. We established that dressing rooms before important games were not warzones. Both teams would have completed their match preparations well before arriving at the ground. Players who had fellow countrymen or former team mates in the opposition camp would drop in for a chat and, if the opposition manager did not like visitors, it would take place in the corridor. Peter went to Nottingham and spoke to a former Scottish international and a friend of Billy's. He remembered the game and recalled chatting to Billy before the match but he could not recall a specific subject. 'Let's be frank,' Peter said, 'It's being said that Billy came in to see you with a view to getting the right result.' The opponent laughed out loud and long and replied, 'I'll be very frank, no-one from Nottingham Forest relished the game at Leeds, we were almost beaten before we left the bus.' He joined the prison service after his career with Forrest ended and was contemptuous of the allegations that Sprake was making.

Sprake also pointed to a game at Newcastle United which was vital for Leeds to get at least a draw to survive in the second division. It was at the beginning of Revie's career in management and it was suggested that the result of that game was fixed. Our exhaustive research, which included visits to the North East, produced no evidence to support that slur. His final allegation was the most interesting as it centred on his debut as a 16-year-old, Sprake having been flown to Southampton in an emergency when the incumbent stopper had been taken ill. Any player would remember his initial appearance in the first team and Sprake said that Revie told the Leeds players before the match that he had arranged for a home team player to be bribed. At the trial Billy MacAdams, who was then a lorry driver, was called to give evidence for the defendant and said, 'Bremner was involved in the fix.' At the time Billy was only 19 and I doubt if the jury gave much weight to his evidence. Mr Justice Bristow told them that the purport of the People case was that Bremner was guilty of three offences of corruption and, in a criminal trial, could have been sent to prison for two years for each offence. The jury did not take long to bring in a verdict in favour of Bremner and reject all the evidence given by Hegan and his witnesses. Hegan had his past life and present situation thoroughly examined and, even today, I am amazed that *The People* gave him and his story any credibility. We even thought that it would be a difficult task to get him into court but he did turn up and merely convinced the jury that he was a person who would say anything.

At the trial, Gary Sprake was placed in the position of

having to withdraw his claims. The pot of gold he received from the *Daily Mirror* for his exuberant revelations did him little good. The goalkeeper who was mocked at Liverpool for a goal when he threw the ball into his own net, provoking a chorus of 'Careless Hands' was sadly remembered for his few spectacular failures rather that the strength and brilliance of many of his performances. Injury forced him out of the game, his health gave serious concern and his marriage of long duration broke up. The camaraderie of Leeds players who enjoyed the glory years and successes has remained strong and forty years on has not dimmed their happy memories of the club and of one another. They meet regularly and speak frequently. Sprake is never invited to their gatherings and is not on the Christmas card list of many of his former colleagues. His name is seldom mentioned. By his actions and false accusations about Revie, he forfeited his right to take his place at the table of those who sit in good fellowship.

Among the lessons I was taught as a solicitor's articled clerk, was to respect a client's pocket as much as his confidence. I was taught that before sending the brief to counsel for a hearing, to speak to your opponent to tell them this fact and to also enquire courteously as to whether there was any possibility of settlement. The reason for that was that the moment the brief was delivered, counsel would receive his fee whether or not the case was settled before trial. As counsel's fee was the largest percentage of the cost, no one wanted to land their client with a bill if it could be avoided. I thought that the Bremner case would be one whereby the defendant's solicitors would have heard of our exhaustive enquiries and probably would have approached the same people as possible witnesses. When I put the question to the solicitor for *The People*, he refused point blank to talk, reiterating their stance. I even proposed each side paying their own costs but they would not even consider it on that basis. Sometime after the sudden death of Billy, in referring to the award for libel another newspaper claimed that Bremner had little confidence in his case because he was prepared to withdraw it.

Our Counsel was Patrick Milmo. He was a junior at the time and Peter, said he was patient and painstaking. The trial was due to last over a week and, as financial resources were scarce and London hotels were expensive, I borrowed the Southgate flat of Liam Brady who was playing for Juventus at that time and Peter and Billy went into residence there. The confidence of the lawyer in the outcome of the trial can be misplaced. In his summing up to the jury which was impeccable, the judge said 'You will no doubt think long and hard, before you find Billy Bremner guilty of corruption.' It did not take them long to decide that *The People* were not justified in making the accusation. The newspaper asked for a stay of execution as they were considering an appeal but none followed and the money and the costs were paid. The anxiety of the allegations and the duration of the proceedings certainly demanded a high price from Billy. The brave, fearless player lost his appetite, smoked more excessively than normal and developed a facial twitch which never left him in moments of stress. But, as he said, 'No-one is going to call me a cheat on the football field and get away with it.' At the time of the trial, he was the manager of Doncaster Rovers and he told the court that he only stopped playing because in away matches he received abuse from the home crowd calling him 'fixer'. He found that difficult to take as did his wife who was taunted when she went out shopping and his children received similar treatment at school.

I was fed on the belief never to underestimate your opponent just as much as not to be fearful of one with a great reputation and, reflecting on the Bremner case thirty years later, I believe there may have been an element of hubris on the defendant's side. When Billy's career in football management ended, he joined the after dinner speaker circuit. Always in demand up and down England as well as in his beloved Scotland, he really delighted in the craic that followed the events, staying into the long hours to talk football with guests. He never tired of meeting the fans but sadly he collapsed after one such engagement and all efforts to save his life failed. His funeral, many of the arrangements being made by his Leeds United colleague and great pal Allan Clarke, was held in a small Roman Catholic church in the village of Edlington near Doncaster, where he lived. It could not accommodate all those who wanted to attend and hundreds were left outside. One of the last mourners to arrive was Sir Alex Ferguson, manager of Manchester United. The previous evening, he had been with his side in Turin and he could have only returned to England in the small hours. Notwithstanding the lack of sleep, he made the effort to pay his respects to one of Scotland's bravest. Billy went to his grave with the affection and admiration of those in the football world who applauded his skill and accomplishments and came from near and far to pay their last respects to a great warrior, an honest footballer who gave everything in his being to his team and to their supporters.

I have always maintained that a skillful artist, let loose on the front cover of the *Holy Bible*, might have it consigned to the top shelf of a popular bookstall. The proof of the adage not to judge a book by its cover was given to me by my clients John Giles and Nobby Stiles – football's most celebrated brothers-in-law.

Stiles was a classical creative midfield player, small in his stature and a hero of the successful 1966 England World Cup team and extremely combative on the field of play. In 2000, the pair had been alerted by a friend that the autobiography of Barry Fry, described as the 'riotous tales from a larger than life football manager' and entitled *Big Fry*, was in the bookshops. The inside front cover flap contained descriptive material as to the contents and read: 'From his early career as a youth apprentice for Manchester United's Busby babes, Fry developed a reputation as a player who knew how to enjoy himself as he found with the likes of George Best, Nobby Stiles and John Giles on a binge of birds, booze and betting.'

The reputation of the late lamented Northern Irishman, Best, with the ladies was well-known and documented. He was linked amorously with Miss Worlds and many famous actresses and models. The respected balding Nobby and the diminutive Giles were not in George's league and their respective spouses, both Irish girls, would not tolerate such behaviour by their men folk. Even worse than that, John Giles was well-known to have a strong aversion to gambling. He neither played cards, went to race meeting and as for booze – forget it. Breweries would close if they had to rely on the support of Giles and Stiles who were irregular and modest drinkers. Inside, there was only one reference to Giles, on page 36, when the author wrote of him cleaning his and Stiles' boots. Nobby is mentioned again on page 34 as the captain of the Manchester United youth team and on page 66 when the author was the manager of Dunstable Town and spoke to the owner about bringing Nobby Stiles and George Best down to play for them. There was no mention of birds, booze or betting. When Giles and Stiles heard of all this, they at first laughed it off. They could not be described as intimate friends of Fry or associates of his, but when the import of the statements sunk in they went ballistic. 'Someone is trying to capitalise on our names with absolutely fictitious stories and are out to make a few bob at our expense,' said Giles who had concerns that there are people who always believe what they read. My opinion was sought and I advised that there could be no clearer case of defamation and I thought it was aggravated by the use of good established sporting names to sell a story which might not have had as much appeal without the promise of the revelation of salacious details. Both Giles and Stiles authorised me to proceed. I made contact with the publishers and very soon negotiations took place which resulted in an apology and cheque for a four figure sum.

On the cover of Fry's book, the collaborator was journalist Phil Rostron. Obviously he could not have authorised the material about which the complaint was made. An amazing coincidence occurred three years later when the same Phil Rostron who, as the chief sports writer for the *Yorkshire Evening Post* followed the fortunes of Leeds United on a daily basis, penned in his column an article attacking the integrity of Giles as a journalist. John at that time was working for the *Daily Express* writing a weekly opinion piece and he also was a respected pundit on Irish television. He phoned me saying that some of his old United friends had read the comments that Rostron had written and asked me to get a copy of the article.

It seemed to suggest that Giles' criticism of his former club for selling youngster Jonathan Woodgate, who had been developed through Leeds' youth system, was affected by him, 'being sore at a former Leeds board overlooking him for a managerial position.' Rostron was turning the clock back over 30 years and much water had moved under the bridge. The truth was that John Giles never applied for the manager's job when Don Revie left Leeds and after the honeymoon with Brian Clough had turned into a nightmare, certainly did not apply to succeed him. John told me bluntly, 'It's a terrible indictment of a journalist to suggest that he has an ulterior motive for his views,' and he was not prepared to accept the allegation from someone he did not know and who had not had the courtesy to even contact him before writing it. 'I don't want damages,' he told me. 'I just want an apology for the slur.' My file on the Fry case had been sent to our repository and I did not make the connection but someone much later down the line told me of it.

We had correspondence with the newspaper and it seemed they were not willing to retract so John gave us the go ahead to start proceedings for defamation and we notified them of our intentions. The newspaper then had a change of heart and agreed to print a statement which read:

> In an opinion column which appeared in the *Yorkshire Evening Post* on February 5th this year, reference was made to comments in a national newspaper column by former Leeds United player Mr John Giles, on the sale of Mr Jonathan Woodgate. The article suggested that Mr Giles may have been affected in his comments on this issue by 'being sore at a former Leeds board overlooking him for a managerial position.' We accept that there were no grounds for this comment. We also now accept that his remarks on the Woodgate issue were based on genuine personal belief. We apologise for the suggestion they were not. Mr Giles has asked us to point out that he never applied for the job of manager at Leeds United and remains to this day on good terms with the members on the Leeds United board referred to.

It was a classic case of making sure you get your facts straight first before committing to paper.

A Lawyer for all Seasons

I became familiar with the strange behaviour of clubs through my association with Leeds United. Manny Cussins, a wealthy furniture magnate with residential building interests was in the chair during most of my dealings and I found myself in dispute with him over those contracted players who were then in the veteran stage. While, perhaps, they had outlived their shelf life at Elland Road, they still had earning potential at lower placed outfits. I fielded a call from Billy Bremner who felt that Mr Cussins was being greedy in demanding a very high fee from Hull City which would inhibit his future earnings if he moved to the east coast. There was a dramatic confrontation at Manny's Leeds home, where we were both invited which became heated.

Manny tried to justify his position by repeating over and over again that Leeds had always paid Billy 'good money' and that he personally had bought a piece of silver designed by Garrods of London for £500 at Billy's testimonial dinner. Billy pulled out from his pocket a cheque book and said, 'Here's my cheque, Manny and I will take the tray.' Manny did not bite but relented and reduced the fee demanded by Leeds to more a modest requirement. John Giles had similar problems which ended with him withdrawing his labour and retiring, which I am pleased to say caused Manny to see sense and reality in his dealings with West Bromwich Albion. John in his recently published biography relates how his disputes with the chairman soured his last days of an otherwise brilliant career at United and never forgave him for his conduct towards him. Years earlier I advised Joe Jordan not to accept an offer from Ajax of Holland which denied Leeds a substantial fee they had agreed which obviously did not endear me to Mr Cussins. When we met socially from time to time, you would hardly think that we were anything but lifetime buddies, he always pinched my cheeks by way of greeting.

I went out of my way to help him and the club when he sacked Brian Clough after 44 days as manager. The club's auditor, Norman Kay, was also the auditor of my own legal practice. Norman phoned me and explained the position quickly, as news of the sacking of Clough had not broken. He asked me, 'Am I right in saying the maximum a club can pay tax free as compensation for loss of office to an employee is £25,000?' I confirmed that was the case and asked, 'What's your problem?' He replied, 'Manny is paying much more than that and has promised that the club will pay Clough's tax.' I advised, 'That could cost a fortune Norman, he's got it totally wrong and you must tell him.' The end result was that Manny took no notice of the advice doing the deal his way, thereby cementing Clough's financial future – as he boasted - and cost Leeds a fortune. It all came out into the public domain later and Norman Kay was embarrassed when people asked him how he could have sanctioned it.

Leslie Silver, a paint manufacturer, was a totally different man when holding the reins at Elland Road. He sought advice, made observations on it and asked for explanations but invariably stuck with it. Bill Fotherby was his right-hand man, a genial extrovert who had been a clothing manufacturer and a member of the United board before he became chief executive there. You could not help but like Bill. He was so optimistic and enthusiastic and, on occasions, had to be reeled back for his own good. He had a secretary who had joined Leeds from a smaller club and he phoned me one day in a very anxious frame of mind. Apparently a player had left England some years earlier for Portugal and played out there successfully and now wished to return to the UK. The Leeds manager at that time, Billy Bremner, wanted him very much. The player had an agent who represented both himself and the club and an all-in price had been negotiated which included a transfer fee, the player's signing on amount and the agent's commission. The Secretary pertinently queried, 'What was the VAT payable on the deal?' I was informed that the breakdown was given by the agent to Leeds and the first thing I did was get a friend from another English club to phone their Portuguese counterpart to find out the fee they required. Then, I tried to check with the enquiry branch at the Customs & Excise as to how they would view the transaction and to get Leeds the VAT registration number of the agent. The first response I received obviated the need to pursue any further enquiries. The Portuguese club required a nominal sum. I spoke to the Leeds United secretary and put him in the picture. The agent had gone to the station with the cheque and I said, 'Get it back or stop it if you can't.' The secretary did, fortunately, retrieve the cheque and the agent left Leeds never to return nor did the very unfortunate player. The press were informed and wrote, 'The transaction did not go through because of legal advice the club had received.' I have to say that Leslie Silver was most appreciative.

I was also engaged by Leeds in the Safety of Sports Ground enquiries. United had an enthusiastic director, retired from his own business life but who put all his efforts into this subject. As the club had been under scrutiny for crowd misbehaviour in England and abroad, Maxwell Holmes was always having meetings with me, preparing reports and observations for presentation to the Government's appointed tribunal. We had regular discussions with the police who were represented by chief superintendent David Clarkson, who I believed was so switched on that he knew every football hooligan within a 30 mile radius of Elland Road. He had worked well with United while preserving the independence of his force but recognising the huge cost of policing which fell to the club. Mr Justice Popplewell, in charge of the enquiry, was courtesy personified and he often rang me for my observations.That was followed by the Taylor report into Hillsborough following the dreadful catastrophe at the FA cup semi-final there. All this work was interesting but not financially rewarding but the liquor licensing application at the stadium was a continual earner and quite complicated requiring a firm knowledge not only of the statute book but the practices of the local magistrate's court. Peter Bell at my office had a mind for detail and a temperament that soothed others and took on this labour with relish.

My work with Leeds United did, occasionally, mean a conflict of interest. From time to time the Rugby Football League used Elland Road for a high profile match and a special licence was required. The beneficiary of the drinks licence was Leeds United and the more the league fans quenched their thirst the more cash went into the football club's coffers. When the bill for legal services relating to these bars was sent to Bill Fotherby, he forwarded them with all their own accounts on to the RFL. Maurice Lindsay, the chief executive there painstakingly scrutinised each and every claim and when he saw these charges he phoned me. Straight to the point he asked, 'Why should the RFL pay these bills, they're not for our benefit?' My reply was equally pointed, 'Maurice, who are they addressed to?' 'Oh I see,' replied Maurice 'They are all to Leeds United.' I was not a party to any dialogue between them – and I would have liked to have been - but I do know my office received a cheque that bore Bill's signature.

14

*

Eddie Waring and the
Death of Hunslet

I imagine there have been more influential and erudite discussion groups in Leeds over the centuries than the one that met weekly at the Queen's Hotel on Fridays.

There was no agenda and certainly no timetable. The drink was included in the fellowship and, in fact, no one actually paid for a round. The head barman would allocate the contributions each of the attendees would have to make at the end of the evening. In the chair was Eddie Waring, the celebrated television personality and rugby league commentator. Eddie's talents away from the sport ranged over a spectacular variety of events from *It's A Knockout* and its continental version *Jeux sans Frontières* to his guest appearances with Morecambe and Wise in their Christmas shows and with *The Goodies*.

Eddie was secretive, no one had his phone number. You would get him at the Queen's Hotel and they would make contact with him if he was not there. No one knew his right age and I recall he was once asked to produce his driving license and I said I would drop it in and he curtly refused. Seldom did his beloved wife Mary appear in public but his son, Tony, was often with him during the day. The evenings were always interrupted by porters appearing at the bar door and miming the answering of a phone and Eddie would depart and return to continue the conversation as if he'd never been interrupted.

The regular coterie were Hector Rawson, a former chairman of Hunslet and the rugby league itself who was a prominent industrialist in the West Riding and who could speak either with an Oxford accent or resort to the local dialect as appropriate; Alan Simpson, a barrister and rugby league fan as well as a steward of the British Boxing Board of Control and a fair bowls player. He later became His Honour Judge Simpson sitting in the crown court at Sheffield. Also present were, Jack Myerscough, a clothing manufacturer and the chairman of Leeds; Jack Lunn, a builder and a member of the board at Hunslet and, occasionally Harry Jepson, a headmaster with serious rugby league connections. Eddie because of his non-conformist temperance background would treat himself to cider but the remainder of the party were whiskey men. There was always a target for someone's humour and it was frequently me. If I had been involved in some court case reported in the press, it would set the ball rolling with Hector Rawson saying, 'Tha'll not win that one lad.' Eddie used to tell me to, 'Fight the good fight.' The politics at rugby league headquarters appeared frequently on the agenda, confirming that folk within the sport were often divided, analytical and self-critical but, to a dismissive outsider, always displayed a united front. It suited the die-hards to believe that all the world was against them and 'the establishment' held them in disdain.

Eddie would say, 'I'm in the chair,' or 'The camera's on me,' when about to pronounce some juicy titbit, rumour or story. The bar was small, 20 people at the most could be accommodated, and he always positioned himself so he could see every one entering into the room. We were always anxious that others might be listening to us so conversations when strangers were around were *sotto voce* and if a person was being slandered we would use initials. Indirectly through Eddie I ended up with a civil case in the Court of Appeal.

Eddie had two friends, Mr and Mrs Creech, who ran a pub in Meanwood, Leeds, called the Myrtle. It was a rather unusual public house as it adjoined a cricket ground and, though it was a couple of miles from the city centre, had the atmosphere of a village. The unfortunate tenants had been sold a jukebox system and entered into a hire purchase agreement. Eddie said they were having aggravation and would I give them some advice. They both came to the Queen's Hotel and I met them with him. They gave me the facts and it appeared that the wretched contraption was always breaking down and the company's service engineers were despairing of ever being able to repair it. For several months it had been idle and unable to be used. The question was what should they do and I told them fearlessly, 'Send it back, stop your payments and say you are rescinding the agreement.' They followed the advice and for months I heard nothing until they then phoned me to say that they had received a summons to appear in Pontefract County Court issued by the finance company. I was in a quandary, I did not know whether my clients could afford to pay the legal costs nor was it a question that I dare put to them. Eddie said, 'If you think they have got a good case, go ahead and if Arthur and Mary cannot pay I'll pick up the tab.' Fortune, they say, smiles on the brave and it did on me in abundance.

The judge was one Ernest Ould, knocking on a bit but he knew all the angles and, as a barrister had been briefed by me. He ran a tidy ship at Pontefract and would travel on the bus from Leeds at nine in the morning, be at the court before ten and, more importantly, had a timepiece that kept him alert so that he could get a bus back to Leeds just after one in the afternoon. He proved the old adage, 'it's not the hours you do but what you do in the hours.'

Very quickly he got to the point; did the machine regularly break down? Yes. Did the plaintiff try to repair? Yes. Did they succeed? No. He found for the defendant saying because of the plaintiff's breaches they were entitled to rescind. We had a few drinks on this success but we did not rejoice for long. Notice of appeal was served on us. Now we were in the 'big league', no instant justice but constructive arguments by those learned in the law and we required someone who could prepare an argument based on legal precedents and were in a higher realm for costs too. I instructed Brian Walsh, later to become the Recorder of Leeds and president of Yorkshire County Cricket Club, and he succeeded in persuading the judges at the Court of Appeal to reject the case, I was saved by the bell again. I learned the lesson – giving free and easy advice off the cuff is a dangerous pastime that can injure health and wealth. On receiving the result Eddie smiled and said that he had, 'No doubt whatsoever at the outcome.'

Eddie never swore or uttered profanities, the farthest he would go was to say, 'he's a real daft B' or, 'He made a BF of himself' but was not averse to a little gentle mickey taking of someone who bordered on pomposity. One of his victims was Hector Rawson's brother-in-law who would occasionally join us. Percy Woodward was the chairman of Leeds United, as the club enjoyed success under Don Revie. Percy had been Lord Mayor of Leeds and it was said that, to him, his term of office did not cease after that year but continued thereafter. He was a ringer for *Dad's Army* character Captain Mainwaring, played by Arthur Lowe. Percy's grumble was that Revie, he never referred to him as Don or Mr Revie, did not show sufficient respect for the Leeds United board in general and him in particular. 'After all Revie wouldn't succeed if we couldn't find the wherewithal,' he would argue. Eddie would gently prompt and prod him, 'How did all this show Percy?' He'd chide. Percy told the tale that when they were about to get off a plane on one of their European jaunts, Revie said, 'Let the players go out first and the directors after,' leaving them at the back of the long immigration queue. 'That was not right,' Woodward complained. Eddie egged him on, 'I would have to agree with you Percy that is no way to treat the directors who have done so much for the club and brought it to its current high status.' It was subsequently reported to us that the next trip was to Glasgow and when the 'fasten seat belt' sign had been turned off, Percy stood up and declared, 'Revie, the directors will go through passports and customs first,' and could not understand why there was a howl of laughter.

There are many stories that come from the court of 'King Eddie', not least the time when he was refused admission to his 'palace'. I had arranged to meet Eddie in the early evening. My progress in entering the Queen's Hotel was blocked by a burly CID officer who I knew. The reason for the refusal was the venue had been taken over by the Variety Club of Great Britain who were having a charity ball and their guest of honour was Her Serene Highness Princess Grace of Monaco, formerly Grace Kelly, accompanied by the celebrated Hollywood star Cary Grant. The hotel had been invaded by the Leeds city police force, their officers being dressed as guests in tuxedos but still looking like policemen, who were providing security for the eminent guests. As I made a tactical withdrawal, I saw Eddie walking towards me with another of our regulars John Smallwood, a partner in the estate agents Dacre, Son and Hartley.

When told of the reason my entry had been rejected Eddie was most annoyed and said, 'They can't refuse me dear boy.' We returned to the hotel and Eddie became engaged in a whispered conversation with the head barman Vince. Eventually, we were allowed into the bar on the undertaking, which Eddie agreed to, that we would vacate at 8.15 prompt. While we were enjoying our drink and the time was approaching eight, the door opened and the serene and elegant pair of celebrities gracefully made an entrance. Eddie rose to his feet - stretching to his full 5 6' - and, in his usual nasal voice said, 'Welcome to Leeds your Royal Highness, can I introduce to you my friends Mr John Smallwood, one of the city's leading estate agents and Mr Teeman, a very well known lawyer.' We both shook hands with Her Grace and then she looked down at Eddie and said imperiously, 'Thank you. But tell me, who are you?' We left promptly.

On another occasion Eddie phoned me and I could tell he was at the Queen's in a call box. He said, 'Look, I haven't got long to talk because I'm on my way to London and I just received a note from the BBC that *Jeux sans Frontières* is taking place in the south of France at a resort called, 'Bowloo'. Eddie's pronunciation in English was often poor but it suddenly struck me that he meant Bealieu. He continued hastily, 'Look Ron, I know that Billy Morris (a local industrialist and well-known bon viveur) knows that area backwards. Find out from him a good place to stay because I think I'll take Mrs Waring with me.' I contacted Billy, at that time the managing director of a company called Troydale Industries in Morley specialising in the production of shoddy cloths, whose son worked for me and told him of Eddie's request. Billy said, 'Look, tell him there's only one place and that's La Reserve.' When Eddie rang back an hour later I dutifully passed on that information. It was a few weeks before I heard from him but then I received a telephone call and the caller was clearly angry. It was Eddie. 'Crickey, that hotel cost an arm and a leg. My expense allowance and my fees were insufficient for the room that Mary and I had. Find out from Billy Morris for heaven's sake why he recommended such a hotel to us?' I phoned Billy and relayed the story. I could hear a hearty laugh. 'Tell Eddie,' he said, 'I don't stay there, I can only afford to have a cup of coffee.'

Eddie was full of aphorisms. He would use them regularly and frequently say, 'To the pure all things are innocent.' In any heated conversation at the bar of the Queen's he would often be heard pronouncing, 'Never explain yourself; your friends don't need one and your enemies won't believe you.' But I remember most of all, the truism he frequently uttered, 'Those who drink the water should remember they who dug the well.' Eddie originated from the Heavy Woollen area of the West Riding where many non-conformists lived alongside other supporters of the Temperance Movement. He liked to believe that his background as a Congregationalist eschewed the partaking of alcohol. I never saw him drink a beer, whisky or any spirits but I did witness him consuming several bottles of cider and he would argue that drinking 'apple juice' was permissible. I learned from him how vulnerable and fragile many in the public eye were, how conscious they were of their own image and how seriously affected by any word of criticism.

In some rugby league circles Eddie was never the most popular of people and, while he accepted that, he still resented those who aired their critical views in public. He felt that he was deserving, if not acclaim, recognition for bringing the sport popularity and to the attention of the nation. It was not forthcoming and that the badge of grievance was worn by him rather sadly. His feud with Bill Fallowfield, iron-handed secretary of the Rugby Football League, was rooted in the official's envy of Eddie and his profile. Bill was a most reliable and efficient ruler of the game but, sadly, could be aggressive and sarcastic to those he disliked. A graduate of one of the older universities, he was insensitive to any person's view other than his own. He resented those who he thought were not as intelligent as himself but who had risen to the higher levels in society. To all intents and purposes, he thought he ran the game and, in reality, he probably did. He would coach the Great Britain team, act as a summariser for television and be the game's international representative. He could not comprehend the popularity of Eddie in the rest of the country and it acted as an irritant that Eddie earned a higher income than he did.

I do not know what motive Fallowfield had for commissioning a report from an organisation called John Caine and Associates into the state of the game, who had not been heard of prior to the publication of their findings. They were based in Manchester and had their moment of fame when the press seized upon its contents. Caine's brief from the Rugby Football League appeared to be quite direct and simple, 'What was the game doing wrong and how could it be improved?' When the report was delivered, to Fallowfield's chagrin, it was damning in general terms but, in a very small paragraph, it indicated that the image of the game was - to some extent - governed by Eddie's portrayal of it. The perception was that the coverage on television reinforced its stereotypical northern background and that the presenter was treating it not as a sport but as an entertainment. That paragraph was the one that was seized upon, not least by newspapers that competed with Eddie for readership as his columns were eagerly awaited and widely read. He became the fulcrum of the argument and debate.

Eddie was mortified; he thought that the end of the world had come. He didn't see how he could be challenged, criticised and abused by all and sundry in the manner that had happened. If I said he was suicidal, I would not be exaggerating. I spent hours counselling him as he stared blankly into space. Eddie considered Caine's reference to him as being defamatory and action should be taken to protect his good name and reputation. I was at pains to explain that the reference to his commentaries was justified as criticism and 'fair comment' and Caine was entitled to freely express himself. I pleaded the fact that the press had picked on the few lines which were very flattering saying that he was known throughout the United Kingdom as 'Mr Rugby League' and told him, 'Forget about defamation Eddie, you don't even know Caine and you couldn't show that he had a personal grouse or grudge against you.'

One of the lawyer's most difficult tasks is to convince a client that the law did not give a remedy for their hurt. I suspect that Eddie sought the advice of the BBC lawyers who expressed similar views for the thoughts of a libel action quickly evaporated. I subsequently spent an evening with Eddie at the Queen's Hotel where we were closeted in the residents lounge with Derek Burrell-Davis, head of the BBC network production centre in Manchester, discussing the situation. Derek had made a special journey over to give Eddie his support. A porter came in and said there was a reporter from, '*The Times* in London' in the hall and he would like to have a few minutes with Eddie. He asked me what he should do and I said, 'I have no doubts at all, you must see him. It shows how serious the attacks on you are being treated.' As soon as the correspondent was admitted, Eddie became his old self, as if he was in front of the camera.

A Lawyer for all Seasons

The article was published on 14th October 1971 and stated:

> Mr Eddie Waring, the Yorkshire born commentator
> who has been the BBC's voice of Rugby League for
> 21 years said that he was hurt and astounded by
> the attack on him by a firm of marketing
> consultants contained in the report commissioned
> by the Rugby League. He said that he was 'taking
> advice' of that report which maintained that the
> BBC's choice of commentator was 'unfortunate'
> and which went on to say 'he may well be
> immensely entertaining and amusing but the
> laughter is patronising and lends support to the
> view of Rugby League held by Midland and
> Southern watchers.' Accompanied by Mr Ronald
> Teeman his solicitor and Mr Derek Burrell-Davis,
> the Head of the BBC network production centre in
> Manchester, Mr Waring spoke frankly and
> disarmingly in a Leeds Hotel about his love for the
> game between 'northern heavyweights' and the
> robust men who played.
>
> 'I am astonished by this report,' he said, 'This
> weekend I will be celebrating my 21st year as a
> television commentator at the Great Britain and
> New Zealand Test Match. I've never had any
> complaints and get tremendous fan mail. Only
> today I received an invitation to address Cambridge
> University Union.' Asked about the section of the
> report which said the game was 'a sport for
> Northern heavyweights with a leaning towards
> brawn rather than brains' Mr Waring retorted
> 'they're a grand bunch of fellows and have just as
> much intelligence as Southerners, Welsh or any
> other heavyweights.' The report said Rugby League
> was played against the background of pithead slag
> heaps in a steady drizzle and was watched by

sparse, flat-capped crowds. Mr Waring commented, 'If I had been criticised for mentioning cranes at Barrow in Furness... well you have shipbuilding there, and if I see a picture of this on the monitor I should talk about them, and I don't think this is deprecatory to Barrow. Neither is there anything wrong if I talk about trains going past with coal on them at Castleford.' Mr Waring grinned then went on, 'For many years there used to be a pit wheel behind the ground at Hunslet I could not by any stretch of imagination convince people it was the Big Wheel at Blackpool. I told the truth about a particular image. I use the language of the North of England and the BBC would not be employing me if they did not think I was doing that.' He said he thought some people listen to comments about remarks he was reported to have made but which he had not made, and he had quoted an example from last year's Challenge Cup Final at Wembley where he recalled that Mr Jack Harding of the Rugby League Management Committee criticised him with being biased, but later saw a rerun of the film and apologised. 'I reflect what is happening,' said Mr Waring, 'and I hope it is entertaining to people who do not know the game, and I also have to satisfy those who know everything about it unlike other sports commentators who report games everybody knows about.'

Mr Burrell-Davis explained that he had travelled to Leeds to see his tailor and to find out if Mr. Waring as an old friend wanted any backing. 'Eddie is not just a commentator,' he said, 'He is *The* commentator, and the five million viewers prove his popularity.' He added, 'Eddie is not patronising. He reflects the game as it is. I remember 21 years ago when I was producing the first programme on Rugby League which was a Test Match. Eddie came up to me knowing who I was and asked if he could sit by me. I had previously found the game a slightly technical bore but this little chap sitting next to me suddenly made it come to life. He did not conform as a commentator, he did not have a posh voice and it may have been a shock to viewers who said 'crikey whose that chap' but we had to let him do it his way, and we have recently signed a new four-year contract with the Rugby League.

Eddie emerged thereafter as bouncy as ever and, to him, restored in the affections of the great British public. Sadly, though, he proved the maxim, 'go at the time when the audience wants more of you, don't outstay your welcome.'

I'm afraid that Eddie did go on too long and his professionalism could be seen to be diminishing as his years advanced. No longer was he the convincing expert giving commentaries that were knowledgeable, he became repetitive and garrulous and made simple mistakes in the identification of players and teams. It was not a surprise to learn that it was caused by the onset of the dementia which eventually claimed him and made his later years most uncomfortable, if not for himself as his conditioned worsened but for his wife, son and many friends. Vanity is a powerful aphrodisiac among those who are on the celebrity bandwagon but Eddie would say, 'All is vanity' and was probably right. Whereas many of his associates - but not friends - were so-called celebrities, Eddie was a genuine star. He rejoiced in the company of great entertainers and, to be fair, he considered himself an equal. Morecambe and Wise in the 70s used him in their famous Christmas Day spectaculars alongside newsreaders and popular artists of the era. Indeed Eric coined him 'the talking trilby'. It was a great joy to him that Mike Yarwood, the celebrated impressionist with a long running, highly popular series, had him as a regular part of his repertoire.

In 1981 his retirement from the commentary box was announced and his final commentary at Wembley was performed under great stress. His friends knew that he had slowed up and had aged quickly but few of us realised that this was the start of his fatal illness. The majority of comments made in the press around that time were in favour of him, gracious and congratulatory on his achievements. Sadly, Colin Welland of *Chariots of Fire* fame, writing in the *Guardian* commented, 'Whilst saying that Eddie was a really nice man, it pains me to see the disservice he was doing to himself and to the game for the blunt truth is that Rugby League has passed by him.' To be truthful, Eddie was vain and ever conscious of his image. He did not court popularity among those who worked in the media but of the BBC, to whom he was ever loyal, he was never critical. If he went to a match at Headingley, when he was not doing the commentary he would sit in the directors' box and not with the press. That hardly endeared him to the rest of the 'stringers' but he still gave his time and energy for player's benefits, and to those of the media posse that he liked, he could be very generous.

When Bill Fallowfield retired from the secretariat at rugby league headquarters, he was succeeded by the personable, cultured Oxford graduate David Oxley. David was full of enthusiasm for the sport but lacking in its nuances and Eddie felt he had an obligation to be not only a prop on which David could lean but a listening post for him to air his problems confidentially. Then, when the League decided to engage, for the first time in the game's history, a PR executive, the young appointee - David Howes - was given practical advice by Eddie to ease him into the role, advising him who was who and where to get help. The Queen's Hotel was Eddie's sanctuary. He did not sleep there but would tell his friends when he was 'in residence' as he put it. Miss Patrick, the head receptionist, was his minder and eyes and ears. 'Mr So-and-So was looking for you yesterday. I told him you were not in and if he wanted you to ring me,' she would typically report to him. Once when in situ, he and I were chatting to a senior BBC executive and during the course of conversation Eddie said, 'Ronald's daughter is going to Liverpool University to study law.' The man from 'Auntie' turned to me and asked, 'Why has she chosen Liverpool?' and before I could reply Eddie answered for me. 'Because there's an Eddie Waring Appreciation Society on the campus.'

Whenever Eddie's name comes up in conversation, even now, I hear critical comments about him and his style. I always point out that his contribution to the broadcasting history of rugby league was immense, witness the fact that it is still being talked about. Who, that saw and heard it, could ever forget the 1968 'Watersplash' Wembley and his evocative and empathetic commentary of Don Fox's historic late, intensely dramatic conversion miss that cost his side the spoils? It revealed his human face and the innate ability he had to convey the feelings of all viewers simply, directly and sympathetically. For evermore Don carried Eddie's description of him as the 'poor lad'. The north's most famous and, possibly, favourite journalist and television presenter Michael Parkinson said that his three favourite commentators were David Coleman, Eddie Waring and John Arlott. Focusing on Eddie he stated that his main asset was his uninhibited approach to commentary - concerning himself with saying exactly what the man standing on the terraces was thinking. To be spoken of in the same breath as the smooth, silky voiced Coleman and the wonderfully poetic doyen Arlott was indeed high praise that Eddie would have loved. Coming from the pen of 'Parky', he would have seen it as an even greater accolade.

Hunslet is situated on the south side of the river Aire in Leeds. It was a thriving, densely populated community of working class folk engaged, principally, in the engineering, printing and clothing trades but it still produced several prominent members of the arts.

Willis Hall and Keith Waterhouse, the authors of *Billy Liar*, among many other literary classics, were educated in south Leeds, as was their friend, actor, Peter O'Toole. The area's rugby league claim to fame was founded in the early part of the twentieth century by its gruesome pack of forwards known at the 'terrible six' who enabled the club to win the unprecedented 'all four trophies' in a single season. A club with strong traditions of service to its local community, it harboured the ambitions of all red blooded youngsters in the area to join its ranks. The redolent colours – flame, myrtle and green - and battle song, 'We've swept the seas before boys and so we shall again,' is, in my view, one of the best sporting anthems, particularly as it is always sung with such fervour and emotion by the passionate devotees.

Things went badly wrong for the club in the 1960s and 70s. The heart went out of it as fast as the bulldozers moved into the adjoining areas to clear the well scrubbed terrace houses and back to backs with the pious hope of regenerating the area. Eventually the directors bailed out, sadly but not gracefully nor with dignity, and they sold the club's prime asset, its ground at Parkside to a developer. Where there was once the famous Mother Benson's Cottage on the ground, there emerged a light industrial unit. All the assets had gone apart from a few players whose enthusiasm exceeded their skills and there was really nothing left except the gallant enthusiasm of Geoffrey Gunney, a player and a coach for over 20 years and rewarded by becoming a Member of the Order of the British Empire. Like in his playing days, he would not give up. He summoned the faithful and spoke to the business community. Two men came forward, Gordon Murray and Stan Whittaker and they recruited Gerry Mason, the successful marketing manager at Comet and myself. We set up New Hunslet, the emblem, fittingly, being a phoenix rising from the ashes.

It was a unique club; no ground, no kit and players that no-one else wanted. The manager of the Leeds Greyhound Stadium, John Kennedy, offered us the use of the venue opposite Elland Road on very low terms, which we accepted. Irrespective of his motive, there would have been no kick off without him. The opening game against Huyton was the battle of the poorest. It, nevertheless, attracted almost 5,000 curious spectators to see Hunslet victorious. When the final whistle blew we made our first mistake, we should have called a halt while we were in front but struggled on, fired by the enthusiasm of the few loyal spectators we had. The pitch was one where the weeds ejected the grass revealing a base of cinders ashes and stones that surfaced regularly. When it rained, it flooded but proved attractive to natural wildlife.

David Oxley noted that when the club was drawn at home to Warrington, in the Challenge Cup, the match was in doubt until kick-off because there was enough water in the middle to start the Varsity boat race. As we were deciding whether to go ahead with what would be a lucrative game, a sport's ground expert John Palmer came along, scratched his head and said the only thing he could think of was to hire a helicopter. 'With a helicopter,' he argued, 'it could gently hover over the playing field and, with the wind generated, would aid the dispersal of the water.' That was the theory but the worry was that the water would be dispersed onto the greyhound track, putting it out of action. That had not escaped John Kennedy's notice who solemnly warned us that if racing was cancelled we could be responsible to his company for thousands of pounds of lost income. We risked it anyway and fortunately very little damage was caused to the track and the match went ahead.

We were then faced with another disaster. Our agreement with the Leeds Greyhound company allowed us to have perimeter advertising when matches were played. It was hardly an attractive proposition for multi-nationals but Gerry Mason's enthusiasm and arm twisting of his suppliers brought a modicum of success in the sale of the hoardings. The stadium however was later taken over by Ladbrokes, who were rapidly expanding their betting shops, casinos and hotels empire. Their chief executive, Cyril Stein, was both ambitious and single minded. We tried to chum them up but they kept their distance and while their manifesto claimed that they catered for all sport's, that did not extend to rugby league football in general or New Hunslet in particular.

The aggravation came when we were assigned an evening match in the BBC 2 Floodlight Trophy. Eddie Waring and company were due to be at our ground, a big day and a nice earner. Unfortunately we were shattered by the groundsman telling us that Ladbrokes' men had arrived and were busily removing our hoardings and replacing them with theirs for the national television audience. That was, in our view, a blow below the belt. Ladbrokes should have phoned and asked our permission to erect their signage where there was available space and, as a friendly gesture, we would have agreed. Instead, we viewed it as a threat to our sovereignty. We contacted them but no one in authority was available and, as always, Mr Stein was unavailable and his PA said that as it was their ground, it was their right to decide who should advertise. We made a speedy application to the High Court for an injunction which was granted and served on Ladbrokes, who had to restore our hoardings and remove their own. We knew deep down at that moment that the bell was sounding for the final round at Elland Road. Ladbrokes refused to renew our license. They even called a halt to the greyhound racing, destroyed the buildings and put in an application for planning permission for industrial development. People from south Leeds were angry and, as a result, the city council refused Ladbrokes permission to develop and resisted a subsequent appeal. Indeed, the ground remains undeveloped. Hunslet became like gypsies and lodged at Batley, then shared the Leeds United ground and finally moved to the South Leeds Stadium where they now play as tenants of the City Council.

I left the board shortly after the problems with Ladbrokes but still kept a close relationship with the directors. Gerry Mason asked me to assist in the negotiations with Leeds United to share their ground. I had to smile because the total crowd supporting New Hunslet would be lost in a small section of the West Stand paddock. Nonetheless, Leeds United were short of money and Gerry Mason put down £50,000 of his own so that the club would have the use of a prestigious stadium and have a sign 'The Home of New Hunslet Rugby League Club' together with their offices alongside the once illustrious football giant. Leeds United, when they got back on their feet, did not want Hunslet in the ground. They made no secret of it and stuck to the letter of agreement but never went beyond it. They enlisted the help of the council who, by then, owned the ground. The council were making noises of support for Hunslet in public but behind the scenes did very little to help and the club had to move on.

15

*

More Characters of Note

John Mellor was the subject of more anecdotes than anyone at the Bar that I knew because of his dour reputation as a 'typical' Yorkshireman. He appeared at the court of Judge James Pickles, another celebrated Tyke, most often by himself. Pickles was from Halifax, renowned for its rugby league team, toffee manufacturers, building society and, he thought, himself especially after he had become a television celebrity. He was a likeable man if he was to your taste; what you saw was precisely what you got. Practicing from chambers in Bradford, he gained a reputation in the county's criminal courts and was made an assistant recorder which, I believe, established his notion that he deserved attention. One of his claims to fame arose when he sentenced a notorious football hooligan to prison.

I knew him only to nod to but when in Leeds he patronised a coffee shop at the corner of Park Square and the Headrow which was ancillary to a tobacconists and I got to know him better. It was there that I witnessed one of his celebrated rants. The lists had just been published of the new crown court recorders, appointed on the re-organisations by Lord Beeching and the name Pickles was not included. All those present received his views and reactions and those who attended later were treated to a repeat performance. He gave a tour de force denouncement of an aggrieved candidate, cast aside because of the prejudice and mean spiritedness of one man Mr Justice Hinchcliffe, who was getting his own back on him. Pickles said, 'I went into his room and I told him to his face what I thought of him.' Later I heard another version told by one of Hinchcliffe's cronies that the assailed thought he was about to be done physical harm. He subsequently became a circuit judge, perhaps heavy handed in sentencing but invariably consistent.

On one occasion, the court's administration provided him with a list of defendants who were expected to plead guilty and whose cases would have been disposed swiftly within a morning by the man they knew as 'Jimmy the Pick'. Those in the dock, however, had not read the script. The first when charged pleaded not guilty and Judge Pickles was compelled to adjourn to fix a trial. The second followed the same line, as did the third. When the fourth was put in the dock the judge smelled a rat. He said to the barrister, John Mellor, defending him, 'I hope your client is not following the same path as the others. It is obvious,' he said testily, 'They know of me and will do anything to get out of my way'. His voice rose to a shouting pitch as he continued, 'Well I have news for them – when they come up for trial they should not be surprised if they meet me again.' Mellor stood quietly, bowed and said gently, 'Will Your Honour allow me a moment or two?' When Pickles agreed Mellor did a neat about turn and walked slowly towards the dock and appeared to have a serious conversation with the accused. Returning slowly to his place he announced, 'Your Honour, he does intend to plead not guilty,' and noting the angry look that came across the judge's face added, 'But I have to tell you Your Honour, he has never ever heard of you'.

Mellor was a delightful man, a contemporary of mine at university and, having his principles to comfort him, shunned preferment and applications for silks. He was born and bred in Morley and died there. Morley rugby union club was his watering hole and its terraces his weekly encampment. After his playing days as a hooker in a pack that no-one wanted to play against, he became a staunch supporter. Morley is only a few miles from Leeds but had its own town hall and council until the day it was taken over by the big city when nothing was ever the same. The independence of Morley equated with John's independent spirit.

I recall Mellor addressing a county court judge courteously but firmly only to be mildly rebuked when the bench interrupted, 'But you've told me this Mr Mellor at least twice.' Mellor replied, 'So be it Your Honour and I will have to do it yet again until I am satisfied that you have understood what I have told you'. He was a man remarkably popular with his peers and indeed he liked nothing more than to sit with younger colleagues at the Town Hall Tavern for a pint and a natter at the close of play. My favourite Mellor story is his appearance in his younger days at the Court of Criminal Appeal in London. Arriving there and about to address the assembled court, the presiding judge said, 'Mr Mellor, is this a serious appeal?' Mellor was surprised but always able to think quickly on his feet countered, 'Your Lordships, when I left Morley near Leeds this morning at six o'clock there was snow on the ground. I could not start my car but walked to the nearest stop and waited for a bus. I arrived at the railway station in Leeds and there was neither heating facilities nor food on the train. I got to Kings Cross and found a taxi to bring me here.' He then paused deliberately, 'I can assure Your Lordships, this is a very serious appeal'.

One of our younger colleagues who learnt much from Mellor was Gerald Lumley. Though not in the same chambers, they clearly enjoyed one another's company which was a little strange as Gerald made no secret of his gay lifestyle. Whereas John was a great family man, Gerald cut a lonely figure who had only a cold flat to return to at the end of the day and that was only when the pub had closed and he had eaten his fish and chips purchased on his way home in a taxi. I was aware that John had hinted that Gerald should form a stable, permanent relationship but it was not to be. Sadly Gerald, always busy and sitting regularly as a recorder in the crown court, was named and shamed by a red top newspaper, photograph and all.

The anger of his friends to this patent set up was loudly voiced and a wave of sympathy cloaked his sad figure. Clearly his judicial career was at an end and, though remaining the relaxed witty friend to all, he obviously suffered. The solicitors who briefed him continued with their support but he lost his enthusiasm and hunger and very soon his neglect saw him living on payments from a sickness policy. He died in his flat in 2010, alone, having inhaled smoke from a fire he had slept through. A fine advocate with a gentle but persuasive manner in the cross-examination of witnesses, he was also a most sought after speaker at sporting dinners. He could be waspish but if he targeted someone who he did not relate to then he gave them a hard time.

My wife, when out shopping, cannot resist entering a 'pound shop'. The fact that she spends a coin on an item that she can get at the corner shop for 50p is irrelevant. Based on the maxim that the poor deserve a bargain while the rich demand one, the various ad-speak-driven, enticing offers of today are merely variations of well known practices and selling arts that go right back to the dawn of trade.

The most spectacular of them all must surely have been the Jewish trader known as 'Five pence ha'penny' who had a cut price shop. I highlight his religious beliefs solely because he took advantage of them. An Act of Parliament allowed a member of the faith to claim exemption from the compulsory closing of shops on Sunday's if he made a statutory declaration that he was an observing Jew and could not and would not work on the Sabbath – from nightfall Friday until nightfall Saturday – in addition to the assorted fasts and festivals. It seemed, *prima facie* to be an innocuous gesture to a community that lived in close proximity and who otherwise might be deprived of shopping facilities at the weekend. 'Five pence Ha'penny' was not a clock watcher and several winter evenings on a Friday he closed as late as 9pm and opened on a Saturday at two in the afternoon, clearly breaking the Jewish Law. The local authority reacted and proceedings were commenced.

Holding their file was an ambitious, enthusiastic solicitor, Ken Potts, later to become their head lawyer and the town clerk. Potts was a winner – so he said –and was believed to have a scoreboard in his office on which was marked 'wins' and 'losses' and there were no ticks in the losses column! He brought his application in an unusual way, by alleging that 'Five pence Ha'penny' had made a declaration, knowing it to be untrue, that he was an observing Jew to gain the necessary exemptions. My employer at the time, Joseph Lester, while entrusting preparation of the defence to me in my first post-qualification year, thought that a Gentile lawyer should appear at court so it could not be suggested that the defence was anything other than objective. I disagreed with him and said so but, as he paid the wages, his view prevailed.

Ernest Ould, a middle-aged, middle-ranked barrister accepted the brief and nothing went past him. Potts and Ould went for each other from the opening bell. If the prosecution made a statement, the defence would object and vice-versa, and the three lay magistrates did not have sufficient strength to keep the combative advocates apart as 'Five pence Ha'penny', by then in his late sixties, sat quietly behind his counsel nodding or shaking his head as points were made and lost. Potts called inspectors as witnesses to prove that the shop was open for trading during the Sabbath, the defendant openly selling cigarettes, chocolate and biscuits. Coins were handed to the shopkeeper and change back to the customer, they said. The chairman asked, 'How much money was spent by the customer?' and before the witness could answer Potts chipped in, 'Certainly more than Five pence Ha'penny, Your Worships'. Ould reacted to that quip with, 'If you want to give evidence Mr Potts, take the oath and go into the witness box.' With such a seemingly strong argument, Potts completed his case.

Ould was quickly on the attack in response, though. 'Your Worships,' he began. 'It is my submission that my client has no case to answer. The unchallenged evidence is that during the Sabbath my client sold goods otherwise prohibited in exchange for money. But we have had no evidence whatsoever,' he declared. 'Not a scrap, to say that it was my client who made the declaration that he was an observant Jew and that is the whole point of this case.' Potts' intake of breath was audible and his colour change almost immediate. It was not the self assured, almost arrogant, combative prosecutor who rose slowly to his feet and muttered, 'Will you allow me a few minutes to consider my response?' Courts, in my view, are always generous to an advocate in distress and a ten minute adjournment was agreed.

Potts began searching for *Stones' Justices Manual*, the

indispensible lawyer's bible looking for precedents for a party that had closed their case being permitted to re-open it. He had no books with him while Ould had his prominently perched next to his file of papers but the prosecutor could not bring himself to ask to borrow it. Potts raced out the room, found the relevant passage and, having recovered his composure, made the submission. After a teasing and tormenting but not compelling response from Ould, the court granted the relieved Potts leave to begin again on this new matter. Then came moments of pure theatre. Potts handed to Ould the statutory declaration at the heart of the contention and the defending barrister took what seemed an age to read and digest it. I was sitting behind him and he turned and showed it to me, took it back after a while and then repeated the process again. After a hugely exaggerated reflection he announced, 'This document, Mr Potts, does not help you. It is said to be made by the defendant and yet is signed only with an 'X' before a commissioner for oaths. How does a court know, or is it expected to guess, that this document was made by this particular defendant?' he questioned.

By this time Potts was clenching and unclenching his fists and, looking at his watch, said, 'I will call the commissioner to give evidence and to identify the man who was the deponent to this declaration.' He went on, 'The time is nearly one o'clock and the commissioner's office is nearby. I will call and ask him to attend at, say, 2.15 if the court agrees that time is convenient.'

When asked, Henry Hyams the oath administrator said of course he would attend but, 'You must obviously *subpoena* me.' Potts duly ran between the offices to get the necessary paperwork and Hyams was duly called at the allotted time. Henry entered the witness box and was well known to the court clerks and magistrates as a regular attender. Suave, well dressed, respected and with a soft accent-free voice, he was conscious of his literary knowledge and artistic background which did not allow him to speak in lay terms. He always felt compelled to display his extensive knowledge of the English language.

Potts began, 'Is your name Henry Hyams?' the reply being, 'So it is.' Potts went on,'Do you see the document which I now hand to you?' Hyams countered, 'Permit me a minute or two whilst I search for my reading glasses – yes thank you, I see it with clarity now.' Potts continued his perusal, 'Is that your name that appears on it?' Hyams confirmed, 'It is my signature.' Potts was showing signs of exasperation, 'Do you see a cross?' Again Hyams was very deliberate in his answer, a drawn out,'I do.' Potts went in for the kill, 'Do you see in court the maker of that cross?' Again his responder took centre stage. 'Permit me Sir to remove my reading glasses and replace them with my viewing spectacles.' The witness then looked around the crowded courtroom allowing his gaze to rest, for a second or two, on each person, the defendant having been asked in the interim by Ould to sit in the public seats. Eventually Hyams said, 'I cannot see him today.'

Potts, by now, was seething and began, 'Now look here Mr Hyams, a man comes to your office, pays you some money and makes a mark and all you can ...' Ould interrupted in a most serious tone, saying, 'Oh no, Mr Potts, we cannot have that. You can't cross-examine your own witness. You must accept his answers.' 'Look,' Hyams interjected. 'Permit me to say to Your Worships, this document was made four years ago. I sometimes see 20 to 30 people a week who avail themselves of the services of a commissioner for oaths. They do not have to produce any identification and I have no lasting association with them. I cannot be expected to remember everyone who comes to my office for that service.' The chairman of the bench then said,

'Of course – we quite understand – thank you Mr Hyams for your attendance.' Denied that identification the prosecution was doomed to failure and Potts left without saying anything to the defence team.

My dear father's birth certificate was similarly marked with an 'x'. He was born on 2nd April, 1892 and died in 1981. It made interesting reading. My Father's parents were immigrants from Poland but married in England around 1880. Unlike most of the Jewish immigrants, grandpa Teeman was clean shaven and spoke impeccable English with no hint of an Eastern European accent. Dad's Birth Certificate was fully completed but in place of the signature by the father there appeared an 'X' and in the space for occupation 'estate agent' was entered. He must have been the first of his profession in the city who could neither read or write.

I still take great pride in a case where I, as David, slew a particular Goliath. In the very early seventies, the Leeds newspapers boasted that we had a local merchant banker in our midst, tall elegant ex-public schoolboy Peter Grimshawe. The city's reputation as a financial centre was clearly growing. Mr Grimshawe liked the highlife, the nightlife and lunches and attracted publicity and money, promising profitable opportunities for private investors.

A very good friend of mine owned a restaurant/disco where the more select members of Leeds society could dine elegantly and unobtrusively. Good food, good wine and good company was his formula for a highly successful business. Members of the sporting community, including Leeds United players, found the atmosphere relaxing and their privacy not intruded. Mr Grimshawe and his friends were also regular patrons and it was not long before his bank became involved. They made a substantial loan at a market rate of interest accompanied by a purchase of a minority of the shares and instituted a consultancy agreement whereby they were to receive an annual fee for providing financial and commercial expertise to the business, which seemed to me to be very expensive. My advice was not sought although when told, I wished my friend well. He also opened, on the north side of the city in a delightful village, an exclusive restaurant in an elegant former mansion, presumably the additional finance coming in handy. I still attended the centrally located venue, almost weekly, with my wife and friends. It was more of a club than an eatery, there was invariably someone you knew there and in mid-week barristers 'on circuit' would often pass a pleasant few hours there. Eventually my friend shook me. He told me he was in financial difficulties as he could not make his repayments to the Merchant Bank and it looked a racing certainty that he would lose his business. He hinted that any help would be more than welcome.

I knew Grimshawe as a nodding acquaintance but this was not my usual sphere of influence. Nevertheless, I started by asking of my friend, 'Where did they get their authority to lend money?' They were not a joint stock bank like those on the high street and I found that they needed a Certificate of Exemption granted by the Board of Trade. I phoned them and they very quickly searched their records and confirmed that none had none been granted to Grimshawes. The only alternative was a Money Lenders Licence which would have been granted by the magistrates' court at Leeds. It was neither a costly or difficult legal procedure but when I checked with Barry Vause, who was in charge of that area, he was able to quickly confirm that they were not one because there were so few in the city at that time. I then checked out the law relating to loans made by unlicensed money lenders and the answer was that they were not recoverable. Grimshawe's, therefore, could not claim repayment much to the relief of my friend, some of his notable clients ringing thereafter to congratulate me. I still have a cutting that was in the *Yorkshire Evening Post* in September 1974:

> Grimshawe Holdings, the Leeds-based Banking and Industrial Group announced losses of £2.2 million, and said it was owed £120,000 by former Group Chairman Peter Grimshawe – but there was little chance of it being paid for some considerable time.

Mr Grimshawe was carried away with his own publicity and the pats on his back from his sycophants who danced attendance on him when he was in his pomp. They soon disappeared and that must have been a great sadness for him. He did not recover and was often spied as a sad, lonely figure wandering around the city centre.

On Christmas Eve 1961, Stuart Simon an 18-year-old who worked as a trainee hairdresser was driving his 'bubble' car along Foundry Lane, Leeds, a road which - though it carried much through traffic - was not very wide. He collided with a saloon car travelling in the opposite direction.

Despite the date, there was no suggestion that either driver had been drinking. Stuart's injuries were horrific, he was in hospital for six months and at the time of the court hearing, confined to a wheelchair. The prognosis was not good but it was believed that with re-training and rehabilitation he could do light clerical work. The accident was investigated by the police who decided the file should be closed marked it NFA - no further action. Stuart's father consulted me and I made several visits to the scene. Stuart maintained that the saloon car came towards him partly on the wrong side of the road having overtaken a parked van and that he was on the correct side. A letter to the defendant, a Mr Perfect brought a denial of liability from his insurance company. This was a classic case of the parties being at issue on the facts and there being no independent evidence available to resolve the position. I completed an application for Legal Aid for without such financial assistance Stuart and his family would be unable to fund the court process. The application was granted and I instructed Mr. Vivian Hurwitz, a barrister who was resilience personified, to advise and draft the 'Particulars of Claim'.

Hurwitz advised that Simon had no more than a reasonable chance of success for even if his version of events was accepted, he had been negligent himself and that contributed to the accident and that the percentage of his liability could be as much as half. The defendant's insurers were represented by Willy Hargraves and Co, a firm who were specialized in resisting personal injury claims and they confirmed, 'No offer will be coming from us.' Harry Brecken, a formidable common law clerk in their office who had the conduct of the case adopted an aggressive attitude. Hurwitz, in conference with the plaintiff said, 'Face the trial with hope rather than expectation.' He advised that we should seek to brief a QC and, with first choice Rudolph Lyons QC tied up, his associate George Waller QC deputised. Though I did know of his reputation, I then had no personal experience of him. At conference the day of the trial, Waller met Stuart for the first time and having only read the papers the previous evening and certainly had no opportunity of visiting the site, he reinforced the view previously expressed by Hurwitz. The defendant's insurers had briefed Henry Scott QC, well known in that branch of the law.

I said to Mr. Harry Brecken, 'Are you still not talking,' and he replied, 'Sorry, your case is a no-hoper.' Another disconcerting indicator was that the trial judge was Mr.

Justice Payne who when counsel had dealt with hundreds of such cases and in his days as a barrister had been regularly briefed by Willy Hargraves to boot. Stuart gave his evidence calmly, admitting that he could have possibly avoided the accident by taking evasive action which was risky but maintained that the saloon car driver was responsible for the outcome. Mr Perfect was a terrible witness. He was nervous, hesitant and contradicted himself. He absolved himself of any liability whatsoever. 'There was sufficient room for Simon to go around him,' he said and it was a no surprise when the judge found in our favour and in his judgment criticized Mr Perfect for, 'Travelling on the wrong side of the road when passing a parked van,' and that it was he who had created a dangerous situation.

Simon was not free from responsibility and the judge assessed his contributory negligence at 20 per cent but awarded substantial damages because Simon's life and enjoyment of its amenities had been gravely impaired. Harry Brecken was furious and he told his counsel to apply for a stay of execution for 21 days so that an appeal could be considered and the judge acceded to that request. Outside the court Brecken was jumping up and down with annoyance, not only at the judge but also at his own counsel. In the eyes of the legal system Stuart was still an infant and the judge also decreed that he should have such a large sum at his disposal and suggested that we should set up a trust fund for him which we duly did, the judge in chambers ordering that the damages be invested for his benefit until he reached the age of 30 and to have the power to make capital advances to him.

Stuart had a girlfriend, a young lady with a mature outlook, absolutely devoted to him. From the day of the accident she hardly left his side. They married and decided to start a ladies hairdressing saloon, where she would work and Stuart could act as manager/receptionist. About three or four years after the accident they found a suitable business in Crossgates, Leeds. Application to the Bank trustees was made for an advance to purchase. To the anger of Stuart, they opposed it because he had not yet shown himself as competent to manage such a business. He listed their qualifications and experience and having bravely pointed out that not all their investments made on his behalf had been successful got the money released, the business subsequently prospering. I quote his case as an illustration that the public funding of litigation brings assistance to needy people who would otherwise have their rightful claims for compensation thwarted. A case is decided not by witness statements on paper but by the challenge to live evidence which can materially affect the presumed outcome.

Mind you, perhaps the court system is best summed up by an anonymously attributed comment from a barrister whose final address to a jury contained this warning, 'Members of the jury, I imagine by now you have decided to acquit my client. If that be so, I trust my few words will not persuade you to the contrary.'

16

*

Where Now for the Law?

It is now fashionable, if not *de rigeur*, for solicitors to have a Sports' Law department. Indeed, the *Leeds Lawyer*, the official organ of the Leeds Law Society, had a paragraph where a local firm announced that they had appointed Robbie Savage, a talented though controversial footballer, as their sports' ambassador. It prompted one wag to suggest that it would be more newsworthy if they announced the appointment of a lawyer to their staff.

Nearly everyone in this celebrity obsessed culture has become a 'jersey toucher' so why should the legal profession be any different? We win a cricket Test Match and the entire team go to 10 Downing Street either fuelled by or plied with alcohol. Everyone likes a winner and politicians like to be associated with the success while financial, commercial and industrial leaders and the like are no different from Joe and Josephine public who patiently line the streets to cheer their heroes home. The amount of money and perceived endorsements, thrown at sports and their stars by institutions was revealed during the banking crisis and caused consternation.

Publically funded Leeds Metropolitan University decided, quite recently before the latest round of swingeing cuts, that an entry into professional sport would advance their objectives. Hardly resourcing direct educational needs of either students or staff, which have always been under funded, they decided to buy a professional rugby union team, Leeds Tykes – a poorly supported 'yoyo' club. The mind boggles at the vanity of those who, knowing that experienced and wealthy owners struggled to keep such clubs alive, believed that they could succeed. Quickly they realised that they were out of their depth, losing over £1,000,000 in the first year and just as speedily sinking in the mire. After parting with millions and likely to lose more, they attempted to retrieve their losses by returning the club to the previous owners and granting them a £1,000,000 a year subsidy. As my Dad would have said, 'You don't have to go to college to make such a mess.'

I learned my trade at the Leeds and District Amateur Rugby League Association which, as the name implies administers the sport locally controlling the activities of both junior and senior clubs. It has a judicial process which rules on disputes between members. They disciplined teams and their players for the entire gamut of alleged wrongdoing varying from abuse of match officials, punching a member of the opposition to administrative errors such as postponing a game without due cause or fielding an ineligible player. I was vice chairman for several years and during the season would be on duty each Monday evening at the church Institute. The quality of advocacy was high, the passions displayed heated and the frequent lack of grace displayed when a party received an adverse decision only lasting a few moments. Often it was found that the trusty rule book did not provide a remedy for a clear wrong, suiting the 'barrack room lawyers' and necessitating amending legislation. Rough and ready justice was dispensed, the principle being that no party should leave the meeting feeling that they had not been listened to. That was sports' law in the raw and at the sharp end and I would commend anyone with ambitions to further a career in that area to join such an association to see it at its basest. The defendants and their club representatives appearing had talents in other, more manual areas but still had the ability to communicate and if, on occasions, they dried up, a member of the adjudicating committee was always willing to draw from them that which they had come to say. That was the breeding ground – seldom entered by professional lawyers – and it gave me an early insight into an important part of good governance of a sport.

Many of the current breed claim to be specialists because they have, on occasion, represented a sporting icon or been introduced to many of them. My practice was built on a much more solid if not exciting foundation based on through working knowledge although I always regretted that despite a Masters degree for my work on the law relating to betting and gaming, it only helped me in appearing at the local Betting Licensing Committee. In both rugby league and soccer I represented clubs, managers and players but not at the same time, though I believe some agents were not averse to allowing interests to conflict. There has always been something of an unsavoury and perhaps sordid nature about deals between clubs and agents. Even though there is a supposed licensing of agents, I firmly believe that no-one really takes a blind bit of notice of the regulations and I would speculate that before long they will be removed. It is no use having a law in the book that is universally ignored especially having examined the details of many such transactions and seen that the agent's bill for the player is picked up by the club. What I fail to understand and no-one yet has provided a plausible explanation, is why a club chairman wishing to buy a player cannot pick up the phone and speak to his opposite number. The transfer from West Ham of Rio Ferdinand to Leeds was brokered by a seriously flawed Norwegian and an Israeli who had only recently arrived on the English football scene. The Leeds chairman gave the Norwegian authority in writing to represent the club with a commission of 5 per cent of transfer fees as his reward on a deal that was essentially done at £18 million. What was so complicated that needed all these intermediaries, where were the complex principles of law or finance or taxation? For over ten years now adverse comment had been made of the actives of agents and they still continue as before. Investigations by football authorities, scandalous reports of bungs and even disputes with the Inland Revenue caused no change. I have had thoughts in black moments that some managers may have received a cut from the agent's commission. I hope I am wrong for many who support the national game would become further disillusioned especially as the considerable sums paid to agents, as recently published, has angered many fans who struggle now to buy their season tickets.

As my earlier sporting clients were ageing soccer professionals ready to embark on stage two of their careers into coaching and management, the terms offered to them or suggested by a potential employer were of major import. Most documents in the legal profession are based on form and precedent. The lazy lawyer – and I have met a few – is nothing more than a copy-cat while the more concerned and informed treat these as skeletons and put the appropriate flesh on the bones to make them bespoke. Thirty years ago if you searched for a precedent of a football manager's contract, you would find it contained in the list of obligations to be performed the duty not only to cut and mark the pitch but to fix the nettings to the goalposts. The first contract I saw from a club was from Bert Millichip, a Solicitor and chairman of West Bromwich Albion and later to become the head of the Football Association. Bert was keen on offering John Giles the position of player/manager at the Hawthorns and sent me a draft contract which was totally unsuitable for use. Don Revie very kindly lent me a copy of his contract with Leeds United, with the financial terms obviously scratched out and that allowed me to draft something more relevant for the Twentieth century. One of the questions I ask budding sport's lawyers applying for a position with me is, apart from the financial salary and bonuses, what obligations would you impose on the employer to protect your client's interests? They are in a result driven industry, the manager's strongest position is when he is appointed and the Industry is governed by insecurity and the constant fear of dismissal. What is equally important as taking the job are its terms of dismissal. The percentage of contracts that are ended before they have run their full course, which runs at about 90 per cent, would be higher still if the club did not pause to think of the high cost for a wrongful termination.

Nowadays, a club dissatisfied with its manager can easily make life uncomfortable and at worst unbearable for its current incumbent by, for example, appointing a director of football or a senior first team coach. With such reduced status, reputation and possibly self esteem, they are hankering after resignation of the incumbent and absolution from compensation to him. Perhaps the manager might have a claim for constructive dismissal but there is no certainty of success in litigation and when the gloves are off, the blows are hard. All the more reason for the knowledgeable sports lawyer to insist on a clause in their client's contract that includes the need to seek his consent first before any appointment in his domain of influence is made. On the other side of the coin, the football industry in particular, is infected by a bug that does not apply in any other avenue of employment and, perhaps, born out of the 'workers' being paid vastly more than their managers. Players are incredibly insecure and seemingly in need of constant reassurance. Often I have heard them say, 'the Gaffer did not speak to me at training today' or, 'The coach asked me to stay out for shooting practice, I wonder why?' and even, 'The local rag said the scouts were looking for a direct winger – that's my position.'

Good management should prevent such myopia spreading and undermining team spirit and, that most elusive of all qualities, confidence. One of the top managers told me he resented his chairman going to his golf club after a bad defeat and being put through the mill by his fellow members because he would be sure to pass it on afterwards. The manager is the public face of the club and receives the praise when results are favourable, and faces the music or is expected to field the flak when they are adverse even though he does not run the business. I designed a clause, which I could justify, which read: The club agrees it will make no comment to the media on playing matters, nor would it permit any other persons so to do on their behalf. It was based on a simple philosophy that the enemy without could always be fought off but the one from within was poisonous and far too dangerous to be let off the leash. If agreed to, the directors would not be inhibited from public comment on financial policy or general football matters but would have to refrain from personal criticism of the team or its management. The relationships within clubs are such that one well known manager once told me, 'Of course we all have a youth policy but few of us are around to see if it is successful.' I said to the press on the occasion when Allan

Clarke lost his job as manager of Scunthorpe that although I had negotiated compensation for him, a government health warning, as on all cigarette packets, should be printed boldly on the a manager's contract. Generally, a club with strong financial backing makes few mistakes but directors of those where the financial muscle is strained lose their equilibrium and, under stress and fan pressure, make poor and costly decisions.

The other area of sport that has created extra work for the lawyer is the increasing incidence of clubs going into administration, a creation of modern insolvency law. The requirements are two-fold, to comply with company law practice and, at the same time, satisfying the rulings of the governing body. I am continually irritated by the cherished privilege that ruling bodies reserve to themselves especially that giving the game's creditors privileged and preferential status. The concept that local traders and the Inland Revenue may only receive ten pence in the pound while rival clubs and playing staff get paid in full is abhorrent to me and should be challenged. Similarly, when clubs owe the Revenue huge sums of money for failure to account for long periods, directors should be personally challenged and made subject to disciplinary process. Furthermore, to re-introduce financial sanity, there needs to be a procedure for the fiscal authorities to notify the Football Association or Football League when clubs immediately fall into arrears with regard to any tax liability. They should then decisively announce that such conduct is bringing the game into disrepute and make it impossible for the directors to continue unless the club pays up immediately.

I am equally concerned that sport generally is becoming global and a club which is in the blood of its local supporters has its heart taken away by a multinational corporation. It seems unreal that Manchester United should be owned and controlled by Americans and their City neighbours at the behest of sheiks; that Blackburn is an Indian concern while Chelsea are owned by Russians. The whim of such people is changeable. This potentially dangerous situation needs addressing by government if the sport cannot deal with it.

I was immensely proud to be elected president of the Rugby Football league in 1996. The sport, dear to my heart, was for almost 100 years governed by bye laws originally found in the Ark and had been dramatically affected by climate changes without anyone noticing, or if they had, the legislators remained masterly inactive. It was a classic case of the tail wagging the dog, with each of the 30-odd clubs nominating a council member and that ruling body then tortuously voting through – or more likely blocking – legislation which may have benefitted the game as a whole but might adversely affect their club.

Some members were determined that, before the new century was ushered in, to have the system updated and I was charged with that onerous task. My appointment was not flattering as there were no other volunteers. It took me several months to deliver and I was helped by the incumbent, innovative chief executive Maurice Lindsay and two experienced administrators, Joe Warham and Harry Jepson. I never pretended that what I drafted would be like the Ten Commandments and handed down from on high but maintained that it was a workable document that would need to be changed and possibly dramatically so when usage revealed its strengths and weaknesses and so it proved when, within ten years, further revisions were made I must confess by a more skilful draftsman.

Creating an independent board of directors to run the sport, which facilitated an amalgamation of its various arms into a single more effective governing body, dragged it into modern business practice. Sport in general can, I believe, learn from the process of change introduced by the RFL. What was a once suitable association of independent clubs governing themselves on the principle of one man one vote was becoming an anacronysm. There was an inequality of assets, clubs became too inward looking and, as a result, policy decisions fragmented. Discipline was difficult to enforce.

How, for example, could you vote to punish a recalcitrant club when you might be the next on the chopping board? The list of deficiencies was endless, it was the classic turkey's-voting-for-Christmas syndrome. The outcome was that there was an inability to provide leadership that was both experienced and objective, that could see the entire picture and could act and not merely react. So the structure governing the league changed from one essentially free of club commitment to one in the interest of the greater good. We might quarrel with the appointees but the principle is correct and I believe it will become a model for other sports. There are now better defined disciplinary processes for example and, whereas there was always the access to justice and fairness, today added to them is the virtue of efficiency. The legal maxim is that justice delayed is justice defeated, I never subscribe to the view that if you ignore something it goes away. All procedures and processes should be and be seen to be, fair and open.

One of the best book purchases I made with a £1 note was, *Sports and the Law* by Edward Grayson, an experienced barrister and noted authority on the subject.

It is only a slim volume and would be lost in a bookcase containing legal textbooks, so I keep it in the top drawer of my desk. In less than 100 pages, the author takes his readers through a catalogue of sporting legal topics and I found it indispensable. He quotes Lord Justice Denning who was on the Bench for an inordinate time speaking on sport's disciplinary procedures stating, 'Justice can often be done in them better by a good layman than a bad lawyer.'

I could not agree more. So often in rugby league the parties suffered by representation from professionals who varied from the average to the incompetent. I remember the occasion when we had up before us the Hunslet under 17s team who were up for a variety of offences. Harry Jepson, a primary school head teacher was their custodian and, invariably, their representative.

Bluntly, they exhausted our patience, regular victors on the field but always losers when they appeared before us. They had to be dealt with severely my colleagues thought, for they were putting the proverbial two fingers up at us and the rest of the game and thought they were untouchable. Despite Harry's eloquence, we expelled them from the League for a year. They were shocked and the rest of the league surprised that we stood up to them. They did not, however, drown in their own tears but picked themselves up and played matches against teams in another league with no problems at all, displaying all the magnanimity of regular winners. When their sentence was over they returned to us refreshed and rehabilitated and continued to make a great contribution to the already high standard of youth rugby in the region.

Harry was born in 1920 and, as befitting a man who has served rugby league at all levels with distinction, deserving of the OBE for his services to the sport and is one of its few Life Presidents. A wonderful raconteur with a sharp memory, at his 90th birthday party he regaled those who joined him in the celebrations with many happy tales. When the party broke up I reminded him of the expulsion. He grimaced when he said, 'It's a hard game, you've got to get up off the ground and start again and that's what we did and we were better for it'. Harry and I have been good friends and colleagues and served on tribunals for years. We have often taken different sides in debates in the Rugby League Council Chamber but even though tough talking went on, it never broke the friendship. We were once guests of a rugby league director who had a box at Market Rasen racecourse. Harry confided in me that he had never in his life placed a bet on the Tote. Not that I was such an expert but I showed him a race card, how to make his selection and then pointed him in the direction of the betting window with his £2. He said he'd got it and I finally mentioned, 'Don't forget Harry, tell the lady you are a pensioner.' I followed him to the Tote and he gave his usual eloquent spiel concluding with his assertion that he was a pensioner. The youngish lady behind the window rebuked him sharply, commenting, 'Well, there are better things to do with your pension money than spend it on the Tote.'

It is over 30 years since Edward Grayson's book appeared and he had the foresight to note the impact of drugs on sport, particularly at the elite, professional end and indicated that the domestic governing bodies at that time had been silent on the subject. While that is still a huge concern, my main worry is the effect that money has which could remove the raison d'etre for sport existing. In their best days, cricket and rugby union epitomized and demonstrated to the world the values sport stood for. Cricket was a way of life, a standard for honesty, integrity and good behaviour. The expression, 'it's not cricket' became a commonly used phrase in the English language to identify fair play. In union, physical blows were exchanged within acceptable boundaries, where picking yourselves up or being helped to your feet were virtues and the losers cheered the winners off the field. The fiercest competitors exchanged handshakes and embraces and often through bruises, aches and pains, shared a glass of ale in the bar later. Now, cricket is under the spotlight for ball tampering, match fixing and abusive behaviour hiding under the name 'sledging' on the field. Rugby union has become synonymous with faking injuries and telling lies to cover up the cheating. Two codes that were the standard bearers for rectitude are now under scrutiny and add to that athletics, where no-one knows for sure whether record holders are genuine or drug assisted.

That is why I urge my profession to become more closely involved in sport of all descriptions and at every level and why law enforcement is as important in their procedures as it is on the streets. It protects the public from deception and those participants who play by the rules and spirit of the game as opposed to the few who chase glory at any cost. Many engaged in the administration and promotion of sport say and do things that would not see the light of day in their own businesses, workplaces and professions. Accepted practice seems to be opposed, on occasions, to morality and good reputations which is again why lawyers in the field should carry around with them the proverbial pinch of salt and accept with care what they are told by those instructing them.

Every sport's governing body should have a professional lawyer working at their headquarters ensuring that there is an awareness that the law has its eyes on all their activities and who is able to provide a skilled legal service to all its members. Local authorities who have licensing obligations and are the nation's largest landowners of playing fields and facilities also need to have a sports lawyer on their staff. The gambling industry, in particular, need lawyers to design controls to prevent abuses. Sport lawyers in their widest possible definition are necessary to protect the interests of the public. Their brief impinges on the lives of those who participate actively, spectate and now even to those who stay at home viewing on television. Ownership of football clubs, the rights of supporters, direct and indirect taxation and the relationship of the rise of in-play gambling are all pertinent issues. Government, however reluctant it may be in saying that there are no votes in sport, will have to provide much more than a powerless Minster who attends merely attends prestigious events.

Sport aficionados know how fragile their particular passion is. How horse racing has insufficient funding, how vulnerable cricket is to illegal gambling and bribery and corruption. How even a sport as supposedly amateur and Corinthian as rugby union used to be has tottered from one scandal to another and that all pervading soccer is answerable to FIFA, a body that is under constant suspicion not least in how it's marquee event, the World Cup, is awarded.

If the government comes in to the arena, organised sports must have more of a defined and accountable role and lawyers will have to have a seat at that table. Sports also have to be accountable for the grant money that government throws at them which is, ultimately, our bequest. The division between professional and amateur structures is becoming increasingly more blurred and clarity is required.

Ultimately, who represents the public in this changing world and debate where once – before vast media revenues – they were key. I suspect no-one does. Expert sports' lawyers with their insightful, analytical skills can help to provide the framework for solutions, if not the answers themselves but only if they are immersed in their area of specialism. We should never forget that sport is inextricably interwoven in the context of the British way of life.

A Lawyer for all Seasons

In my long and varied career I have come across a number of legal personalities whose lives enriched their colleagues and are but remembered with affection when tales are recounted of their exploits.

Peter Taylor was a rugby playing piano player who in addition was an excellent advocate starting from chambers in Newcastle and ending up as the Lord Chief Justice. He never lost his humanity and common touch and when he climbed the ladder of success, he may have overtaken his friends but he never forgot them. It was as a newly appointed wearer of the silk gown that I first briefed him in Leeds which until then was territory seldom invaded by him as a junior member of the Bar.

At our first conference before trial I quickly appreciated his grasp of the considerable number of papers that had been placed before him and of the issues involved. He carried a conference book and read from it a series of questions to both the client and myself. They were deliberately pointed and if some could not be answered he asked that further investigations to be made. He was never ruffled, and always appeared to be in control. His facial expressions did convey his feelings, a grimace behind his hands or a quick raise of the eyebrows and a broad smile were parts of his armoury.

I only saw him hesitant and uncomfortable on one occasion at the celebrated Leeds Police trial, where he had to patiently sit on his hands for days on end until successfully making a submission that his client had no case to answer. I think his attraction to Leeds was its Victorian town hall with its majestic concert auditorium which housed from time to time the Leeds International Piano competition which he patronized. The Steinway was an irresistible attraction and at most intervals in a trial he would retreat to the piano stool and elegant sounds of sonatas and fugues could be heard in the corridors to the court. Peter had family connections to the city, his mother being born and educated there. One Monday morning he greeted me on his return to Leeds with a tale of dining with his mother on the previous Friday night and she had told him that she sat next to my father at elementary school. When I told my dad he did remember her as Mary, a pretty ten year old. Later, Prime Minister Margaret Thatcher appointed him to enquire into the dreadful Hillsborough disaster when Liverpool football fans looking forward to a sporting afternoon found death and devastation round the corner. I had experience of tribunal enquiries into football grounds and when I read one of his observations I appreciated that he was advising himself incorrectly and I sent a note to him to that effect.

Contemporaries say that the duel between him and the shamed Scottish civil servant and man of letters Pottinger, charged alongside disgraced architect John Poulson in a sensational corruption trial was a masterpiece of the art of cross examination. Pottinger believed himself to be a man of erudition. Peter Taylor QC, although number two in the prosecution team, conducted a verbal duel, the rapier smart wit of the defendant being repelled by the cool, nagging persistent and penetrating questions of the barrister who secured the conviction and sentence of a lengthy period of imprisonment.

As a Leader at the Bar frequently instructed by the Crown, probably his most publicised case was when Jeremy Thorpe MP, the leader of the Liberal party, was charged along with three others of conspiring to kill a man who claimed to have had a homosexual relationship with him. The committal proceedings were held in Minehead Magistrates Court in Somerset. Sir David Napley, a former President of the Law Society, appeared for Thorpe. Napley had, along with his forensic skills, a great gift of attracting publicity. The satirical magazine *Private Eye* gave him the full treatment not least because he had written a book entitled *Techniques of Persuasion* to help beginners in the profession but demonstrated in that court that he had failed to heed its advice.

The obviously wounded Napley devoted several pages in his memoirs *Not Without Prejudice* to defending himself. 'The article was of course highly libellous,' he wrote. 'It presented me as both incompetent and negligent. I realised if I were to sue I could have taken them to the cleaners,' he continued. He chose not to do so but did give a qualified character reference to Peter Taylor. 'Taylor, with only one minor lapse from grace conducted the case against Thorpe with scrupulous fairness, integrity and in accordance with the highest traditions of the Bar.'

Within the profession, this long preliminary hearing was deemed to have set back the movement to allow solicitors to have the same right to represent defendants in the High Court as do members of the Bar, a subject dear to my heart. I was a campaigner for solicitors right's, though personally not wishing to pursue them to the optimum. I spoke out, wrote letters and published articles as a spokesman for my side of the argument. The last time Peter and I met was at a Buckingham Palace garden party. Seeing me in my finest attire he came over. 'How on earth do they allow you in?' he asked with a smile close to a grimace. Whether he accepted my explanation that it was because of my rugby league connections I do not know.

THE STORY OF FOOTBALL:
via the Moors, Dales and Wolds of England's largest and proudest county

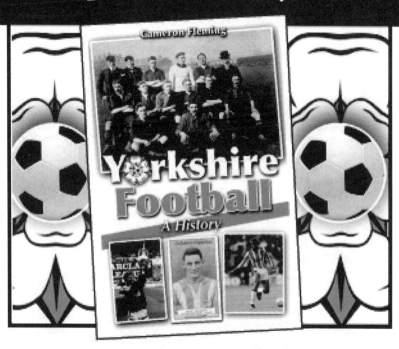

YORKSHIRE FOOTBALL
- A HISTORY
Cameron Fleming

ISBN: 978-0956252654

Scratching Shed Publishing Ltd

If you enjoyed this, you'll love these from Scratching Shed Publishing Ltd...

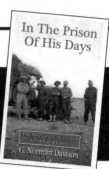

Scratching Shed Publishing Ltd - Bringing history to life

Off The Ropes
The Ron Lyle Story - by Candace Toft

In a life as tough and brutal as his bouts, Ron Lyle had already served time for second degree murder before he began his boxing career. Later, he was the supposedly third-rate fighter who had Muhammad Ali beat for ten rounds; the guy who knocked George Foreman down four times; and the guy who was arrested for murder a second time. **ISBN: 978-0956252623**

Reluctant Hero
The John Holmes Story

The OFFICIAL and FAMILY-APPROVED biography of the late Leeds and Great Britain rugby league legend John Holmes. Uniquely told by his brother and nephew, it is littered with anecdotes and reminiscences from friends and former team mates. The definitive life of one of the code's greats.

ISBN: 978-0956252647

1895 & All That...
Inside Rugby League's Hidden History - Tony Collins

As one of rugby's leading historians, Professor Tony Collins knows his onions. Here, for the first time, is a collection of his rarest pieces - each as entertaining as it is informative - in which subjects as diverse as the RL/Aussie Rules merger of 1933, the myth & reality of the great rugby split & the history of black rugby players are tackled.

ISBN: 978-0956007599

Scratching Shed Publishing Ltd

Scratching Shed Publishing Ltd is an independent publishing company founded in May 2008. We aim to produce high-quality books covering a wide range of subjects - including sport, travel and popular culture - of worldwide interest yet with the distinctive flavour of the North of England.

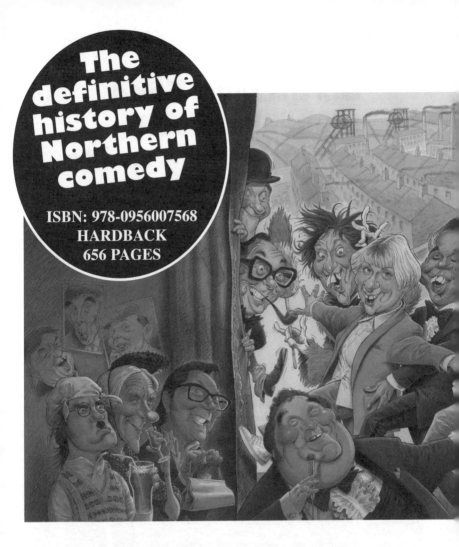

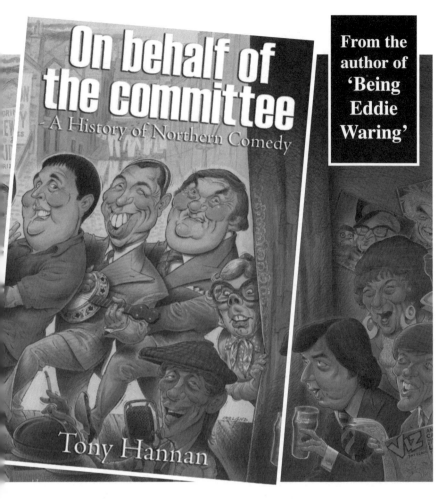

On behalf of the committee
- A History of Northern Comedy

From the author of 'Being Eddie Waring'

Tony Hannan

From the Industrial Revolution to our own comfortable 21st century digital age - via music hall, Variety, working mens clubs, radio, cinema & television - Northern-born comedians have consistently been at the heart of popular British comedy culture, tickling the funny bone of the entire nation.

This witty and informative book questions why that should be so, all the while charting an entertaining course through the careers of George Formby, Tommy Handley, Gracie Fields, Frank Randle, Al Read, Jimmy James, Hylda Baker, Jimmy Clitheroe, Les Dawson, Morecambe & Wise, Bernard Manning, Alan Bennett, Monty Python, Victoria Wood, Ken Dodd, Chubby Brown, The Young Ones, Vic and Bob, Steve Coogan, Caroline Aherne, the League of Gentlemen, Johnny Vegas, Peter Kay and many many others. Along the way, it also wonders why such a huge contribution to the British entertainment industry should be so often under-appreciated.

Mostly, however, it is a rich celebration of British comedy history & confirmation that you really do have to laugh - or else you'd cry...

Past deeds. Present voices.

Introducing Rugby League Classics - an ongoing series of historically significant rugby league books - rediscovered, rebranded and republished in paperback, often after having been long out-of-print.

Each edition comes complete with the original manuscript intact, and contains a wealth of new and updated material, including an introductory overview written by a relevant modern-day expert, evocative photographs, appendices, an index and the modern-day recollections of those closest to the book's primary subject, i.e. family members, former team-mates and other contemporary figures.

It is anticipated that at least two such titles will published every year, covering a wide range of eras and celebrated rugby league personalities.

To stay right up to date with news of all our latest releases, simply drop an email to **news@scratchingshedpublishing.com** and we will add you to our mailing list.

Rugby League Classics

OUT NOW - Numbers 1-5

- Gus Risman
- Lewis Jones
- Eric Ashton
- XIII Winters, XIII Worlds
- Eddie Waring

COLLECT THE SET!

Visit our website:
www.scratchingshedpublishing.co.uk

Scratching Shed Publishing Ltd

Treasure the old. Embrace the new.

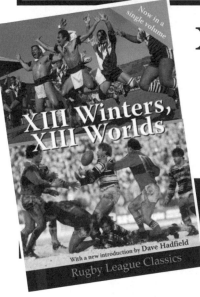

A sports autobiography like no other....

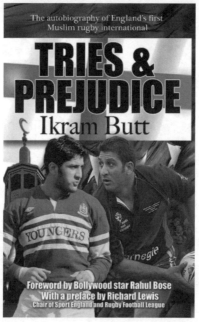

The autobiography of England's first Muslim rugby international

TRIES & PREJUDICE
Ikram Butt

Foreword by Bollywood star Rahul Bose
With a preface by Richard Lewis
Chair of Sport England and Rugby Football League

In February 1995, Ikram Butt became England's first Muslim rugby international in either code - blazing a trail for British Asians.

Since then, the former Leeds, Featherstone, London, Huddersfield and Hunslet rugby league star has continued to campaign for wider Asian involvement in sport and in 2004 was a prime mover in the formation of BARA - the British Asian Rugby Association. From the start, BARA had a vital social as well as sporting function. How could it not, in the wake of such 'War on Terror'-related atrocities as 9/11, 7/7 and the reported alienation of Britain's disaffected Asian youth?

Now, for the first time, Ikram Butt has his say, telling of his upbringing in Headingley; his own experiences on the wrong end of the law; the potential conflict between personal ambition and religion; racism in sport; run-ins with coaches and short-sighted officials; and, most recently, his regular visits to the House of Commons and pioneering development work in the UK, India and Pakistan.

Tries & Prejudice is by turns amusing, controversial, humane and eye-opening. It provides long overdue food for thought for politicians, the public and sports governing bodies alike.   ISBN 978-0956007537

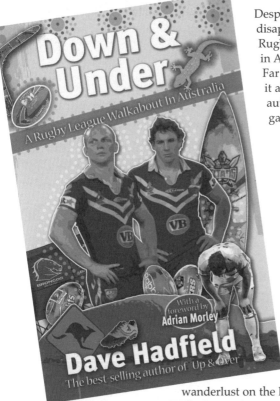

Stay up to date with all our lastest releases at
www.scratchingshedpublishing.co.uk